The
ENGLISH
WIFE

BOOKS BY ANNA STUART

The Berlin Zookeeper
The Secret Diary
A Letter from Pearl Harbor

WOMEN OF WAR
The Midwife of Auschwitz
The Midwife of Berlin
The War Orphan
The Secret Message

THE BLETCHLEY PARK GIRLS
The Bletchley Girls
Code Name Elodie

The
ENGLISH WIFE

ANNA STUART

bookouture

Published by Bookouture in 2025

An imprint of Storyfire Ltd.
Carmelite House
50 Victoria Embankment
London EC4Y oDZ

www.bookouture.com

The authorised representative in the EEA is Hachette Ireland
8 Castlecourt Centre
Dublin 15 D15 XTP3
Ireland
(email: info@hbgi.ie)

ISBN: 978-1-83618-675-5
eBook ISBN: 978-1-83618-674-8

This book is a work of fiction. Whilst some characters and circumstances
portrayed by the author are based on real people and historical fact, references
to real people, events, establishments, organizations or locales are intended only
to provide a sense of authenticity and are used fictitiously. All other characters
and all incidents and dialogue are drawn from the author's imagination and are
not to be construed as real.

*For Stuart – my very own Winston (only a lot more handsome).
Thank you from the bottom of my heart for all your support, help,
and love.*

xxxx

PROLOGUE
MAY 1941

CLEMENTINE

I stand, alone, on a Whitehall rooftop and stare into blazing London below. It's like looking into hell. I'm here to put out incendiary bombs before they take hold, but this tiny act of salvation feels futile for a city burning beneath the Luftwaffe onslaught. I kick my right foot against my metal bucket to be sure the sand is still loose within it, and adjust the fire extinguisher in my arms, feeling for one dislocated moment as if I'm cradling one of my babies. They're long since grown up, but they need protecting still, as all London needs protecting in these dark days.

Ahead, anti-aircraft lights criss-cross the night skies, seeking the planes that dart and slide between them. I catch the flash of bomb doors opening and watch, tensed, as the dark shapes fall, surely too ungainly for the deadly explosions they're about to rip through innocent homes. I'm too high up to hear the cries of distress, but they echo in my ears all the same. I've heard them too many times to ignore, spoken too often with people emerging from a shelter to see their precious home a pile of rubble or, worse, a pile of rubble and limbs, their families shattered with their houses. The Nazis are trying to break our spirit; we cannot let them succeed.

A plane flies so close overhead that, if I look up, I might see into the eyes of the pilot trying to destroy our world. I do not look up, not even when a bomb lands close enough to shake my rooftop perch; I will not give him that satisfaction. But I *do* look back, checking death is not dancing on my patch, not burning into the Treasury building, or the Admiralty, or Number Ten itself, the heart of Britain's lonely fight. I must be sure it is not burning into our home, is not striking at Winston Churchill, the man resisting Hitler's black tide, the man it is my duty – and my joy – to keep standing.

It is a heavy charge.

This time I'm lucky (though luck, in the spring of 1941, is all relative) and the bombs burst in a spray of sand across Horse Guards Parade and whump into the allotments that were once St James's Park. Someone's vegetables will have been blown out of the soil and that, as rationing tightens everyone's belts, is bad luck enough, but no one is dead.

This time.

There is silence. Or, rather, there is stillness in the skies. Down on the streets, people scurry to help the injured, knowing how easily it could be them. The wail of an ambulance wobbles as the driver negotiates a torn-up road. A hiss of water from a fire engine hits flames and they crackle angrily. Only the devil is having fun in the hell of London right now – the devil and his Messerschmitt henchmen. I think again of my children and pray they are safe, then feel guilty for wishing the bombs might land elsewhere. What right do I have to expect special treatment? I'm in Downing Street, at my husband's side, to protect all Britain, not just my tiny corner of it.

A telltale drone alerts me to a renewed rash of black across the seeking beams of light – the Luftwaffe are coming again, as relentless as a stormy sea. The worst thing, as I watch them draw close, is the fear that these overhead attacks are a precursor to something much, much worse. My gaze is pulled past the planes, past London, to the dark blank beyond, where a skinny strip of sea creates the last barrier to the relentless waves of Nazi attack across Europe.

I put a hand to my head, trying to wipe out everything I know, for on dark nights like this it's almost too much to bear. I've seen the maps stuck to the walls in the War Rooms far below me. I've seen the mass of pins marking the myriad Luftwaffe bases in poor, occupied Europe. I've read the precious 'enigma' of Hitler's commands, broken by the brilliant minds in Bletchley Park, and I'm not sure if this knowledge is a blessing or a curse. We have watched, in horrifying detail, as all fall before the Nazi tanks and guns – all bar us. But for how much longer?

An incendiary drops mere feet away, and I leap up, rushing to the sparking metal tube and dumping my sand upon it with a nod of my head. 'Take that, Hitler.' It's a small act, but a million small acts can offer a huge defence. All across London, and the other brave cities of our isolated island, others are doing the same, united in a determination to stay free, and that knowledge gives me strength; I am not, in fact, alone on this rooftop. Drawing myself up to my full height, I ready my extinguisher once more. Hitler will not take Britain; not on my watch.

PART ONE

ONE

CHARTWELL, SEPTEMBER, 1938

CLEMENTINE

Clementine Churchill peered out the long windows of Chartwell's dining room and across the rolling gardens to the family swimming pool, glowing pink in the last rays of the September sun. If she squinted into the low light she could almost see ten years into the past, to the children splashing around, encouraged by Winston in one of his more exuberant moods. She could almost see a brightly coloured ball bouncing between them and light dappling through the trees to sparkle on the water. If she tried really hard, she could almost see herself sitting in a deckchair, offering pennies for well-executed dives and holding out towels when the children ran to her for warmth.

It had been a happy time, one she hadn't appreciated to the full and now longed to recapture – the embodiment of family contentment, of fun, of peace. But peace was becoming an increasingly precious commodity in Europe, and in Chartwell too.

'Hitler lies!' Winston bellowed, and Clementine turned

reluctantly from the idyllic view to the group of men huddled around her dining table. 'He promises peace, but that's conditional on us letting him take as many countries as he chooses and imposing his hateful brand of fascism upon them. What sort of peace is that?!'

Clementine leaned against one of her perfectly upholstered dining chairs to steady herself. Her husband was right, but only the few men clustered here, in their country home, were listening to him.

'The cabinet just don't seem to appreciate the vastness of Hitler's plans,' one of their guests moaned.

'Quite!' Winston agreed. 'Have none of them read *Mein Kampf*? Because I have and it's not pretty!'

That wasn't, Clementine thought, strictly true. *She* had read it for him, her well-schooled German almost as good as her perfect French. She'd sat patiently translating every line as Winston had paced his study, muttering furiously at the phrases that caught his imagination – which had been almost all of them. And, to be fair, he would remember it better than she. He always did.

'His plans are clearly laid out,' Winston raged on. 'He intends to take over central Europe for his blasted Aryans and eliminate anyone who doesn't fit his very precise mould. Sudetenland will never satisfy the greedy dog. He wants all of Czechoslovakia, mark my words, and then Poland and the Low Countries. France, if he thinks he can get it, which he does! And what's after France? *We* are, that's what! Why can't Chamberlain see it?'

The men mumbled agreement into their wine and Winston sank into his seat, turning despairing eyes on Clementine. She saw the fierce, furious passion burning within them for the fate of this pretty island of theirs and felt her heart turn over.

'He just doesn't want war, Winston,' she said.

A tear welled in her husband's eye. 'But he will get it all the same, my dear. If you let a mad dog into a room full of juicy steaks, you cannot expect him to be satisfied with a nibble of the nearest morsel. He will tear through every single one. Meanwhile, the damned appeasers think talks and compromises will stop the man.' He leaped up to join her at the windows, waving his cigar imperiously towards his beloved Kentish Weald as the sun cast her final rays across it. 'God help us, that fool Chamberlain will have the Wehrmacht at our door within weeks.'

Clementine sighed and wondered if she could retire to bed yet. Hitler was a monster, but she sometimes wondered if ranting endlessly about him on the borders of Kent was achieving much. But then, to be fair, Winston was desperate for the power to do something – anything – and Chamberlain, not surprisingly, wouldn't let him anywhere near his peace-seeking cabinet.

She moved closer to him, feeling her hair touching the ceiling and cursing herself for opting for a high bun, then Winston for insisting on a ceiling that couldn't contain even a basic hairstyle. The floor of the dining room – part of an extension they'd added to the mish-mash house when Winston had bought it – should have been far lower, designed to create a gracious ceiling space and lead onto the lawns beyond the long windows, but when Winston had registered that he couldn't see what he was already calling 'his view' of the Weald, he'd ordered it raised. The result, besides a considerable addition to the already vast bill, had been a room she called 'poky' and he 'cosy'. It was not, as she often pointed out, *his* head that scraped the ceiling (for the very good reason that she was taller than him, even without her heels), but the view was, she had to admit, excellent.

It would be less so swarming with Nazi tanks.

Resolve renewed, Clementine squeezed Winston's arm and led him back to the table, waving for the port to be brought over. The men he had gathered in their dining room were the few brave enough to insist that Hitler was planning war and she must give them her every support. She just wished she didn't feel so very alone in doing so.

'Please come for the weekend,' she'd begged her sister, Nellie, on the telephone the other day.

'I'd love to, darling,' she'd said, 'but all this ranting against Hitler has got very tiresome.'

Winston had overheard and snatched up the telephone. 'This is the problem, Nellie,' he'd snarled. 'The world is going to go to the dogs because people are too bored to care!'

'Perhaps then, Winston, you should be less boring about it,' Nellie had told him tartly.

Clementine had privately applauded her sister for her nerve, but Winston had stormed off, wrapped up in his fury at a world that would not listen.

'Please come, Nell,' she'd said, 'or I'll be left all alone with him.'

'You married the man, Clemmie. You knew what you were getting into.'

Which was true, of course. Right before Winston had proposed to her thirty years ago, he'd told her he wanted to be prime minister one day. He'd offered the information as they'd walked around the gracious grounds of Blenheim Palace, not as arrogance, but as a warning – this is what you're in for if you say yes. She'd understood completely and when they'd stepped into the pretty Temple of Diana and he'd finally plucked up the courage to ask for her hand, she'd agreed without hesitation. She'd been excited by his ambition; she still was.

It just wasn't so easy these days.

'At the very least, we must prepare,' Winston was saying to his fellows. 'We must rearm.'

'What we need,' one man said, 'is America.'

'They're not interested,' another moaned.

'I think Roosevelt is,' Clementine put in.

Winston looked gratefully at her. 'I think you're right, Clemmie. But he answers to the Yank in the street, so the question is: how do we engage them?'

Ronald Tree, an American-born member of their small gang of anti-appeasers, leaned forward. 'There's a new guy in town, Winston. A young radio reporter, name of Ned Miller. You might have heard him. Made quite a stir broadcasting the Anschluss live from Vienna.'

'Yes!' Winston strode round to place a hand on his friend's shoulder. 'Mighty fine broadcasting. Every detail told, every sense awakened. Felt as if I was there myself.'

'Well, he's in London, working for CBS. His wife too.'

'His wife broadcasts?' Clementine asked, interested.

'He means his wife is in London, dear,' Winston corrected.

But Ronald shook his head. 'No, no, his wife broadcasts too. Jenny Miller. She's good. Women's stuff, you know – fashion and housekeeping and the like – but people enjoy it.'

'Women enjoy it,' Winston scoffed.

'Which is rather the point,' Clementine told him.

He snorted, then offered her the briefest of smiles. 'I suppose it rather is. But how on earth does it help us?'

'Because,' Ronald said triumphantly, 'they're both keen interventionists. Honeymooned all over Europe and love it. Do a lot of telling America this is their war too.'

'Excellent!' Winston clapped his hands, a glimmer of a smile bringing welcome light back into his eyes. 'Let's meet them. Let's have them for dinner. Soon. All hands to the pump, what, Clemmie?' His smile, as ever-ready as his tears, was wide now.

Clementine made a note of these young broadcasters, then rose determinedly. 'I'd love to meet them, Winston,' she said. 'And now, if you'll excuse me, gentlemen, I shall leave you to your deliberations.'

The men all leaped to their feet, full of fake protestations of disappointment, and she made her escape. Winston escorted her gallantly to the door and leaned in to kiss her goodnight.

'Are we frightful bores, Clemmie?' he asked softly.

'Frightful,' she agreed.

'But you understand why it matters so very much? We cannot let that mad dog take Great Britain, Clemmie, we cannot.'

'I know, Winston,' she agreed, kissing him back. 'I just wish it wasn't you that had to do it.'

'Me too, my dear,' he agreed, 'me too.'

But he was already turning back and she knew he didn't mean it. She'd known from the day he'd slipped his ring on her finger that he wanted to lead the country. And he would be good at it, she knew he would, but it would be hard. As she retreated to the safety of her pretty bedroom, one question buzzed around in her head: Winston was desperate to save the country, but who was going to save Winston?

TWO

THE HOUSES OF PARLIAMENT, 28 SEPTEMBER 1938

JENNY

'1099?' Jenny Miller looked up into the arched timbers of Westminster Hall, trying to bend her brain around the date. 'This was built in 1099? That was...' She fought to do the math – almost seven hundred years before her country had been founded. Could that be right? She looked to Ned, who squeezed her hand.

'Don't say it, honey! The Brits love reminding us what a whippersnapper country we are.'

Jenny smiled back at her husband. 'Young, energetic and upcoming?'

'You've got it!' He looked around. 'Though I admit, I do love all this ancient grandeur. And I sure as hell don't want to see Europe stamped all over by Herr Hitler.'

His hand tightened around hers and she pressed closer to him, knowing exactly what he meant. They'd had a glorious honeymoon touring the continent three years ago and she'd been stunned by the beauty of the cities – and their diversity. Now they were living in London and truly getting to know their

European cousins, and the thought of Hitler stomping his homogenous Nazi eagle across so many beautiful cultures was heartbreaking.

'Why is no one doing anything to stop him?' she asked, looking around. 'All this history, all this power – don't they want to protect it?'

'A few of them do, which is why we're here, remember?'

Jenny nodded. Ronald Tree, a generous man who'd taken them under his wing since their arrival in London last year, had brought them to the Houses of Parliament to meet someone called Winston Churchill. They would find him inspiring, he'd said. He was one of the few MPs prepared to speak against appeasement and he was keen to meet them.

'Winston's mother is American,' Ronald told them now.

'Meaning he's prepared to shoot his mouth off?' Ned laughed.

'Maybe, but more that he's keen to ally with those of us from across the pond.'

Ronald's parents were both American, though you'd never be able to tell. Born and raised in Britain, he had the cut-glass tone and manner of an English gentleman. He strode easily through the ancient hall at the heart of London, weaving between the many men striding up grand steps to turn into the House proper. The stark, open stateliness gave way to an almost church-like magnificence of soaring Gothic columns, marble statues and vast wall paintings. Jenny didn't realise she was gaping until Ned pushed her mouth gently shut.

'It's so... elaborate.'

Ronald smiled. 'That's the Victorians for you. This place isn't as old as it looks.' He leaned conspiratorially in. 'The Brits are as capable of faking it as the Yanks sometimes. All this was built in the mid-1800s, after the original was destroyed by a fire, but it was designed to look fully Elizabethan to fit their ideas of the dignity of governance.'

'Elizabethan?' Jenny whispered to Ned. Over here, they threw these eras around as if everyone understood them, which she supposed they did.

'Queen Elizabeth I's time – 1500s, I think.'

'When we were still all...'

'Don't say it!'

She laughed. 'Sorry.'

They'd reached the end of the painted court and now stood in a stunning circular section, even more cathedral-like than before, complete with mosaics of saints above the arched door-ways. Jenny stared as men darted carelessly beneath, chatting and waving papers as if this were any old office.

'Can you imagine what our younger selves would say if they could see us now?' she whispered to Ned.

'They'd really think we'd made it!' he whispered back, squeezing her hand.

They'd met each other on the way to the National Student Federation Congress in the fall of 1931. Ned had been its ardent young president, Jenny an earnest economics student, and they'd both been burning to change the world. They'd got talking on the train and never stopped. The next day he'd invited her out for breakfast, paying a fortune for strawberries to try and impress her. It had done, so much so that she'd eaten the lot despite not really liking them. She'd liked him, though, and miraculously, given the number of women following him around the halls and corridors of the conference, he'd liked her too. The rest, as they said, was history – though not as much history as they found surrounding them right now.

'Should we have gone into politics?' she asked him, feeling guilty for allowing themselves to be pulled into radio and away from true activism.

'There's more ways to change the world than being a congressman,' Ned said firmly. 'Or a Member of Parliament for that matter. And, look, we're here anyway!'

She nodded, glad of his optimistic certainty.

'Do you like it?' Ronald asked eagerly.

'It's very... holy,' she said.

Their host clapped his hands. 'Holy! Excellent. The religion of government! Winston will be delighted with that. Now, come along, let's get to the bar and find him. Ooh, not that way, that's the Lords. Red carpet, see. Green for us commoners.'

Yet more terminology Jenny did not understand. She hurried after Ronald, trying to work out what he meant. A few weeks ago, he and his wife, Nancy, had invited them to Ditchley, his 'place in the country'. Thankfully Ned had warned her to pack her best frocks because this 'place' had turned out to be a cream-stoned mansion set in elegantly manicured grounds, with soaring halls and reception rooms fit for royalty. If that was a commoner's home, then goodness only knew how a lord lived.

Jenny had been raised in a nice home in Connecticut, with all the advantages of a happy family and a liberal education. She'd considered herself well-off and had been very ready, with Ned, to work her way into being even more so. In America they respected that, and maybe over here too, but true wealth, like something they called 'breeding', apparently needed history to count.

It was perhaps bound up with having a monarchy. One of Jenny and Ned's first assignments had been covering the coronation of King George VI and Queen Elizabeth. Jenny had never seen as much pomp in her entire life but now it seemed that Parliament, even on a normal day, was almost as grand.

'Here we are. What can I get you?' Ronald asked.

Perhaps, Jenny thought, this section was for commoners because they had to fetch their own drinks. Maybe the lords got waiter service like – well, like everywhere in America. Ned asked for something called a bitter. Jenny wondered if she should be ladylike and have a soda, but she couldn't remember what they called that over here and, besides, there were so many loud people she needed something stronger. She asked for a gin.

As Ronald elbowed happily through the thickening crowd around the bar, Ned steered Jenny to the patio doors and she was grateful to step onto a long, paved terrace running the length of the glorious buildings above the vast Thames. Ronald had told her there were six hundred and fifteen Members of Parliament and it felt as if every single one of them was in the House today. Words buzzed around her like stings: 'mobilisation', 'conscription', 'war'.

Last week, Chamberlain, the prime minister, had flown to two sets of talks with Hitler, agreeing to him taking Sudetenland from the Czechs, as if this was his to do. The Czechs, sure enough, had had something to say about that and were mobilising. Chamberlain had, in turn, called out the British fleet and Jenny felt excited to be at the heart of the action. And a little scared. War was a terrible prospect. Her mother wanted her home 'safe', but, as she and Ned kept trying to explain, if Hitler kicked off, *nobody* would be safe. Even so, it did feel shockingly close right now.

The buzz was loudest around several tables nearby and Jenny looked curiously over as Ronald arrived with her gin.

'Chamberlain,' he told her. 'Gearing up to declare war.'

'I thought he didn't want war?'

'He doesn't. Few do, and who can blame them? People don't want to send their husbands and sons into battle again. Neither do I. It will break Nancy's heart if our boys are sent to Czechoslovakia or Poland to face the Boche guns, but – God help us – if they don't, they may end up fighting in Dover. I think even Chamberlain can see that now.'

Jenny swallowed. She glanced up at the glorious building behind, imagining it draped with swastikas. Was it really that close?

'I'm sorry,' Ronald said. 'I'm frightening you. Where *is* Winston? Ah!'

He turned to look inside where a voice was rising above the hubbub, strident and certain: 'Did you hear he wants Czechoslovakia "broken up" now? Broken up! Bollocks! Pardon my French. Actually, don't pardon it. And it's not French. It's good old Anglo-Saxon. Make the most of it – you won't be hearing it in these noble halls much longer if we don't get off our arses and do something!'

The voice rose on the last words and all around fell silent before it. Jenny edged to the door and saw, in a slight gap in the bustling bar, a short, wide man with a baby-smooth face curiously at odds with the cigar being wafted angrily in front of it. *This* was Winston Churchill?

'Excellent,' Ronald said. 'He's here. I can introduce you.'

'Are you sure now's a good—?'

But Ronald was pushing through the crowd, Ned hot on his heels, and there was little choice but to follow.

'You know what Herr Hitler is?' Winston was asking the crowd, though not even pretending to pause for an answer. 'He's a bully. A classic, schoolboy bully, thinking he can push everyone around if he shouts the loudest.'

'He's not the only one,' someone called, and there was laughter.

Mr Churchill didn't flinch. 'Do bullies understand "negotiation"? They do not! They understand force. Stand up to him and he'll back down.'

'I'm not sure he will,' said a quiet voice, and Jenny saw a tall woman at his side. She wore an immaculately tailored, fur-trimmed suit with a chic hat and stunning pearls, and held herself with perfect poise. Jenny was not surprised to see Winston incline his head in a small bow. Was this the queen?

'Quite right, Clemmie dear, not at first, but he will eventually.'

'Clementine Churchill,' Ronald whispered. 'Winston's wife. They must think it's a big day if she's come to watch proceedings.'

'She's beautiful.'

'Yes. Strange, isn't it? Word is, Winston used his golden tongue to talk his way into her, er... her favour.'

Jenny grinned. The British were so damned reserved.

'Into her bed, you mean? Still, he obviously thinks the world of her.'

Ronald flushed. 'He does, he does. We all do. You'll love her. Come on!' He plunged boldly into the small space before the mismatched couple. 'Winston! Good to see you. You too, Clementine, looking as divine as always. I've brought those people I told you about – the broadcasters.'

Jenny flushed with pride. She'd only done a few broadcasts so far, but it was lovely to share the designation with Ned. Not as lovely, mind you, as it would have been to share a child with him, but God had not seen fit to bless them, despite their best efforts. She felt a familiar pang, but reminded herself that if she had children she would not be here now, and brushed it aside as Winston gave them his disconcertingly piercing consideration.

'You're the chap from Vienna,' he said to Ned.

'That's right, sir. Terrible time it was.'

'You gave us a wonderful flavour of the Anschluss. Shame no one was listening – properly listening, I mean. People around here think it's a show, a drama over the sea with no impact on us. We're an island, you see, a complacent little island, but you saw the planes, yes? You saw the Luftwaffe?'

'I did, sir, and they're terrifying.'

'Not until they're over one's own head, it would seem. Still, you've picked a propitious day to visit the House. You will see war announced, mark my words. Hitler is marching on Czecho-slovakia, the fleet is out, and it is time to declare our hand!' Again, his voice raised as if he were preaching at a lectern not standing in a group of friends. His wife put a hand on his arm and he gave a loud harrumph but drew himself back in.

'My wife, Clementine – *teen*, mind, not *tine*, like your song about the miner. She hates that song, don't you, dear?'

'Delighted to meet you, Mrs Miller.' Clementine stepped past her blustering husband, holding out a hand, slim and cool, but with a surprisingly firm grasp. 'How do you find our parliament?'

'Magnificent,' Jenny said, but before she could elaborate, an elderly man in a black suit and silver regalia stepped into the bar, bearing a silver tray with a small envelope sitting innocuously in its centre. 'Telegram for the prime minister. Telegram for Mr Chamberlain.'

A hush fell on the crowded room and they all watched as Neville Chamberlain appeared and took the envelope with studied calm. He read it once, twice, a third time and then he looked up, his eyes sweeping the MPs and their guests, a small smile playing across his lips.

'I have been invited to Munich to confer with Herr Hitler, Monsieur Daladier and Signor Mussolini.'

'Confer?!' The roar came from Winston, so loud Jenny physically flinched.

Chamberlain stepped towards him. 'Confer, yes. He has agreed to postpone mobilisation. It is clear, surely even to you, Winston, that Hitler does not want war either. We have called his bluff and he is backing down. Force is, perhaps, a blunter weapon than you believe, sir.'

The MPs roared approval and Chamberlain wafted the telegram like a white flag. 'This afternoon's session is adjourned. I must to Munich to secure peace in our time.'

The roar grew and Jenny curled against Ned, feeling the desperate need of the crowd.

Winston Churchill was purple with rage. 'Hitler will lie!' he shouted after Chamberlain, but even his strident voice could not be heard above the cries for peace. Jenny saw him turn to his wife. 'Hitler will lie, Clemmie.'

'We'll see, Winston.'

'We will. We bloody well will! He will make fools of us all. Ronald, this way. We need to assemble the troops.'

'Delighted to meet you, sir,' Ned tried, but Winston was gone, summoning his straggle of believers as the rest of the House surged after Chamberlain.

'I'm so sorry.' Clementine pressed Jenny's hand. 'You catch us at a bad time, as you see. You must come to dinner when things are calmer. If things are *ever* calmer.' She turned towards the door.

'You're not staying with your husband?' Jenny asked.

'Goodness no. He'll be far too busy.'

'What can he do?'

Clementine Churchill fixed her with piercing blue eyes. 'Nothing at all, my dear, save rant that the entire government policy is wrong. We can only pray that, in this, *he* is the one who is wrong, but I'm afraid, in my extensive experience of my husband, that is rarely the case. Good day.'

And with that she was gone, heading out of the Houses of Parliament as Winston dived deeper inside, taking Ronald with him, and leaving Jenny and Ned standing adrift in the emptying bar.

Jenny turned to her husband, her head whirling. 'Should we go back to America like Mother says, Ned?'

'We most certainly should not, honey,' he shot back with a smile. 'Things are just getting interesting!'

It was the broadcaster in him, alive with the seductive call of a story. Jenny put a hand to her stomach, wishing there was a child in there she was obliged to protect, but there was no child and no obligation and she must step up and trace the fate of this uncertain country on the edge of teetering Europe as best she could.

THREE

CHATEAU DE SAINT-GEORGES-MOTEL, AUGUST 1939

CLEMENTINE

Clementine threw herself into a deckchair, feeling the glorious ache of well-worked muscles and the even more glorious glow of victory.

'Good game, thank you, Mary.'

'Not so good for me, Mummy. You tore me apart in that final set.'

'You lost concentration, darling.'

'Can you blame me? Did you see those yummy gardeners going past?'

'Mary!'

Her daughter winked cheekily and threw herself onto the ground, her tennis whites bright against the lush grass. Clementine rang the bell on the table for tea. This really had been the most perfect holiday at their friends' kindly loaned chateau in Saint-Georges-Motel. Barely two hours' drive due west from Paris, it was nestled into the ever-rolling countryside of lower Normandy as if nothing as vulgar as a city existed in the world – not Paris, not London and certainly not Berlin.

Clementine tutted at herself. She was not meant to be thinking about Germany. The whole point of this blissful week had been to *stop* thinking about Germany. It had been nearly a year since Chamberlain had brought back 'peace in our time', but it had been no peace for Clementine, with Winston still raving on about Hitler's lies and the damned Führer doing his best to prove him right. Here, however, with Winston absorbed at his easel, and Mary to play tennis with, it was easier than almost anywhere else.

'I think I like skiing better than tennis,' Mary said, her eyes closed against the bright sun. 'It has that divine rush of speed.'

'Only once you've trekked your way up the mountain,' Clementine pointed out.

Mary sat up. 'I read the other day that they're installing lifts in some resorts. How jolly would that be?'

'Very,' Clementine agreed.

She and Mary had taken up skiing three years ago and although Clementine also loved the rush, it was very hard work trekking high enough for a decent run, especially when you were in your fifties. Still, she'd persisted, both for the challenge and because it had been wonderful spending time with her youngest daughter.

'Ooh, cake!' Mary cried now and ran to help the maid bring the tea tray across the lawns.

Clementine watched indulgently, sending up a prayer of thanks for her uncomplicated youngest child. She had not, she knew, been the most devoted of mothers when her first three were young and worried that it showed now.

Diana, her eldest, had married a peacock of a man who'd lasted barely a year before showing his true, horribly drunken colours. Extracting her had been unpleasant, but successful, and at least now she was happily married to Duncan Sandys, with two little ones to keep her endlessly occupied. Clementine sometimes felt that Diana's fussy parenting was a living rebuke to herself for her more distanced approach. And perhaps a fair one.

Randolph, their only son, had been indulged by a father delighted to have an heir to the Churchill name, and had proved far too much of a handful for any of the succession of nannies they'd employed over the years. Then there was Sarah, her second daughter, whose childhood had been marked by crippling shyness. She'd overcome it via the curious method of taking to the stage, and was actually rather good. Clementine had nearly burst with pride when she'd watched her opening show in Manchester back in 1935.

Unfortunately Sarah had created a drama of her own, running off to America after a handsome vaudeville star eighteen years her senior. Still, they were back in Britain now and Vic was a decent man – for a comedian – and he cared deeply for Sarah. Clementine sometimes thought it was in a rather fatherly way, but perhaps both girls had been trying to find a version of their father. Just as Randolph was trying to *be* him. And who could blame them? When you were used to such a man about the house, so many others would feel quiet. Not that there was anything wrong with quiet every once in a while.

Clementine looked over to Winston, deep in concentration at his easel. He'd sailed through parenthood, dipping in to play raucously with his children, then out again whenever politics called him back. He saw them through rose-tinted spectacles and only faced their wilder tendencies when absolutely forced to – and then usually by despatching Clementine to sort things out. It must be very relaxing. Thank heavens, with Mary, she'd seen sense and employed Cousin Maryott as her youngest daughter's constant housekeeper and companion – a pseudo-mother with a soft, patient personality far more suited to the job of raising small children than Clementine's. Though, of course, it had taken tragedy to force the issue...

She sighed, but then saw Winston cock his head on one

side, as dainty as a bird, to analyse the effect of his brushstrokes, and felt her heart turn over with love. He'd joined them three days ago, fresh from touring French defences at the invitation of Monsieur Daladier, and today was the first day he'd calmed down. It was good to see.

'Tea, Winston,' she called.

He looked up and waved acknowledgement. Setting his paintbrush carefully down, he lumbered towards them, wiping his fingers on his smock. She watched him fondly, glad he was here safe. He'd come close to offending the French by suggesting their precious Maginot Line – the long run of static defences protecting their eastern border – would not be equal to German firepower. Clementine prayed he was wrong. She loved France. Not Dieppe, maybe, not since the family tragedy there, but much of the rest of it, and she knew the whole country was watching Germany with the wariness of a mouse trapped far too close to a tiger.

Clementine drank her tea crossly. Hitler intruding again! She should take a leaf out of Mary's book and live for the moment. She tore her eyes back to her daughter, who was eagerly helping herself to chocolate gateau.

'Don't get that on your whites,' she cautioned.

'Too late!' Mary wiped shamefacedly at a smudge of dark brown on her pretty dress. 'Tell you what, why don't I finish this and then go and slip into an evening gown.'

She smiled innocently – far too innocently.

Clementine frowned. 'Why? What are you planning?'

'Nothing much.' Mary twisted a ringlet into her hair. 'It's just that René and Julian have offered me a lift into Dreux for this divine dinner dance tonight and I thought you and Papa might like me out of the way so you can talk, you know, politics and stuff.'

'Did you indeed?' Clementine shook her head. Mary, at nearly seventeen, had a nose for a party. And why not! Clementine had enjoyed a few in her younger days, had, in truth, been engaged twice before Winston came along, though she did not consider herself a good model for Mary. 'You must be back by midnight.'

Mary laughed. 'Midnight? It'll barely have started. I'll be back by two, I promise. Or maybe three...?'

Winston chuckled. 'Let the girl go, Clemmie. There could be precious little time to enjoy ourselves ahead.'

There it was again – Herr Hitler intruding, however hard you tried to keep him out.

'Fine, fine. Have fun.'

Mary gave a squeal, kissed her and, wolfing down her cake, shot off towards the chateau. Clementine handed Winston his tea and he sank into a chair at her side with a sigh of contentment.

'Nice to have a bit of time to ourselves, hey, Clemmie?'

'Wonderful. I feel like royalty in this chateau.'

'You're the queen of my heart, my dear.'

She brushed this away, embarrassed. 'I hear the king and queen's trip to America went well.'

'I believe so, though no one tells me anything.'

'Because you backed Edward VIII in the abdication crisis.'

'In wishing to marry the woman he loved. Is that such a crime?'

'If you are the king of Great Britain and she a double divorcée, yes.'

Winston groaned and selected the largest slice of cake. 'Well, it all seems to be working out now. I hear tell they had a picnic with the Roosevelts, on a rug, with hot dogs!'

Clementine blinked, surprised. She knew Elizabeth Bowes-Lyon and doubted the dignified Scottish aristocrat had enjoyed the experience. But she had got on with it, as they all had to get on with things these days.

'The visit will be a big help if we need to get the Americans on board,' she said.

'*When* we need to, Clemmie.'

Guiltily, Clementine remembered the young American broadcasters she'd met in the House amidst the chaos of Chamberlain's Munich telegram – the Millers, was it? She'd suggested they come to dinner, but done nothing further about it. She would, she resolved, but first she could surely enjoy her brief holiday without fretting over home affairs?

'At least the king and queen understand the situation,' she said placatingly.

Winston humphed. 'They do. Perhaps they're getting over their love affair with bloody Chamberlain.'

'Winston! Respect. It's hardly a love affair.'

'They had him onto the palace balcony like a bloody hero when he came back from Munich with his stupid paper full of lies.'

'Because everyone wanted to believe in peace and the king doesn't like to see his subjects suffer.'

'Then he shouldn't nurture a damned appeaser,' he growled.

She pushed herself to her feet, hoping to forestall the perpetual subject. 'Another cup of tea?'

Winston nodded grudging assent and she reached for the pot but then noticed the head butler bursting from the chateau, clutching a note. Her heart sank.

'Clemmie! The tea!'

Winston leaped to take the pot and Clementine looked down to see she'd poured Earl Grey all over the petits fours. She stuttered apologies as she watched the servant make his panting approach.

Winston hurried to meet him. 'Qu'est-ce que c'est passé?' he demanded in deplorable French. 'What's happened?'

'Beg pardon, monsieur,' the butler gasped out, 'but I have an urgent telegram for you. From Whitehall.'

Winston waved paint-covered hands. 'What does it say, man?'

The butler blanched. 'It says, sir, that Russia and Germany have signed a pact. A non-aggression pact. It says you must come home immediately. It says...' He drew in a dramatic breath. 'It says there will be war.'

The next day, Clementine found herself sitting with Mary in a Paris taxi as it crawled between the Gare Montparnasse and the Gare du Nord, both of them rigid, their eyes fixed on the teeming streets. Winston had headed off within an hour of the message arriving the day before, desperate to be at the heart of the unfolding action, but Clementine had seen no reason to be overdramatic and followed at a more measured pace. Not that there was anything measured about Paris.

The French capital was alive with troops. No official mobilisation orders had yet gone out but standing units were being moved east towards the Maginot defence line at the devastating news of the Russo-German pact. All year, Winston had been urging the government to draw Russia into an alliance, but efforts had been half-hearted and it seemed Marshal Stalin had had enough and gone over to the devil.

'Why on earth would a communist leader align himself with a fascist one?' Mary had wailed to her father last night.

'For one reason only, my dear girl,' Winston had said. 'Poland.'

'Poland?'

'Yes, you know – great big, fertile country with the misfortune to be sat between Germany and Russia. They've been trying to carve her up between them for centuries. Now they're at it again. They'll be invading within days, mark my words. Good God! I *told* Chamberlain to get the Russians on board and now look, bloody Hitler's done it instead.'

He'd been apoplectic with rage and Clementine had been secretly relieved when he'd left for his flight home. She still yearned, with every fibre of her body, for her husband to be wrong about the Führer, but it was ever more apparent that he was not. Even Paris knew it.

'It's a tragedy,' Mary said, pressing her face against the glass as they passed a young couple caught in a longing clinch. 'All these young men off to the front. Even those who've completed their national service are going back. René's going to join up and Julian said he would too, though only to avoid ribbing.'

'What a reason to go to war.'

Clementine put a hand on her daughter's knee and Mary pressed it. She had gone to her party last night, saying the boys wanted to dance while they still could, but clearly no one's heart had been in it for she'd come home barely past 1 a.m.

'At least they'll be safe behind the Maginot Line,' she said.

Clementine didn't want to contradict her but she'd heard far too much of Winston's exhaustingly detailed assessment of France's precious defences to trust in it.

'It would have worked a treat in the Great War, Clemmie,' he'd said, pacing at the bottom of her bed. 'But now... The German tanks will roll over the French so-called fortifications without even breaking sweat. There's one general over there, De Gaulle, who knows his stuff and has been trying to get anti-tank regiments together, but he's an imperious sort and no one cares to listen to him.'

'Sound familiar?' she'd asked, but he'd been too caught up in the absorbing world of military tactics to notice. It was probably as well; it had been churlish of her.

The taxi finally pulled into the Gare du Nord, thankfully clear of troops. Obviously, the French weren't sending them north to the Ardennes where, according to Winston, they would be most needed. *Please*, she thought once more, *let him be wrong*, but she knew he was not and the world, it seemed, was starting to know that too. Summoning a porter, she took Mary's arm and threaded her way towards the trains to the coast, and home.

FOUR

DITCHLEY PARK, OXFORDSHIRE, 28 AUGUST 1939

JENNY

Jenny looked around their palatial bedroom in Ronald Tree's magnificent mansion and couldn't quite believe she was here, in the peace of the English countryside, with Europe, surely, on the brink of war. The Churchills were joining them for the weekend and she was both excited and nervous about meeting them again. Thank heavens for her new dress! She glanced in the ornate mirror and was delighted to see an elegant society woman looking back. She'd found this gold sateen gown second-hand from the newspapers but the seller could not have worn it more than once for it was immaculate. And magical! For once her petite frame was almost stately and the sharp lines of her face less pixie and more queenly.

She smoothed down the bias-cut skirt, trying to enjoy the fine fabric and not let her hands linger on her belly whose dull ache matched the one in her heart. Another month; another chance gone. What was wrong with her? Everyone else seemed to pop out babies as soon as they got married, but she and Ned were approaching their fifth anniversary with nothing more than her monthly pains to show for it.

'You look beautiful, honey.' Ned put his arms around her waist from behind, running kisses down her neck, and straining to reach the plunging neckline.

She snuggled back against him, enjoying the attention and not wanting to break it with her news. That hurt every month too – having to tell him, yet again, that he wouldn't be a father. She knew how much he wanted it and couldn't help feeling that little ones in their nest would keep him at home, despite the frantic news from Europe calling him so frequently to work. Still, the world's affairs were more vital than her domestic ones right now and at least she was free to cover them alongside him.

'Shall we go down?' she asked as his attentions grew more amorous.

'Would it matter if we were a few minutes late...?'

'A *few minutes*?' She laughed.

'Well, you do look very delicious, my golden girl.'

She spun in his arms to kiss him. 'As do you, but I think that was the Churchills I heard arriving. I wouldn't want—'

It was enough. He was out of her arms immediately and smoothing her lipstick where he'd smudged it with his kiss.

'You're quite right. Let's to dinner, my lady.'

He proffered his arm and she took it, casting a last glance in the mirror at the elegant pair they made. They were two broadcasters together, living their dream in Europe, and that was what counted.

'Jenny! Ned!' Ronald drew them forward the moment they stepped into the drawing room. 'Let me introduce you. This is Nellie Romilly, Clementine's sister.' A petite, dark-haired woman, who looked very unlike tall, white-haired Mrs Churchill, waved from where she was pulling a rug around an elderly man's legs. 'And her husband, Bertram.'

Jenny just about managed to hide her surprise as she wished the thin-faced man good evening.

'Nellie nursed Bertie in the Great War,' Ronald's wife, Nancy, filled in.

'And ever since,' Bertram Romilly said with a wan smile. 'She's an angel.'

'She hasn't much choice,' said Mrs Churchill crisply.

'I'd rather tend my dear Bertie than your Winston and all his demanding dignitaries,' Nellie retorted. She came over, clasping Jenny's hand in a hearty shake. 'Pleased to meet you, Mrs Miller.'

'And you,' Jenny said, looking uncertainly between the sparring sisters. 'And you too, Mrs Churchill.'

Clementine Churchill took Jenny's hand in the slender but firm grip Jenny remembered so well from the Houses of Parliament.

'We met before,' she said in her beautiful English voice, 'but had no time to talk properly. I do apologise. Things were rather... hectic that day.'

'Hectic!' Winston exclaimed, holding his empty flute out to the butler circulating with a champagne bottle. 'Tragic is nearer the mark, Clemmie. That was the day bloody Neville went waltzing off to Munich to dance to Hitler's tune – which was not, mark you, a waltz at all!'

'As you said at the time, Mr Churchill,' Ned said keenly.

'As I said at the time, Mr Miller, for all anyone cared. And now look – Germany has allied with Russia and they're sharpening their knives to carve up poor Poland. Years, I've been warning everyone, but they didn't want to believe it possible that we could head to another war so soon.'

'Can you blame them, Winston?' Clementine said. 'We lost so many.'

Jenny looked at her curiously. Clementine Churchill was only fifty-four but she'd lived through so much.

'You must have been very young in the Great War,' she said, trying to work it out.

Clementine gave a startling snort of a laugh, quite at odds with her elegant appearance. 'Bless you, my dear, I was in my twenties, married and with three children – and a fourth barely days after the Armistice.'

Jenny's hand went instinctively to her stomach.

'Are you well?' Mrs Churchill asked.

Jenny flushed, mortified to be caught in her petty concerns. 'Quite well, thank you. Just, you know, the thought of war.'

'Oh, I do know. It's a tragedy when a few cold-hearted men rip up the lives of millions of innocents in their quest for power.'

Jenny blinked.

'Beautifully put,' Ned said. 'Have you considered going on the radio, Mrs Churchill?'

Again that laugh, gloriously brash and sudden. 'Good Lord no. Who'd want to listen to me?'

'Mrs Roosevelt broadcasts to America every Sunday night. And has a daily column in the papers.'

'She does? Why?'

'Because people are interested in what she has to say.'

'Ah,' Winston interposed, 'but Mrs Roosevelt is the wife of a president. My dear Mrs Churchill is the wife of a nobody, a man who, despite being right about every single move Hitler has made since 1933, is not even in the cabinet.'

'For now,' Bertram said. 'Surely Chamberlain will see sense soon, Winston?'

'As the people do,' Ned put in. 'I hear them talking about it in the streets, discussing it in the pubs. They know Hitler must be stopped. The nation is speaking and you, sir, are their voice.'

Winston beamed, his cherubic face turning a delighted pink. 'Thank you, young man. It's kind of you to say, but what use is a voice without power?'

Ned smiled. 'As a radio broadcaster, I would suggest that a

voice *is* power.' Winston stared at him, fascinated, and with a glance at Jenny, Ned went on. 'Radio goes deep into people's homes, into their lives, into their very hearts. That, surely, is both a power and a privilege.'

'Well said, by Jove! Very well said.' Winston clapped him on the back. 'See, Clemmie, I told you we needed the Americans on board.'

'I'm not sure we're quite the ones you need, sir,' Ned said.

Winston grinned. 'But you're all the ones we've got for now. Right, what's for dinner, Nancy, my dear? I could eat a horse.'

Dinner was not, thankfully, horse, but a series of delicate dishes that Jenny, still feeling sick and headachey, was embarrassed not to be able to enjoy fully. She saw Clementine Churchill watching her closely and was sure she thought she was being insulting to her gracious hosts but she simply could not eat as much as the quality of the food merited. The only person who ate less than her was Bertram Romilly, who didn't look as if he'd been able to get a decent meal down in ten years.

Jenny sipped at her wine and excused herself to the lavatory twice. Ned looked at her with concern but, thankfully, Winston Churchill held forth so loudly and so eloquently throughout dinner that her paltry contribution to the conversation went largely unnoticed. Afterwards, however, when the ladies withdrew (actually withdrew to another room, like in Jane Austen novels), it was a different matter.

'What did you think of the trifle?' Nancy Tree asked, pouring coffee. 'Cook was keen to try loganberries but I wasn't sure. Are they a little tart?'

'I thought it was delicious,' Jenny said.

'You barely touched it,' Clementine Churchill pointed out, quite correctly.

'I was very full from all the other amazing food.'

'Which you also barely touched.'

Jenny felt heat flush through her, pulsing from her aching belly. 'I'm sorry, I just...'

Mrs Churchill placed a warm hand on her knee. 'I'm not criticising, merely concerned. Are you not feeling well, my dear?'

Jenny flushed further. The older woman's blue eyes were looking at her with genuine concern and she felt tears prick in response and blinked them furiously away.

'You should have said. We women have much to put up with, do we not?'

'I...'

Now the tears did come, but Mrs Churchill was not fazed. Passing Jenny an embroidered handkerchief, she sat quietly at her side until she'd recovered her composure.

'Now, how about you tell us what's wrong?'

'It's silly.'

'I very much doubt it. You don't seem like a silly woman. Come, a problem shared is a problem halved.'

It seemed crazy. These sophisticated English women did not need to hear her petty troubles, but Nancy was so calm and Nellie so kind and Mrs Churchill's manner was so accepting that somehow it all came pouring out – how much she wanted a baby and how, month after month, her body confounded her.

'There now,' Mrs Churchill said. 'That wasn't so hard, was it? And it's not silly in the slightest. Of course it's going to hurt that God has not so blessed you – yet – but you're young and you have a fine husband and a happy marriage. There is plenty of time.'

'I'm nearly thirty,' Jenny said, tears threatening once more.

'Many women have babies well into their forties,' Mrs Churchill said. 'I worked in hostels and hospitals in the Great War and saw grandmothers giving birth. The worst thing you can do is worry about it. Now, I shall fetch you two painkillers, Nancy will pour you a nice strong brandy, and all will feel much better, trust me.' She patted Jenny's knee again and was gone, sliding from the room with barely a rustle of skirts.

Jenny looked after her, astonished.

Nancy laughed. 'Mrs Churchill is a woman of surprises, Mrs Miller.'

'I thought she was cross with me for dishonouring your delicious food, Mrs Tree.'

'Clementine? Oh no! She'll never be cross with you if you're genuine. It's fakes and shams she hates.'

'And people who drone on and on and on...' Nellie added with a laugh. 'Lordie, Winston was on fire tonight. I pity your poor husband, Jenny, for my brother-in-law will be going for hours more if he thinks he has a willing audience.'

'Ned will be more than willing. And Mr Churchill does speak very well.'

'Thank heavens for small mercies! Sometimes I don't know how Clemmie puts up with him.'

'Because she's a woman of surprises?' Jenny suggested.

Nellie laughed again. 'Exactly right! My sister has many interests, even if she insists on putting them second to his, God bless her. Have you seen her play tennis?'

Jenny shook her head.

'She's a marvel,' Nancy said. 'She used to win tournaments all over Europe when she was younger.'

'Not all over *Europe*,' Nellie objected.

Nancy waved a careless hand. 'Well, all over France then, though the pair of you are virtually natives there.'

'Natives?' Jenny looked curiously at Nellie, but Nancy was still going.

'She's got a fabulous golf swing, too. Beats Ronald most times, which infuriates him. And she can ski. That's to say, Mary says she can ski. You wouldn't catch me anywhere near those nasty cold mountains to find out.'

'She sounds swell,' Jenny said, dazed.

'She is. Stunning taste in interior design and what she can do with a small budget would amaze you.'

Jenny laughed. 'Surely she's never had to deal with a small budget?'

'Oh she has!' Nancy glanced to Nellie. 'Tell our guest where you grew up, Nell.'

'Dieppe,' Nellie supplied, adding happily, 'the seedier end.' Jenny goggled and Nancy let out a tinkling laugh. 'There's far more to Clementine Churchill than meets the eye, Mrs Miller. You should ask her to tell you about hunting dragons.'

'Dragons?' Jenny looked from Nellie to Nancy, her head whirling. Were they teasing her?

But no. Clementine swept back in and sat herself down with a casual, 'Not so much dragons, dear, as large lizards.'

'Do tell.'

'If you take these.' She passed her two tablets and waved the maid for a glass of water.

Jenny swallowed them obediently and looked to her for the story.

'It's not nearly as dramatic as Nellie makes it sound,' she started. 'I was invited on a yachting trip to the Pacific islands a few years ago by Walter Guinness, Lord Moyne, who was hunting down Komodo dragons and tuatara lizards for London Zoo. I was merely a hunting assistant, you understand, and, quite frankly, a useless one. On the day of the main hunt, climbing high into the tropical jungle, I was overcome by the heat and had to turn back for the boat.

'Walter offered to come with me, but he was hot on a trail and I had no intention of ruining the mission. Besides, the path was quite clearly marked – or so I thought. It turns out one palm tree looks very much like another, especially with most unladylike sweat in your eyes. I ended up horribly lost, silly ass, then caught my footing on a trailing vine and twisted my ankle. I think I may have blanked out, for the next thing I remember is a great big Komodo hissing at me from barely feet away.'

Jenny gasped and Clementine chuckled.

'It wasn't ideal. They're fierce creatures with teeth like knives.'

'What did you do?'

'Made a noise like hell rising! Startled it away and brought Walter's second officer running.'

'Did he catch it?'

She shook her head. 'Clever thing was long gone by the time he crashed into the clearing. I offered myself as bait another day but Walter was far too gentlemanly to take me up on it, and one of the big ones would have been very hard to get on the ship anyway. They caught five youngsters in the end. London Zoo were delighted. I believe several of them are still there. You should visit.'

'I will,' Jenny agreed eagerly. 'What an amazing journey.'

'It was. I've been very lucky. Winston and I get many kind invitations to stay in all sorts of exquisite places, like Ditchley here.'

She raised her coffee cup to Nancy, who smiled.

'Always a pleasure to have you, Clemmie. Winston too, though I fear the nation is going to claim him soon.'

'You think he'll be PM?' Nellie asked.

'I think he should,' Nancy said. She looked at Mrs Churchill. 'Would he want to be?'

'He'd love to,' she agreed instantly but her words were tight and her shoulders, beneath her silk gown, equally so.

Jenny, her belly soothed by this intriguing woman's kind tablets and her heart by her even kinder words, leaned forward in concern. 'And you?' she asked. 'Would *you* want him to be?'

Clementine gave a long sigh. 'I'm not sure that matters. He told me, when he proposed, that he wanted to be prime minister one day.'

'The old romantic!' Nellie laughed.

'Not in the actual proposal, Nell, as well you know.' She looked back to Jenny. 'It was a little before. We were walking the gardens at Blenheim, you see, round and round and round. It turns out he was trying to get up the courage to speak, but for once it was failing him.'

'So he told you he wanted to be prime minister instead?' Jenny asked.

'We were talking about life goals. He was trying to warn me, to explain to me the sort of life that he wanted so that I was... abreast of all the facts before he laid his suit before me.'

'Laid his suit!' Nellie laughed. 'You do talk rot, Clemmie.'

Jenny didn't think it was rot; she thought it was fascinating.

'How old was he?' she asked.

'Thirty-three, and already the youngest cabinet minister in a hundred years. He was making quite a name for himself and he wanted me to know how committed he was to the political life.'

'And goodness, isn't he just!' Nancy said. 'Plenty of men would have given up and let it go after ten years out of ministerial position.'

'But not Winston,' Clementine agreed. 'Which is simply him keeping his promise. So, you see, Mrs Miller, I can't complain.'

'*Won't* complain,' said their hostess, 'which is why I have to do it for her. If Nellie is an angel for looking after dear Bertram then Clemmie is a saint for sticking it out with Winston.'

Clementine shook her head. 'Don't listen to them, Mrs Miller. Winston can be awkward at times, but he's passionate and driven and consistent. If he thinks he can be prime minister, then I'm still as here for him as the day I said, "I do".'

'That's lovely,' Jenny said.

Mrs Churchill smiled but her sister rolled her eyes.

'It *is* lovely but, Lord help you both, Clemmie. If he's right about Herr Hitler, then what a time to become prime minister. I wouldn't wish it on my worst enemy!'

'What will be, will be,' Clementine said primly, but Jenny felt the strain in the words as, through the door, the sound of the men's voices raised in fierce debate cut the peace of the evening.

Sitting in this beautiful mansion, it was hard to imagine Great Britain at war, but if the Churchills were right, that was exactly what would happen. And the Churchills, she was learning, were usually right. She and Ned had come to England to report on the drama of events unfolding in central Europe, but those events were now heading inexorably their way and her adopted country might soon be a war zone.

FIVE

MORPETH MANSIONS, LONDON, 3
SEPTEMBER 1939

CLEMENTINE

Clementine had rarely felt more helpless in her life save, perhaps, that dark time in Dieppe all those years ago. And of course when Marigold... She shut her mind to the dark thoughts; they wouldn't help anyone. The world was seething and there seemed little they could do to calm it down. She watched Winston, standing with his nose pressed against the window of their Morpeth Mansions apartment, straining to see the roofs of his beloved Whitehall shimmering in the sun of this late-summer Sunday morning, and her heart ached for him.

For them all.

She glanced to the clock. Ten minutes to eleven; ten minutes to Chamberlain's deadline to Germany; ten minutes for the power-crazy Führer to withdraw his troops from Poland, or it would be war. Hitler had invaded Poland three days ago and today the whole country would see that Winston's endless 'ravings' of the last decade had been right. Hitler had played them all for fools, buying time to arm himself to the teeth while everyone else had half-heartedly polished up a few rusty guns. Now they had to take those guns into the fight against the lethal Messerschmitt planes and Panzer tanks.

Clementine smoothed her frock, a short-sleeved black day dress that felt suitably sombre for the news they were expecting.

'Shall I turn on the wireless?' she suggested.

Winston glared at the radiogram. He hated having to hear this news with the rest of the country, but hated even more being in the House and excluded from the cabinet room, so here they were, sitting like countless other couples to hear the fate of their country.

'I suppose you'd better.'

Five to eleven.

Clementine rose and turned the dial. A crackle of static filled their drawing room as she tuned it to the new Home Service, but the airwaves were empty.

'Course Neville won't broadcast bang on the deadline,' Winston growled. 'He'll give Herr Hitler at least fifteen minutes to change his mind. Idiot!'

'There will be administrative issues to resolve...' Clementine started, but stopped herself. He didn't want to hear. She sat down again, fiddling with her pearl earrings as she willed the news to come.

A voice broke into the room, but only to tell them to tune in for an important announcement from Downing Street at 11.15.

'What did I tell you?' Winston pointed his cigar at her. 'Right again.'

'I never said you were not, Winston. Now sit down. You're making me nervous.'

'*I'm* making you nervous! That's rich. Me, not Herr Hitler?'

Clementine rolled her eyes. 'Don't be insufferable, Winston, you know what I mean.'

He sank into the armchair with a harrumph. 'I don't even

know why we're listening. We know what's going to happen. We've known it for years.'

'But this is still it. This is still the moment. Hush now.'

He sat back, quiet for once, then suddenly leaned over and clasped her hand. 'You know, Clemmie, don't you, that I don't want war?'

She looked at him, surprised. 'Of course I know, Pug.'

He smiled at the endearment. Shy at expressing their newfound devotion for one another when first married, they'd retreated into pet names, she his sleek 'Kat' and he her faithful Pug. The terms had stuck and, even now, rarely a note was passed between them without a cartoon picture of their little love-animals.

'Thank you, my Kat,' he said, taking her hand. 'I wish others understood me as you do. They call me the warmonger in the House, but I never wanted war. I simply knew it was coming.'

'I know.'

'Being right about it is painful. I'd far rather have been wrong.'

She clutched at his hand. 'I know!'

'Still.' He bounced back with his usual irrepressible style. 'At least Neville will have to have me in the cabinet now. Won't he?'

'There'll be an outcry if he doesn't. Hush, here it comes.'

Winston set his cigar in the ashtray and sat, straining towards the wireless, his hand holding Clementine's so tightly she feared her fingers might crack.

'This is London speaking,' the voice said. 'And now we have an announcement from the prime minister.'

Neville Chamberlain's voice leaked into their drawing room, calm and measured. 'This morning, the British Ambassador in Berlin handed the German government a final note stating that unless we heard from them by eleven o'clock that they were prepared at once to withdraw their troops from Poland, a state of war would exist between us. I have to tell you now that no such undertaking has been received, and that consequently this country is at war with Germany.'

There was a pause and then more words, an outpouring of instructions and recommendations. Clementine heard phrases like 'air-raid shelter' and 'gas mask', talk of theatres closing and sports being suspended, but none of it went in. This was like a death. Years ago, she'd sat at her mother's bedside with her sister Nellie for endless hours. Lady Blanche had drawn in persistently weaker breaths but even so, when the last one had finally come, it had been a shock. It felt the same way now.

'That's it then, Pug.'

'That's it, Kat. Here we go again.'

Still they sat there, welded into their home in what might be the last minutes of normality, until, with a fearful shriek, a siren wailed out.

Winston leaped to his feet. 'Air raid? Already? Come, Clemmie.' He yanked her up after him.

'To the shelter?'

'No, my dear – to the roof. Let's see what the Hun has in store for us.'

They panted up the stairs, but on the roof they could only see fat barrage balloons floating over the city like oversized children's toys. The siren was still wailing and people were scurrying for shelters, but the skies remained serenely clear and blue. Directly below them a man in a Great War uniform with an air-raid warden band wrapped proudly around his upper arm, called officiously up at them to 'get the hell down from there'.

'Doesn't he know who I am?' Winston demanded, then tutted at himself. 'Of course he doesn't. Nobody knows who I am.'

That was patently untrue, but Clementine was not about to indulge his histrionics with the Luftwaffe due.

'He's just doing his job, Winston. Let's go to the shelter.'

For months, the London authorities had been designating Tube stations, cellars and underground restaurants as shelters in the event of war. She and Winston had been informed by an officious elderly warden of the location of their closest one, but it felt unreal that they were actually using it. And so fast.

'I'll need supplies,' Winston grumbled, dashing into the apartment to snatch a bottle of his favourite Hine cognac, before leading her to the street shelter.

A one-time wine cellar, it was dank and crowded, filled with a babble of frightened chatter. No one paid them any attention, save two young lads who reluctantly obeyed their mother's order to 'squeeze up and make space for the nice couple to sit'. The door was open to let others inside but no sound of an aeroplane engine penetrated their cellar, no bombs shook the earth above them. Before Winston could even crack the cork on his cognac, the all-clear sounded.

'False alarm,' the warden said cheerily. 'I guess someone on the controls panicked. All home, folks. Hope no one's dinner's burned.'

Clementine followed two women, whose main concern seemed to be whether their Yorkshire puddings would have gone flat, and felt a rush of love for the British people. She had no firm idea what might be about to happen, but she did know they would meet it with the resilience and steady humour of a country well-used to rain spoiling their parade. She was turning to say this to Winston when his valet pulled open their apartment door with the telephone in his hand.

'It's for you, sir. Number Ten.'

. . .

Half an hour later, Clementine sat fidgeting in the car outside the iconic black door of Number Ten Downing Street, trying to imagine the conversations going on inside. Chamberlain had conceded quickly that he needed her husband, but what would he offer Winston? What would Winston take?

He'd held several ministerial roles in the past. First, secretary of the Board of Trade at just thirty-three, then home secretary in the early years of their marriage. That had come with all the pain of the suffragettes. Winston had not agreed with votes for women – the cause of many an argument – but mistreating them had gone against every chivalrous bone in his body. Not that they'd realised that. She could still remember the time he'd been attacked in Bristol railway station. The suffragette had almost whipped him under an oncoming train while his so-called bodyguards had stood there, stunned. It had been left to Clementine to vault a clutch of cases and grab him back from the brink. Later, curled up in bed together, he'd told her, 'If all women were like you, I'd definitely give them the vote.' It had been a classically Winstonian compromise. These days she might have responded to it with indignation on behalf of other women without her privileges but, back then, only a year into marriage, she had simply kissed him.

Then, of course, he'd been first lord of the Admiralty, in charge of the whole Royal Navy. He'd loved that. And he'd loved Admiralty House, right on the corner of Horse Guards Parade, at the heart of Westminster. The four-storey building, built of fine yellow brick, was grand but ridiculously impractical to run. His salary had been reasonable but the housing costs, including the dozen staff, had fallen to them and, with little personal money and two small children, it had been hard.

Clementine twiddled her ruby earring round and round. Money had always been tight back then. If she was honest, it still was. Winston earned a small fortune from his books, but he spent a large one on fine wines, fancy underclothes and endless 'improvements' to Chartwell. *Please,* she sent into Number Ten, *don't let it be first lord again.* Admiralty House was a burden they could do without.

The last time, despite her husband's love of the position, had ended in a disaster that still haunted Winston in his sleep. Even now, he would sometimes creep into her bedroom in the darkest hours of the night with a whispered request for a hug. Those were the times she knew he'd been woken by nightmares about the Dardanelles.

The Dardanelles were the channel from the eastern Mediterranean into the Black Sea and had been key to a bold plan in 1915 to take Turkey and provide a southern base from which to attack Germany. It should have worked, *would* have worked if the army and the navy had been prepared to put away their schoolboy differences and coordinate their attacks. Instead, they had delayed and game-played themselves into a trap that had cost many innocent men their lives – and Winston his position. He had been the boldest proponent of the Dardanelles scheme, and those most at fault had been sharp enough to palm it off on him. It still hurt.

Please don't let it be first lord, Clementine begged again.

With a rattle of seeming response, the door of Number Ten swung open and Winston came out, bobbing and smiling. Camera bulbs popped and he offered the journalists a cheery wave then slid into the car at her side.

'So?' she asked.

'Good news.'

'Yes...?'

'You need to pack.'

'Chancellor?'

'No.'

'Foreign minister?'

'No.'

'Home Office?'

'No, thank heavens.' He grabbed her hands, bouncing on the seat in excitement. 'It's first lord, Clemmie. First lord again at last. Is that not wonderful?'

'Wonderful,' she agreed faintly and shook a silent fist at the skies.

God and the government were, it seemed, conspiring to confound her – as usual.

They lunched at their daughter Sarah's apartment in Westminster Gardens, all the family called in to hear Papa's news and converging in noisy chaos. Sarah and her husband, Vic, drew every new arrival eagerly inside, plying them with cocktails mixed with all the drama of their chosen profession, but with a notable lack of teamwork. Watching closely, Clementine could see Sarah moving gingerly around her husband and her heart squeezed. She must talk with her second daughter about her married life, though Lord knows when there would be time if she had to move into Admiralty House.

Diana, her eldest, arrived with Duncan, shepherding their two children loudly, then Randolph sauntered in from his apartment below Sarah's, bringing his fiancé, Pamela Digby, and drawing attention away from the little ones. Theirs had been a whirlwind romance, Randolph proposing a mere eight days after he'd met the girl and, perhaps more tellingly, not much more since he'd proposed to another – and another, and another – in a run of frankly desperate propositions once he'd signed up to the Oxfordshire Hussars, his father's old regiment.

'I need a wife, Mummy,' he'd said. 'There's going to be a war and Papa will be devastated if I die without siring a Churchill heir.'

'Papa will be devastated if you die at all,' she'd told him, which was true. The girls were always complaining that, despite Randolph creating the most trouble for and paying the least attention to their father, Winston still doted on him. It was the son thing – so pathetically traditional of him. It disappointed Clementine if she thought about it too closely, so she did her best not to. 'And *I* will be devastated,' she'd gone on, 'if you take on a wife to whom you are unsuited. Look what happened to poor Diana, divorced within a year.'

'Pam is nothing like Diana,' Randolph had declared firmly.

'How do you know? You've barely been seeing her a month.'

'I've been seeing her long enough to know she's jolly good fun.'

From what Clementine had seen of her prospective daughter-in-law, that was certainly true. Pam was a bouncy, plumply pretty nineteen-year-old with sparkling eyes, a wicked smile and an easy manner. She'd grown up with her parents, Lord and Lady Digby, on their estate of Minterne Magna in Dorset, and Clementine had feared she would be gauche, but the girl was a natural socialite. She watched her now, teasing Vic into mixing her an extra-strong cocktail with a gay laugh, and prayed Randolph treated her well. Only time would tell and perhaps marriage – and war – would settle her son.

The noise levels grew but Clementine eagerly watched the door for the final family member and was relieved when Mary burst in, full of hugs for everyone. She threw Diana's children in the air, asked her soon-to-be sister-in-law about wedding plans, and slung a protective arm around Sarah's shoulders as Vic began grumbling about the theatres closing. Her youngest child was utterly without rancour or resentment, Clementine thought, and sat more easily in her chair as Winston took centre stage.

The announcement that he was first lord was met with predictable squeals of enthusiasm. None of the rest of the family ever doubted Winston's abilities. Only Clementine questioned him. But, then, someone had to or family life would be flung into total chaos rather than simply walking its usual teetering precipice.

'Mary!' Sarah said. 'You shall live in the Admiralty – how grand.'

'I don't know about grand,' Mary countered, 'but it's right next to Horse Guards Parade. I'll be able to see the horses from my bedroom window every day. Will they let me ride one, do you think?'

'Course not,' Randolph said. 'They're professional fighting beasts, not little girls' ponies.'

Mary turned puce but before she could protest, Pamela said, 'Randy, don't be so mean. Mary is a talented rider. She jumped that huge hedge at Chartwell, remember, the one your horse baulked at.'

Randolph gasped, Mary clapped, and Clementine could have kissed the newest nearly family member. Perhaps this marriage would work out after all.

'Shall we have luncheon?' she said, before the arguments could break out again. 'Something smells delicious.'

'Beef stew,' Sarah provided.

Clementine glanced out the window at the warm September skies, wishing it could have been a nice light salad, but Winston rubbed his hands together delightedly.

'My favourite.'

That, of course, was why Sarah was serving it and, to be fair, today was Winston's day. Besides, with war officially declared, meat might become horribly scarce so she should enjoy it while she could.

'A toast!' Winston proposed as they skirmished for places around the table. The family raised hastily filled glasses, faces upturned to their father. Winston thought a moment and Clementine feared they would be in for a long speech but instead he drew in a deep breath and, looking fondly around, said two simple words: 'To victory.'

'To victory,' everyone chorused.

Clementine sipped her drink. Champagne seemed wrong with the first air-raid sirens ringing in their ears, but there was nowhere to live bar the present and, for now, with her family together, and just about getting on with each other, that was a good place to be.

'Will people evacuate, do you think?' Sarah asked, glancing to Vic.

'If they've got any sense,' Vic said. 'Especially those with relatives in America.'

'Like you?' Randolph said.

'Yes, but like all of you too. Your grandmother must still have family over there, so why not just—'

'No!' Winston said, stamping his foot.

Vic jumped. 'No? Just like that?'

'No one in my family will be leaving Great Britain. What would it say about their belief in the ability of their government to keep them safe?'

Vic flushed. 'I hadn't thought about it like that.'

'Which is why I am in charge of the country, and you are not.'

'Not entirely in charge, Winston,' Duncan pointed out. 'You're not the prime minister.'

'Not yet,' he shot back. 'But I *am* in the cabinet and our position is clear – we need the Americans over here, helping us, not over there harbouring runaways.'

Clementine supposed he was right and made a mental note to keep an eye on the movements of the wider family. She thought of the charming young couple she'd met at Ditchley, Jenny and Ned Miller. She must seek Jenny out, make use of her clear talents and ensure she felt welcome in the country she had so bravely espoused in these troubled times. There would be much to do on the home front and—

'Goodness, Mummy,' Mary said into her thoughts, 'does this make you the first lady of the Admiralty?'

'Oh no—' she started, but Winston cut across her protests.

'Your mother,' he said, in his usual grand style, 'is the first lady of everything!'

And then they were all raising glasses and toasting her, and she felt herself blush with pleasure at their undeserved praise – and resolved to match up to it, come what may.

SIX

FULMER CHASE MATERNITY HOSPITAL, BUCKINGHAMSHIRE, FEBRUARY 1940

JENNY

Jenny drew her notebook from her bag with determination. She'd been invited to the opening of the Fulmer Chase Maternity Hospital by Mrs Churchill and, of the many journalists present, was one of only two women. She must be a focused CBS reporter, not someone desperate to be in the situation of the six women in the beds before her. She made a brisk note:

> *All patients look comfortable and happy in the sparkling maternity hospital at Fulmer Chase, content to be cared for in their confinement while their husbands are bravely leading the troops into battle in France.*

Tapping her pen against her teeth, she considered the best way to frame the report when she recorded it for the radio, then wrote again:

> *This hospital, specially created for the wives of officers so their husbands can give their all for the country without worrying*

about their precious families back home, is the brainchild of Mrs Clementine Churchill, wife of the first lord of the Admiralty.

She stopped, feeling a tug of annoyance. The hospital *was* wonderful and Mrs Churchill *was* wonderful for setting it up, but her recent untimely interference in Jenny's new project had been less so. With the war now six months old and mired in strange inaction, Jenny had joined the American Committee for the Evacuation of Children to get at-risk British youngsters across the Atlantic. Their safety was the paramount concern but there was a hope, too, that their appearance in the States would force Americans to see the realities of war and offer more help. This was something Winston Churchill was desperate for, which is what had made it so galling when, last week, his wife had stepped in to stop five-year-old Sally Churchill, her great-niece, from taking up her place on a ship to the States with her nanny.

It had been horribly dramatic, with a car screeching up to Waterloo station to snatch Sally's passport and forcibly prevent her boarding the train to the coast. The press had reported it in lurid detail under unhelpful headlines like *First lord blocks children leaving for safety in America*. It had been most embarrassing for the organisation and especially for Jenny who, she had to admit, had been rather flaunting the fact that she'd met the famous couple.

She looked across the ward to where Mrs Churchill, elegant in a fitted dress with a peplum hem was talking to one of the lucky soon-to-be-mothers. She was asking earnest questions and really listening to the answers, and Jenny couldn't understand why such a caring woman would stop her niece moving to safety in the States. She started to move forward, but was distracted by a rush of noise at the door and looked curiously over to see an attractive woman in the most beautiful fur coat arriving on a trill of laughter.

Journalists crowded around and Jenny recognised Pamela Digby – or Pamela Churchill as she was now. Her wedding to Randolph Churchill last October had been all over the press as the 'first war wedding' and they'd been pictured at various events ever since.

'Isn't this place just darling!' Pamela exclaimed, wafting immaculately manicured hands around the ward. 'Such lucky women, getting to give birth here.' She looked around and then dropped in, 'Maybe I'll do so myself if dear Randolph is posted overseas...'

The surprise announcement set off a furore of questions and Jenny saw the pretty young woman draw back her fancy fur coat and run her perfect hands over what was still a very flat stomach. Her heart lurched. The other reporters pressed for more on the Churchill baby – 'a boy, bound to be' – and the due date – 'sometime in October, so let's hope this beastly war is over by then' – and Pamela's father-in-law's reaction – 'He's over the moon, bless him. Another Churchill for the world!'

Jenny made a few desultory notes, but it was hard to feel the delight everyone else was noisily expressing. 'Envy is a deadly sin, Jenny,' she chided under her breath.

She reminded herself that Ned was a far nicer husband than boorish Randolph Churchill but still couldn't help staring at Pamela's midriff, so easily filled with a child after only a few months of marriage. She fled through to the next ward, but came slap-bang up against three rows of cosy cots. In the nearest one a tiny baby was sleeping, its hands splayed like starfishes above its head. The blanket was blue and a label on the side proclaimed him to be Ernie Jonathan Proctor, Fulmer Chase's first newborn. The mother was recorded as Maisie and the father as Sergeant Ernest Proctor, currently serving at Vimy.

Jenny made a note of the details – the personal angle was

always effective – and tried very hard not to imagine a minia-
ture Ned Miller lying there waiting for his proud father to come
and see his newborn son and heir. Her arms ached to hold the
tiny bundle and she dropped her pen, sending it clattering to
the floor. The infant startled, its blue eyes flying open and its
starfish hands twitching in fright, and Jenny held her breath,
ashamed of herself. Little Ernie, however, simply pursed his
lips, let out a tiny sigh, and went back to sleep.

'Gorgeous, isn't he?' an older man said, stepping up to
retrieve her pen.

'Gorgeous,' she agreed, checking his badge: Reggie Green of
the *Daily Mail*.

'Mind you, they always are when they're asleep,' Reggie
went on. 'My three were angels in their cots – devils the rest of
the time. Do you have children?'

'No. That is, not yet.'

'Career girl, hey?'

'Not really, I—'

'Is your husband happy with that?'

A flush of anger rose beneath her skin. 'Very happy, thank
you. We work for CBS together.'

'CBS! Ah, you're American.' Reggie let out a throaty cackle.
'That explains it. Things a bit more "modern" over there, are
they? Here, we like to support our women to stay at home and
raise a family.'

'As do we, thank you very much. I just—' She cut herself off.
She did not need to justify her life choices to this presumptuous
old hack. Plucking her pen from his meaty fingers with a crisp,
'thank you', she strode away.

'Where you going?' Reggie asked, apparently unable to believe
she'd had enough of his opinions on her reproductive status.

'To interview Mrs Churchill,' she shot back.

'You won't get close, love. She's very busy.'

'Don't worry, she'll talk to me. She invited me personally.' She gave him her sweetest smile and headed back into the pre-natal ward, making straight for Mrs Churchill. Reggie Green was watching and she wouldn't give him the satisfaction of seeing her fail.

'Mrs Miller!' Mrs Churchill shook her hand with a broad smile. 'I'm delighted to find you amidst this pleasing crowd at last. I'm so glad you could make it. What do you think of our little venture?'

'It's marvellous,' Jenny said truthfully.

'Winston is delighted with it – says it'll stop the men being distracted from their duties in the field. I'm sure that's true and obviously an advantage in the war, but my thoughts were all for these poor women stuck here alone at a frankly terrifying point in their lives.'

Jenny warmed to her instantly. It was impossible not to, though that didn't mean she wasn't still annoyed about the incident at Waterloo. She cleared her throat, wondering how best to broach the issue of young Sally Churchill.

'Children are so important,' she started.

'They are,' Mrs Churchill agreed. 'And mothers even more so. It's a hellish business giving birth – breaks your body apart and does more or less the same thing for your life.'

Jenny blinked at the vehemence in her tone. 'I wouldn't know,' she said dully.

'Oh my dear, I'm so sorry!' Mrs Churchill took her arm. 'How tactless of me. I didn't think. Unforgivable.'

'Not at all.' Now Jenny was embarrassed. 'I'm here to do a job.'

'Of course, and I'm sure you'll do it very well indeed, but that doesn't stop you being human, with natural reactions. Why don't we ask Maisie if you can hold Baby Ernie? They say that gives the body a bit of a reminder of what it's there for. That's to say...' She put a gloved hand to her mouth. 'I'm not getting this right, I'm sorry.'

'Not at all, you're trying to be kind.'

'Trying but not succeeding. Tell you what, shall we have some tea? My new cook at the Admiralty, Mrs Landermare, has sent down a batch of her finest fruit cake, sweetened with Chartwell honey. You must try it. She's working wonders with rationing. Winston is over the moon we've found her – says he can't possibly make important decisions on an empty stomach.'

'I'm sure he's right.' Jenny was feeling overwhelmed. She'd forgotten how kind Mrs Churchill was, though she'd not been kind to her great-niece, not at all. Jenny had to ask her about that, but right now it was rather nice to be escorted personally through to the teas past a gaping Reggie Green. No doubt he'd be sniping to his fellow hacks about unnatural women reporters but she doubted anything she could say would change that and at least she'd have personal quotes from the first lord's wife for her broadcast.

Teas were laid out in the post-natal ward, occupied, so far, only by Maisie Proctor. Little Ernie had woken and was nestled at her breast, discreetly covered by a snowy shawl. Maisie's mother was bustling proudly around and Jenny felt another pull of longing, this time for her mother, far away in Connecticut.

'How are you getting on in London?' Mrs Churchill asked.

Jenny turned to her, unreasonably out of sorts once more. 'I was getting on very well.'

'Was?'

'I've been working with the American Committee for the Evacuation of Children.'

'I see.' Mrs Churchill looked wary, as well she might. 'An interesting project.'

There were people crowding around, understandably keen to talk to Mrs Churchill about the hospital, and Jenny knew she had to speak now.

'And one you will know all about, Mrs Churchill. I believe you, er, interjected personally last week.'

Clementine Churchill gave her a sharp look. 'You're referring to my great-niece, Sally Churchill? I most certainly did. I'm sure what you are doing is excellent for many young children, Mrs Miller, but not for my family.'

'Because?'

'Because Winston is part of the cabinet, part of those making crucial decisions about the progress of the war. Running away implies a lack of confidence in those decisions. The royals are not going, are they? You don't catch the queen sending her princesses off to Canada as if her country is not good enough for them, and we feel the same. Sally fleeing would have undermined Winston's position and I cannot have that.'

Jenny stared at her. She did have a point, she supposed, and she felt her anger dropping, though only a little.

'It's not fleeing, surely, but evacuation? Thousands of children are doing it.'

'Not *my* children,' Mrs Churchill said again. 'It's just not our way, I'm sorry. My mother taught me long ago to stand up to your enemies and it's a lesson that has stuck.'

Her chin had gone up and her eyes had hardened and Jenny sensed a personal hurt.

'What sort of enemies must your poor mother have had to have to teach you such a lesson?' she asked lightly.

Mrs Churchill's chin rose further. 'My father,' she replied crisply, then she was striding forward saying, 'Come on, before the fruit cake is all gone.'

Jenny understood the subject to be dismissed. She respected that and she was not going to be like creepy Reggie Green, prying into someone else's world, but she couldn't help but be fascinated, both by Clementine Churchill's past and her plans for the war ahead. She truly hoped she would get a chance to know more of both.

SEVEN

ADMIRALTY HOUSE, 7 MAY 1940

CLEMENTINE

Clementine gripped the telephone receiver tightly, feeling torn. At the end of the corridor, Winston strode past his secretary, tapping his watch and saying they had to get to the House. After a winter of suffocating inactivity, Hitler had jumped at last, attacking Scandinavia, taking Denmark in a day and marching all over Norway. German forces were massing on the Dutch and Belgium borders, pushing the Allies back. France, as Winston had once said, would be next, then only the thin strip of the Channel would protect Great Britain. Chamberlain was facing a vote of no confidence and Westminster was demanding a coalition government under either Winston or Lord Halifax. It was a critical time – but not just for Winston.

Clementine tried to concentrate on what her sister was saying at the other end of the line.

'It's not like I didn't know it was coming,' Nellie wept. 'Poor Bertie has been ill for so long.'

'Ever since the Great War,' Clementine said gently.

Nellie's grief for her husband vibrated down the phone line;

she needed her sister, but the timing was terrible. Clementine fiddled with her diamond stud earrings, feeling one of them worrying loose, like everything else. She should leap on a train to Nellie's estate in Herefordshire to comfort her and help with arrangements for Bertram's funeral. That was her duty and she wanted to do it, of course she did. Except that Winston...

She fondly watched him fussing over his choice of hats. For the last thirty years, Clementine had stood at his side as, together, they'd fought for his political advancement. How, at the very point it might all be coming to fruition, could she abandon him?

'I'll come as soon as I can,' she assured a still weeping Nellie. Her sister had never been as resilient as Clementine – or Kitty. If only their older sister were here to help, Clementine thought longingly, but she'd been lost to them long ago and it was all down to her.

'How soon will that be?' Nellie asked.

'Soon. Let me go now and I can get things organised.'

She put the phone down and went to say good luck to Winston. He was still in a fluster over hats, but stopped when he saw her face.

'What's happened?' He came over, taking her hands and looking into her eyes, everything else forgotten.

Oh, she loved him then.

'It's Bertram...'

'He's gone? Oh, my dear, I'm so sorry.'

He held her fast in his steady grip and Clementine leaned against him, tipping her head onto his shoulder and letting his care soothe her. She could sense the secretary fidgeting behind them but Winston paid him no attention.

'You must go to her, Clemmie.'

'But you—'

'Are a big boy and can cope alone for a day or two.'

'But the vote, the leadership...'

'Will take days to thrash out. You know what us politicians are like. It takes endless pontificating to make a minor decision let alone a great big one like this.' He took her face in his soft hands and planted a kiss on her lips. 'It's your sister, Kat, she needs you. I will manage.'

'Really?'

'Really.' He smiled. 'Go while you can. If this nonsense happens to unfold our way, I'll be a demanding pain in the posterior for as long as it takes to whack Herr Hitler into oblivion.'

'Thank you, Winston.'

He tutted. 'Thank you! Goodness, I'm not that selfish, Clemmie. Not all the time anyway.' He winked and kissed her again. 'Give Nellie my love, will you, and tell her I'm so sorry I can't be there.'

And then he was gone, whisked off to the House to fight for his dream, while Clementine turned her reluctant steps to Herefordshire.

Colonel Bertram Romilly was buried in the churchyard of St Thomas à Becket, Huntingdon, with all honours. Clementine stood tight at Nellie's side as he was piped into the church by the Scots Guards, but, to her shame, it was hard to stop her thoughts straying to what might be happening in Westminster.

Chamberlain had survived the vote of no confidence but by so few votes that it had been a pointless victory. The heated session had ended, so Winston had gleefully reported, with Leo Amery, in a Cromwellian flourish, berating the beleaguered prime minister to, 'In the name of God, go!' The House had adjourned at 11.30 p.m. amidst chaos and the next day Chamberlain had been openly jeered. His resignation was expected and Clementine chafed against the fates that had taken her away at this nexus in her husband's life.

'Chamberlain wants Halifax,' Winston had said yesterday, the phone line crackly, though not as broken as her husband's voice when he'd added, 'so does the king.'

That hurt, she knew. Winston was an ardent supporter of the monarchy but King George had been wary of him since he'd foolishly supported the then King Edward during the abdication crisis. It would be a long way back into royal trust.

'He will learn what a good man you are once you're in power,' she'd assured him. 'Far better than Halifax.'

'Halifax is lazy,' Winston had agreed, buoyed up again. 'He doesn't want the pressures of the job.'

'That's hardly a valid reason.'

'No.'

There was a full choral mass after the committal and Clementine, despite her rigid schooling in etiquette, struggled to stop herself twitching through the endless psalms. At last, they were released to a nearby hotel for the welcome balm of wine and shared memories, but Clementine was ever alert for a bellboy with news of a phone call and almost jumped on the lad when he finally appeared.

'Mrs Churchill? Telephone for you.'

She took the call standing in a small booth in the lobby. The bellboy brought a padded chair and she felt obliged to sit on it, though she was far too agitated to settle.

'How was the funeral?' Winston's voice was calm. Too calm, perhaps?

'Beautiful. Very well done. The pipers were magnificent.'

'Good, good.'

'And you? What news with you?' The pause was unbearable, but then came a low, throaty chuckle. 'Winston, are you...?'

'Not yet, my dear. There is still pontificating to be had, but we are close. Halifax says it would not be right for a peer of the realm, unelected by the people, to stand as their leader in this time of crisis.'

'Then surely you—?'

'The decision has gone to Attlee to approve.'

'Attlee? What has it to do with the leader of the opposition?'

'They are the opposition no longer. This is to be a coalition government, so we must... coalesce.'

Clementine fiddled at her earrings – sombre jet studs. 'How will he make his decision?'

'He is taking it to Bournemouth.'

'Bournemouth?' Clementine's head spun.

'Where the Labour Party are in conference. They will decide tomorrow. Clemmie...' His steady calm broke. 'Will you come home? Will you come home to me?'

'Of course. Oh, Winston, of course I will. I'll get the first train in the morning.'

'Nellie won't mind too much?'

'Of course not.'

Nellie did mind, but there was nothing to be done about it.

'The world needs you, Clemmie,' she said, flinging herself onto her favourite chaise longue once they were finally alone, 'so who am I to hold you back for my petty concerns?'

'The world needs *Winston*,' Clementine corrected her melodramatic sister.

'But Winston needs you and that, in the end, amounts to much the same thing. You must go, sister, and with my blessing.'

'Thank you, Nell.'

'I shall be exhausted anyway, after all this sadness. I shall probably take to my bed.'

Clementine was not to be drawn. 'It is probably best,' she said. 'And I will be back soon.'

'Back in Herefordshire? I very much doubt it. You, my dear, will be moving into Number Ten.'

It sounded ridiculous in Nellie's petulant tones but the next day, leaping out of a taxi at Admiralty House, she found Winston getting ready to go out, fussing over his hats, as if he had simply been suspended in the cloakroom for the three days she'd been away.

'Clemmie!' He pulled her inside. 'You're just in time, for I am off across the park.'

'To the palace?' she gasped.

'The very same. Chamberlain has resigned and the king has summoned me.'

'To ask you to form a government?'

'Either that or to offer me a job as his butler.'

'Winston! Don't joke.'

He held her close and she felt, to her astonishment, that he was shaking.

'Wait for me, Clemmie.'

'Always.'

She did not have long to wait. He was back within the hour and she was behind the door to meet him, barely restraining herself from rushing onto Horse Guards Parade like a young girl.

'So...?'

'So, Mrs Churchill...' He took her in his arms. 'You are now the wife of the prime minister of Great Britain and her empire.'

'Oh, Winston!'

'I told you, did I not, when I was trying to pluck up the courage to ask the gorgeous, willowy, astonishingly fascinating creature that you were – and still are – that I would one day be prime minister.'

'You did,' she agreed, remembering him, unusually flushed and tongue-tied, leading her round and round the vast Blenheim estate under louring skies, before finally rain had forced them into the pretty Temple of Diana and he had declared his hand. 'And I believed you.'

'Your faith is stronger than mine, Kat, for I lost it in those dark years of the thirties, when I seemed to be railing into a void.'

Clementine closed her eyes and saw him, framed against the windows of the Chartwell dining room, shouting against appeasement until her head rang with the echoes of his anger.

'This, surely, is not how you would have wanted it?'

He clasped her close. 'Of course not, but it is what I have been handed and I will do it to the very best of my ability – with your help.'

'I am here for you.'

'I have been a pain.'

'You have been *in* pain. Now, at least, you can act.'

'Now, at least, I can *lead*. The rest will be up to the ability and bravery of the fine men of this country.'

'And women.'

He smiled. 'How can I doubt it. You women are stronger than any of us dare to imagine. And you the strongest of them all.'

Clementine did not think that true but if he did, that was what counted. She looked around, unable to believe they were leaving the Admiralty so fast, though this time up the road to Downing Street. At last! She had not, in truth, accepted his marriage proposal because of promises of greatness, money or fame. She had accepted it because his passion for life and his curiosity about the world had awakened hers. It was now about to be tested to its limits.

'God help us, that fool Chamberlain will have the Wehrmacht at our door within weeks,' Winston had shouted into the Chartwell night two years ago. He'd been ahead of himself, but correct all the same. The Wehrmacht were in Holland, Norway and Belgium and knocking, indeed, at the door of Great Britain – the door it was now up to them to hold fast.

EIGHT

ADMIRALTY HOUSE, 25 MAY 1940

CLEMENTINE

It was the tinkle of breaking china that alerted Clementine that all might not be well with the new prime minister. She paused in her supervision of the packing of Admiralty House and made for his office to find him standing behind his desk, staring at the wall, which was splattered with a tea stain from the cup now lying in myriad pieces on the polished wood flooring.

'Did that help?' she asked.

Winston turned and grimaced. 'It did not.'

'Would you like to discuss it?'

'No.' He sank into his chair, kicking at the broken china.

'I see.' Grabbing a discarded cardboard box, she moved forward to retrieve the pieces. 'Would you, then, like simply to tell me about it?'

He groaned. 'There's too much to tell.'

His face was creased with worry and his eyes shadowed; she hated to see him that way.

'Come, Winston,' she said gently. 'You have the words to tell anything.'

He humphed. 'I know what you're doing, Clemmie. You're flattering me into capitulation.'

'Is it working?'

He gave a reluctant smile. 'A little. But everything is so tangled it's hard to know what to focus on first, let alone how to frame it for someone else.'

She set the box down on his desk and reached for his hand. So many times over the years she'd seen him tortured with concern for the world and it tortured her too. She sought for a way to reach him and then it came to her.

'You reminded me the other day of when you proposed to me.'

'I did,' he agreed. 'Happiest day of my life.'

'Eventually, yes, but if I recall correctly you were in agonies beforehand. We had to walk three times around the lake before rain eventually sent us into the Temple of Diana and forced your hand.'

'True.'

'So, maybe, if you can drag yourself away from Westminster, you could let your imagination transport you back there. We are in the temple, you and I, sitting on a limestone bench, with the rain as a shield from the rest of the world. Can you join me?' His eyes misted and she knew he could see it too. She pulled him gently to his feet. 'Good. So, now, talk to me. Just to me.'

His eyes fixed on her. 'Very well, but it will not be pretty.'

'There is a war on, Winston, nothing is pretty.'

'You are.'

'Hush! Talk to me. Is it the poor boys in France that are worrying you?'

Tears twinkled instantly in his eyes. 'I fear they are trapped, Clemmie. The French command has been in chaos and they have missed the chance to order the retreat southwards. I did not realise. We have a map room here in the Admiralty that tracks all our ships, but there is nothing like that for the infantry. We have four divisions stranded in France and I'm blind to their positions. I was there in the Great War, Clemmie. I was stationed around Dunkirk. I know that land, but I do not know what is going on there right now. How, then, am I meant to make decisions?'

'You must trust those on the ground, those who, like you in the last war, are dedicated to their men and our cause.'

He drew in a long breath. 'You are right, of course. Lord Gort says the Germans are cutting off the escape route across the Somme, leaving our boys trapped around Arras. He says the only way out is over the Channel, and I'm sure that's true but I cannot see how we can get more than a tiny proportion of them home.'

'You got the garrison back from Boulogne yesterday,' she reminded him.

'We did and I was glad of it, but I fear it was a mistake. The Germans have already seized the city and are marching on Calais at pace. We are going to have to order the garrison there to hold just to buy us the time to get at least some of our men out of Dunkirk.'

'You will ask them to fight to the death?' Clementine gasped.

'I will ask them to fight until surrender is the only option. We must hope they can hold for a few days or every soldier in France will be lost. And even then...'

She squeezed his hands. 'We have the best navy in the world, Winston. Is that not what you've always told me? We must be able to evacuate some men from a well-established port?'

'*Some* men, yes, but three hundred and fifty thousand?'

She gasped. 'That many?'

'If they make it as far as Dunkirk, yes. Poor buggers.' He clasped her fingers so tightly the ends paled but she bit back her protest. 'I am prime minister now, Clemmie – those lives are in my hands.'

'And they are the best possible hands. What plans have you made?'

He eased his grip. 'We are working on "Operation Dynamo" to send ships across to fetch them back. Vice Admiral Ramsay is in charge.'

'He's a good man.'

'And a vigorous one. He has Admiralty officers scouring the south for vessels, not just naval ones but any we can requisition. This morning he took charge of forty Dutch schuits that were in our ports when the Netherlands surrendered. And the Shipping Ministry is scouring boatyards from Teddington to the south coast for suitable craft.'

'There then. The boys are not just in your hands, Winston, but in those of many capable men. You must trust them to do their job.'

'True, true. Thank you, wife.' He gave her a small smile. 'I like this temple.'

'As you should.' She leaned in to kiss him but his brow was still creased. 'There's more?'

He let go of her hands and strode around, pacing in a tight line as if he were, indeed, cocooned in a mock-Greek temple in the heart of Blenheim's vast gardens.

'Halifax,' he said eventually.

'Lord Halifax?'

'He wants peace.'

'Don't we all?'

'He wants peace *now*. I have been with the war cabinet several times today and all is in uproar. We must decide, you see, if we wish to continue.'

'With the cabinet?'

'With the *war*, Clemmie.' He came back to her. 'It's important. If we do not feel we can stand alone, there is little point in mounting a dangerous rescue mission. We might as well simply surrender and have our boys taken prisoner unharmed.'

'Surrender?' she whispered. It felt like the dirtiest of words. 'But, Winston, you have only just become prime minister. You have only just taken up the fight. How can you—'

'I know!' It came out on a wail. 'You think I don't know? I do not want to give in and I'm sure most of the men are with me, but Halifax is talking to the Italian embassy. He wants us to use Mussolini as a go-between with Hitler. He says that with Holland and Denmark and Norway fallen, Belgium surely about to surrender and the French crumbling, we must face the fact that the war is hopeless. Hitler is too strong.'

'So, what, we just give in to him?'

'We do a deal. The Nazis get continental Europe and we get autonomy.'

'You want that?'

'No! But I am duty bound to consider it if that is what my war cabinet wish. Hitler has called a halt to the attack around Dunkirk and Halifax believes that is to give us room to negotiate.'

She stared at him and for a moment she was not in his prime ministerial office, not even in a make-believe temple in Blenheim, but in the dining room at Chartwell with Winston railing against anyone foolish enough to trust the Führer.

'You've always said Hitler doesn't negotiate, Winston.'

He stared at her for some time, but then she saw the mist almost visibly lift from his eyes.

'True!' he cried. 'I *have* always said that, and I've been proved correct every time. You are right, Clemmie, I must be strong. I must stand up and insist the cabinet does not give in to these milksop ideas of appeasement once more. I must drive them to resilience.'

Clementine put up a cautious hand. It was good to see him fired up, but he must be careful. His leadership was newborn and fragile. Halifax was backed by many of the Tories and could yet oust Winston as prime minister.

'Perhaps, my dear,' she said carefully, 'you should think less about *driving* them and more about... *carrying* them.'

'Carrying them?'

'With the strength of your personality and the force of your words. Show them the best way in all its glory, and let them choose it themselves...'

'Show them?'

'Construct it for them, as we have constructed this temple.' She gestured at the empty air around them.

'These four Ionic columns?' he suggested with his wave.

'Exactly. And the Greek friezes above our heads, and the glorious, green, English gardens leading down to the lake in front.'

'And the beautiful young woman agreeing to be my wife?'

She stepped close and wrapped her arms around his neck. 'Perhaps we keep that for ourselves?'

He put his arms around her, stroking her back. 'You are not just beautiful, my Clementine, but wise. I will battle on as you suggest, with resilience and courage.'

'And tact?'

'And tact. Or as much of it as I can muster.' He kissed her. 'The king is calling a national day of prayer on Sunday to ask for God's intercession. I fear he doesn't trust me, Clemmie.'

'Maybe he just wishes to offer you holy backing?'

'Humph. I prefer to put my trust in the navy than the Almighty.'

She kissed him. 'How good then, my love, that with the king's help, we can have both.'

He nodded, but his eyes were misting again as the Temple of Diana fell away and the dark clouds of the real world crowded back in on them. 'Frankly, Clemmie, we're going to need all the help we can get.'

30 MAY 1940

Four days later, Winston's eyes were clouded again but this time with tears of joy. 'Look at this!'

He strode into the drawing room, thrusting a morning newspaper under her nose, and she saw the bold picture on the front page. It must have been taken from the deck of one of the hundreds of ships plying their way back and forth across the Channel, and showed a flotilla of mismatched boats bravely ferrying soldiers off the beaches north of Dunkirk to the large vessels sitting at anchor in the deeper waters.

Once the first ships had set sail on 26 May, the Admiralty had put out a general call for help and Britain's sailors, professional and amateur, had rushed to answer. Now, alongside the destroyers and minesweepers of the navy sailed liners and cruisers, fishing craft, tugboats and tiny motor launches. With the piers of Dunkirk bombed to pieces, they were invaluable in breaching the gap between sand and sea, and men were escaping in their thousands.

In the foreground of the picture, a group of soldiers in torn uniforms smiled broadly into the camera. Behind them, low cloud hung over the flat-calm sea, making the picture dull but, far more importantly, the waters safe for all types of craft and the skies awkward for Luftwaffe planes. On the first day of Operation Dynamo, fewer than ten thousand men had been embarked and Winston had been tearing out his few strands of hair, but the next day it had been up to seventeen and today they were transporting over fifty. That was fifty thousand men and boys returned to their homes to live and to fight another day.

'You did it, Winston.'

'*They* did it,' he corrected. 'The men you told me to trust did it, and they're still doing it. We won't stop till we get every last one of those troops back to Blighty. That'll show Halifax what fighting spirit truly is.'

She placed a finger over his lips. 'Don't be churlish, Winston. You won that battle too.'

After two exhausting days of political wrangling, the majority of the wider war cabinet had roared their approval of Winston's desire to fight on, and Halifax had been forced to concede his petty desires for a backroom peace. The wisdom of this had been proven when he'd shamefacedly come in the next day with news from the Italian ambassador that Italy was poised to declare war and Mussolini had no intention of helping anyone, least of all the French or the British.

They were on their own, but at least they now had their forces back to stand and fight.

'Tea?' Clementine suggested, indicating the tray on the side table.

Winston scoffed, as she'd known he would, and, grinning, she waved the maid forward with the iced bottle of Pol Roger she'd requested the moment she'd seen the news this morning. Winston rubbed his hands gleefully.

'That's more like it, Clemmie. And only the two of us to share it too!'

He reached eagerly to take the bottle from her, but behind them the butler coughed.

'What is it, Sawyers?' Winston demanded crossly.

'Not *it*, sir, but *who*.'

'What on earth...?'

'The king, sir.' He stood back to usher King George into the room, adding, 'And the queen.'

Clementine nearly dropped the bottle. 'Your royal highnesses.'

Winston gave a smooth bow and Clementine hastily dipped into a curtsy, feeling like a fool clutching wine to her chest at eleven in the morning.

King George, however, strode forward, saying, 'Excellent! It seems you have perfectly anticipated our desire to celebrate.'

'It seemed appropriate, sir,' Clementine stuttered, gesturing to the newspaper picture.

'Quite right. Over a hundred and fifty thousand off the beaches, I'm told, and more to come. It's a miracle.'

'It's a defeat, sir,' Winston pointed out.

'But a victory within a defeat, Mr Churchill. God heard our prayers.'

Winston bowed again. 'It would seem so, sir.'

'And you, Prime Minister, have united our nation. This' – he tapped the picture of the small boats – 'is the British spirit. This is what you have harnessed, Winston, and this is what, with God's continued help, will see us through the war.'

Winston looked as if he might be about to cry and Clementine stepped hastily across him towards the queen, to allow him a moment to recover.

'A glass of champagne, ma'am?'

'Absolutely.' The queen took a chair with a sparkling smile. 'Pol Roger is my favourite!'

'Mine too, ma'am,' Winston said, regaining his usual aplomb. 'And it will be an honour to share a glass with you.'

'Goodness, Mr Churchill,' she shot back, 'I hope I get my own glass.'

Clementine burst out laughing and gladly surrendered the bottle to Winston, sliding into the indicated seat next to the queen. She'd seen Elizabeth Bowes-Lyon plenty of times at balls and fetes when she'd been a young debutante, out on the scene a mere ten years after Clementine, but that was before she'd been queen of England.

'I'm so pleased to have you in our home, ma'am,' she said.

'And I'm pleased to be here. We have much in common, Mrs Churchill.'

Clementine looked at the petite royal and struggled to see what she meant.

The queen gestured to their husbands, pouring frothing champagne into crystal flutes. 'We must both keep men vital to the nation standing, must we not?'

'We must,' Clementine agreed, feeling warmth steal through her at the thought of someone understanding her role so clearly. 'My husband longed to lead but has not found this first month easy.'

'My husband longed *not to*,' Queen Elizabeth replied crisply, 'but is finding it easier with yours at his side.'

'Truly?' Clementine swallowed, feeling the swirling undercurrents of the abdication crisis pulling at the happy moment. 'Winston has always been a great admirer of King George, ma'am, even if that was not, at one point, totally apparent.'

The queen leaned over and patted her hand. 'That's in the past. The time for division is over. Britain must stand together now.'

'Alone?'

'Together!' The queen took a proffered glass and raised it. 'To bringing our men home.'

'To bringing our men home,' the others echoed gladly.

Clementine took a cautious sip of the champagne, for she felt giddy already. She was truly the prime minister's wife, truly part of the group leading the country, and she felt rich with joy and heavy with responsibility. The men were coming home from France, but how long would it be before Hitler chased after them? How long before this war was not just knocking on their door, but kicking it down?

NINE

JENNY

'I'm talking to you from Dover where the battle of Britain is in full flow above her iconic white cliffs. Just over my head, a Spitfire swoops round in a daring manoeuvre and opens fire on the Messerschmitt trying to carve its way into British skies. The German tries to dodge but he's no match for the daring British pilot and his right engine bursts into flames. The plane turns, slowly at first and then in a death spiral towards the blue sea below. The crowds on the cliffs cheer in triumph.'

Ned nudged at Jenny. 'What do you think?'

She stretched out sleepily. They were lying in bed listening to Ned's broadcast from two days ago and the words felt strangely dislocated against the summer sunshine slanting into the room between the curtains.

'I think you look like a Greek god.'

'Idiot!'

'I do.'

She reached for him and he kissed her, but then pulled back.

'Really though, the broadcast – what do you think?'

'It was excellent, Ned. Very evocative.'

He squinted at her. 'Were you listening or are you just saying that to shut me up?'

She sat up indignantly. 'I was listening, Ned. I was listening just then and I was listening live too. I was tired, after all day in the evacuation offices, but I stayed awake specially and I loved it. Well...' She frowned. 'Not loved it – who could love listening to men fighting each other in the skies – but I thought it was really well done. I felt like I was there.'

He smiled shyly. 'That was the idea. Some of the other reporters say it's wrong, that it's dramatising war, turning it into entertainment, but I think it's making it real for people.'

'I agree.' She pulled him down, snuggling into the crook of his arm. 'The broadcasts you did from Dunkirk were the same. I'd never have believed what a sight it was without you there telling us about the fishing boats and the paddle cruisers and all those other brave sailors bringing the soldiers back across the Channel. And when that boat sank in front of you...'

He clasped her tight. 'It was horrible, Jen. Those young lads flailing around in the water. We must make sure our children learn to swim.'

Jenny froze. 'You still...' She swallowed. 'You still think we'll have children?'

He looked at her curiously. 'Of course. Why wouldn't we?'

'Well, you know, it's been nearly five years now. And—'

He kissed her quiet. 'And we'll just have to try harder.'

His hand stroked down her back and she arched into him.

'Yes, sir!'

He chuckled and kissed her more deeply but just as her body started to sing at his touch, the phone shrilled into the apartment.

'Leave it,' she murmured against his lips but she already

knew he wouldn't. No reporter could ignore a call, especially in wartime.

'Won't be long.'

He slid out of bed and ducked into the living room. She'd made it as cosy as possible with warm, cream walls, bright cushions and her favourite Navajo Indian rug, and had clearly done a good job as many of the CBS reporters chose to base themselves back here of an evening. They lived just down the road from Langham Place, home of BBC Broadcasting House, and the CBS offices across the way, so it was a handy location, especially for those broadcasting to America. The regular slots were midnight and 3 a.m. British time, leaving an awkward couple of hours in which no public house was open, so the Miller apartment had become the perfect alternative.

Since Hitler had romped through Belgium and the Netherlands and entered France, the thirst for news back home was high. For the Americans, Jenny thought ruefully, it was a drama. Over here, with the Luftwaffe taking to the skies over the Channel every day, and invasion an increasing likelihood, the battle for Britain was a stark reality. Sometimes Jenny stayed up, glad of the company in these worrying times, but more often than not, worn out from her conventional hours in the evacuation offices, she slid off to bed leaving her husband and the other men in a fug of cigarette smoke and whisky fumes.

Last night had clearly been a big one, for a stale smell wafted through the door, and she hoped Ned's call would be routine and he could come swiftly back into the far cleaner haven of the bedroom.

'Of course,' she heard him say. 'One moment please.' He darted back. 'It's for you, Jen.'

'Me?!' It was never for her. She wasn't important enough for CBS and it was too expensive for her parents to call from the States.

'Yes! Hurry up. It's Mrs Churchill.'

'Goodness!' Jenny leaped up and ran through. Snatching the receiver from the side table, she composed herself a second and then said, 'Hello?'

'Mrs Miller? Mrs Churchill here. So sorry to disturb you so, erm, early.' Jenny glanced at the clock and saw to her shame that it was gone 10 a.m. No doubt Mrs Churchill had been up for hours.

'Not a problem at all. Can I help you?'

'I rather hope you can. Fulmer Chase is so popular that we are unable to accommodate the mothers for the three weeks we feel is ideal to let them recover and get on their feet with Baby.'

'I see,' Jenny said, though she didn't really.

'This week a benefactor has donated a considerable sum with which to purchase a second house to transfer the women after the immediate post-natal period.'

'That's very kind of them.'

Jenny looked around her mess of a living room and wondered what on earth Mrs Churchill was getting at. She seemed unusually hesitant.

'Isn't it? I've seen a house I think might be suitable but I'd, well, I'd like a second opinion.'

'Very wise. Wait – mine? You want my opinion?'

'If you are free.'

'Of course, but why me?'

'I'm told you have an economics degree, so thought perhaps you had sound financial sense.'

That was true and with top grades too, though she'd learned not to say that over here. (It was, apparently, blowing your own trumpet, though Lord knows why, if you had a trumpet, you shouldn't blow it!)

'I have a degree,' she admitted cautiously, 'but I'm no expert on houses.'

'Oh.' Mrs Churchill sounded forlorn. 'Well, if you're not interested...'

'I didn't say that,' Jenny said hastily. 'I'd love to come and look around, if you think it would help.'

'You would? I'm so pleased.' Her voice bubbled up. 'I can drive us. Hallam Street, isn't it? How about I pick you up in half an hour?'

'Erm, yes. Thank you.'

'Until then!'

And with that, Mrs Churchill was gone. Jenny stared at the receiver as if it might be able to explain what had just happened but it stared blankly back.

'What was that about?' Ned asked, wandering through, his pyjama trousers hanging tantalisingly low.

Jenny groaned. 'I'm really not sure, but I need to get dressed.'

'Right now?' he asked, trying to take her in his arms.

'Right now!' She laughed, and wriggled free to run for the bathroom. She had no idea why the prime minister's wife wanted her company, but she sure as hell wasn't going to be late.

She was standing on the road in her best summer frock when Clementine Churchill pulled up in a fine red Napier exactly half an hour later.

'Thank you so much for joining me,' she said, throwing open the door.

'It's my absolute pleasure. What girl wouldn't want to spend someone else's money on a house?'

Mrs Churchill gave her braying laugh. 'Well quite! Though it seems none of my girls feel the same way.'

'Really?'

'They're all very busy,' Clementine said, a little defensively. 'I was hoping Nellie could get involved but she hasn't really got over losing her husband yet. She's always been rather needy.'

'Needy?'

'You think I'm heartless? I probably am. I learned very young to rely on myself and tend to expect others to do the same. My children don't thank me for it.'

'I don't believe that's true.'

'Perhaps. Although Diana absorbs herself in her own children, as if to show me how I should have done it.'

'I'm sure that's not the case. She's probably just overwhelmed.'

Mrs Churchill smiled at her and swerved, just in time, around an oak tree. She drove rather fast, Jenny noticed, and surreptitiously gripped the side of her seat.

'You're far kinder than me, Mrs Miller,' Mrs Churchill went on, smiling at her. 'And I think, if it suits you, it's time you called me Clementine.'

'Truly? I'd be honoured.'

'Please don't be. Honour sounds so formal and my idea is quite the opposite.'

'Thank you. You'll call me Jenny?'

'Happily. And I'm sure you're right about Diana. Small children are exhausting and bringing them along today would have been terribly tiresome. Sarah would have loved to come, but she's joined the WAAF, and Mary has gone to stay with a friend for the school hols. She did suggest I wait until she was back but I'm very keen to get on with it.'

'Of course.'

'And praying we get a chance to put it in action before the Germans come.'

Jenny gasped. 'You think they'll invade?'

'I think they must since we have refused any pact.'

'Pact?'

'A neutrality pact, an agreement to stay out of Hitler's way in return for immunity from attack.'

'Like America?' Jenny said heavily.

'Something like that, yes.'

'But we've said no?'

'*We?*' Clementine asked lightly.

Jenny flushed. 'In the matter of the war, I consider myself English.'

'And we're very glad to have you, but you must be sure to think of yourself as American if it... comes to it.'

Jenny caught the heavy darkness in her tone and swallowed. 'You know something, Mrs... Clementine?'

'I know too many things,' Clementine said wearily. 'But, yes, there are... indications that Hitler is preparing to invade and if he does so, you should go home. Fast.'

'I thought you didn't believe in fleeing?'

'Not while there's hope, but once there is not, refusing to do so is foolish. I am not a fan of the last stand; life is too precious to waste on a lost cause. Ah, but look, I think this is the road. Let's stop all this nasty talk of invasion and focus on babies, shall we?'

Must we? Jenny wanted to say but it sounded callous.

'Will your daughter-in-law give birth at Fulmer Chase?' she forced herself to ask.

'Pam? I did suggest it, but Winston is certain the baby will be a boy and considers Chequers more appropriate for his heir.'

Jenny winced. 'Do you think,' she asked tightly, 'that men feel the need for an heir more sharply than women?'

'Oh yes,' Clementine bumped over a roundabout. 'They have this thing about "carrying on the name". Nonsense, of course. I believe the name you carry is not as important as the way you carry yourself. But then, us women are conditioned from early on not to rely on our name so perhaps we understand that more clearly.'

'A very good point,' Jenny conceded. 'And that's why men want boys?'

'Presumably. Winston gets on far better with our daughters than our son, but he dotes on every foolish thing Randolph does.' Jenny gaped at Clementine who gave her a sudden, broad wink. 'You think I shouldn't talk so honestly about my children?'

'No. I like it. It's just surprising in a Brit.'

'Ah!' Clementine laughed again. 'Well, you see, I grew up in Dieppe and the French, I find, are a pragmatic race, not afraid to speak the truth. Perhaps that rubbed off on me. I apologise if I seem uncouth.'

Now it was Jenny's turn to laugh. If there was any word that less applied to the elegant Clementine Churchill, it was 'uncouth'. She opened her mouth to say so but was stopped by the prime minister's wife screeching to a halt outside a gate.

'Here we are. Fircroft, it's called. Sounds promising, does it not?' Clementine got out and smoothed down her outfit, a beautiful Kitty Foyle dress in navy blue with shining cream collars and cuffs. 'The house isn't very grand, but I'm told it's solidly made, which is what we're after, isn't it?'

'Absolutely,' Jenny agreed, though Fircroft was far grander than any house she'd ever lived in.

An estate agent was waiting eagerly at the gates, clipboard in hand, and rushed forward to welcome them.

'Mrs Churchill, I'm Mr Samson. I'm honoured to meet you, truly honoured.'

She gave him a firm handshake. 'Very kind of you, Mr Samson, but this is business as usual. The house is empty, yes?'

'It is.'

'Excellent. If you don't mind, then, my friend and I will look around by ourselves.'

He clearly did mind but there was little he could do, for

Clementine was already sweeping forward. Jenny rushed after her, tingling at having been called her friend.

'We'll start upstairs,' Clementine said, pounding upward until they reached the attic rooms on the third floor, clearly once servants' bedrooms. 'Useful,' she observed, looking into each and every one. 'Perfect space for mother and baby.'

'Though a long way up for any nursing staff.'

'True. See, I knew I brought you for a reason, Jenny.' Clementine grinned at her. 'That is a much more sensible comment than we'd get from the estate agent, who'd be full of the "aspects" and the "potential for improvement".'

She'd put on a smarmy voice and Jenny laughed. 'You know estate agents well?'

'Far too well. My mother was forever on the move – on the run, some might say – and a politician's career does not offer his family the chance of a stable home.'

'But you have your country house – Chartwell, is it?'

'Chartwell, yes. We do. Something of a mixed blessing but it's closed up for the war now we have Chequers as a country residence, so let's not dwell on it. What do you think of this bathroom?'

'Potential for improvement?' Jenny suggested.

Clementine roared with laughter. 'Quite right. A few new tiles and some linoleum on the floor and it will be perfect. Come on, next floor.'

The second floor was a mass of larger rooms. Jenny followed Clementine, making notes, both for the benefit of decision-making and because this could be an excellent CBS feature. She'd made several broadcasts recently and the channel officials had been so pleased that Ned had taken her to apply for a licence to stay out after midnight so she could fill the prime American slots. He'd long since been granted this roving pass for his important war work but he hadn't seemed that happy about her acquiring the same privilege.

'Don't you like your wife working with you?' she'd challenged.

'Course I do. I'm just not happy with her being out late. There're all sorts of bandits roaming the blackout and I want you safe, gorgeous.'

He'd kissed her and she'd felt bad for doubting him, but worried that, whatever he said out loud, he wanted her at home giving him babies. That wasn't happening, though, so better she got on with the important work of telling Americans about this terrible war.

'Right then.' Clementine interrupted her thoughts, stopping on the central landing and looking around. 'If we put two mothers to a room, maybe even three in this front one, we can fit, what...?'

Jenny glanced at her notes. 'I make it fifteen.'

'Excellent. We can take twenty-eight at Fulmer Chase. The mothers are there for two weeks and the idea will be to move those who wish to go to Fircroft for one more. They can learn to bathe baby and get into a feeding routine and, hope-fully, a sleeping one too, so that both go home fit and equipped to enjoy life together.' Her face had taken on a dreamlike quality.

Jenny looked at her closely. 'It sounds idyllic. Is that what you had with your babies?'

'Good Lord no!' Clementine strode to the window and peered out at the garden. 'Unkempt,' she observed, 'but pleas-ingly large. Plenty of room for prams beneath those trees.'

Jenny wasn't going to let her off that easily. 'What *was* your experience?'

Clementine sighed. 'Different with each baby, of course, but characterised almost exclusively by a lack of the sort of peace and quiet I'm trying to establish here. Actually, with Diana, my eldest, I did have quiet but no decent nurse and I was bewildered by her. Winston was terribly busy with the

Trade Boards Bill, and I had no idea what to do with myself, even less with Diana. In the end I ran away.'

'From the baby?'

'I'm afraid so. I left her with a wet nurse and went to Brighton with my mother and Nellie.' Clementine fiddled with her earring and threw Jenny an embarrassed smile. 'Unforgivable of me, really. Can't think why Mother permitted it but I wasn't very well. I recovered soon enough and fetched Diana down but it wasn't the perfect start and she never lets me forget it.'

'But you learned,' Jenny said cautiously, trying not to show her shock, 'before you had Randolph, I mean.'

'I learned,' Clementine agreed heavily, 'not that it helped. He was the much-wanted boy so I was drowned in gifts and attention, but then Winston was asked to entertain the king of Portugal and fifty guests at Blenheim so I had to heave myself out of bed and be sure that was all sorted.'

Jenny made a sympathetic noise, though she couldn't imagine such a vast royal party. 'And your next baby?' she asked.

'Sarah? Sarah was born in October 1914, three months into the Great War. Winston was first lord of the Admiralty so there was little time for rest. Plus, Nellie went and got herself imprisoned by the Germans and would insist on aggravating them, so it was all we could do to get her safely home.'

'Aggravating them?' Jenny squeaked, trying to imagine all this. She'd been four in 1914.

'Chalking anti-German propaganda on the cell walls, mainly. Her German was very good, like mine, and she could be quite... anatomical.' Clementine shook her head, though she was smiling at the memory.

'You can speak German?' Jenny asked.

'Yes, but don't tell anyone. It's rather frowned upon these days!' She chuckled. 'Shall we look at the ground floor?'

Jenny followed her new friend down the stairs. 'Tell me you had an easier time with your next baby,' she said as they headed into the big kitchens.

'Not really.' Clementine bent to check the ovens. 'Marigold was born in 1918, four days after the Armistice, not that it brought much peace to *my* household. Winston was furiously trying to stop everyone Kaiser-bashing. He said that being too hard on Germany would only lead to trouble in the future, and he was right, was he not?'

'Sadly so,' Jenny agreed, though that wasn't what interested her. 'Is Marigold Mary's full name then?'

Clementine's shoulders tightened. 'No,' she said shortly and moved into the pantry, clattering cupboards open.

Jenny watched, feeling awkward. She sought for the words to ask more about what she assumed was a lost daughter, but it was clear from Clementine's taut shoulders that such a question would not be welcome.

'Are you all right?' she asked tentatively.

'Quite fine, thank you.' The older woman slammed the last door and came back as if there had been no interruption to their conversation. 'Mary was born just before a general election and Winston got appendicitis. There was nothing for it but to pack her up and head off to Dundee to campaign on his behalf.'

'Dundee? In Scotland?'

'Correct. He didn't get the Essex constituency until later.'

'You went all that way with a newborn baby?'

'I did. She was very popular with the voters, though sadly Winston was not. It was post-war and everyone had had enough of hardship and thought Labour would bring them prosperity. There was little I could do, however hard I tried.'

'I'm sorry. At least Winston recovered.'

'True. And his illness was most convenient. The drama of nearly losing him made me forgive him for Chartwell.'

'Forgive him...?' Jenny felt as if she'd been dropped into a dizzying swirl of places and people. Just listening to what Clementine had had to deal with felt exhausting, so Lord knows how she'd actually lived it.

'For buying it while I was lying in with Mary.'

'As a present?'

'For himself, yes. I'd already told him I didn't like it.'

'But he...?'

'Bought it anyway. He took the older children down while I was recovering from the birth and, of course, they loved it. He brought their enthusiasm back to bolster him when he admitted what he'd done.'

'He bought a house without your agreement?'

'That's right, and a rather big house too. Beautiful, of course. That's to say, the house isn't that beautiful, but it's set in glorious grounds and the views over the Kentish Weald are quite stunning. The first time I saw it, I felt as if I were living in an aeroplane.'

Jenny was confused. 'So you *did* like it?'

'I liked it with my heart but not with my head. It was a clear money pit.' Clementine shook herself. 'That's not fair. We've had many, many very happy times there. The children adore it and so does Winston, so I try my best to do so too.'

'But you wouldn't have chosen it yourself?'

'Never. I'd have had somewhere far more modest. But modesty is not something Winston understands. And he did insist on me having the top floor of our extension as my bedroom where I still, if I can forget the money, feel like I'm in an aeroplane when I look out the windows. So I can hardly complain, can I?'

'No, but—'

'And,' she said briskly, the subject clearly closed, 'I can choose *this* house. What do we think, Jenny? Will Fircroft do for our post-natal mothers?'

'I think it's perfect,' Jenny said. She had little idea but

Clementine was sure and her job seemed to be to back her up in a way that too few people apparently did.

'Excellent. Mr Samson!' she hailed the estate agent, who bounded over. 'We might be interested, if the price is right. What can you offer...?'

And with that, the personal story was gone, and the elusive Clementine Churchill was all business once more.

TEN

CLEMENTINE

'To young Winston's very good health!'

Winston raised his glass and, around the table, Clementine, Diana and Duncan did the same. Pamela had given birth to her baby four days ago and had obligingly provided a son, promptly named Winston. His grandfather was over the moon and was eager to get to Chequers – the official prime ministerial country residence – to meet the child for himself. In the meantime, this must be the hundredth toast Clementine had drunk to the newest family member.

Pamela was doing well and Randolph had reported himself proud and pleased with his son, though not, apparently either proud or pleased enough to have been anywhere near Chequers for the birthing. Rumour had it he'd been out partying but Clementine was trying not to listen. He'd returned to his regiment now and she was desperately hoping that the army would somehow settle him.

'Delicious stew.'

Winston had already polished off his entire helping and

started to dip a finger into the last of his gravy before, with a glance to Clementine, stopping himself. She handed him a piece of bread and he eagerly applied it to his plate. Tonight, for an unusually intimate family dinner, Mrs Landermare had treated them to Winston's favourite and he was fulsome in his appreciation. Now he sat back and patted his stomach, bulging comfortably beneath his new all-in-one suit.

A few months ago, Clementine had shown him an article in one of Mary's magazines about a new item of clothing they were calling a 'siren suit' – a single garment, similar to the overalls worn by boilermen, designed to be pulled on when the air-raid siren sounded, so one could make it to the shelter in warmth and decency. They were intended for women, but Winston had been most taken with the idea and acquired one for himself. He'd found what he happily called his 'romper' so comfortable and practical that he wore it most of the time and had already ordered more.

'That beef should sit warm in the stomach for later,' he said happily.

'You're going out?' Clementine asked, with a spike of alarm.

'I feel I should.'

She fiddled at her earring, a drop pearl that felt reassuringly smooth but all too fragile. Last month, giving up their battles with the noble Spitfires over the Channel, the Luftwaffe had switched to blitzing London. They came every night, with fearsome ferocity. Buildings cracked apart, fires raged and far too many lives were tragically lost. There weren't enough shelters, or ambulances or fire engines and the call had gone out for volunteers. Clementine was urging women to help wherever they could, for Hitler could not be allowed destroy the precious heart of London – or those within it.

Resistance was all, and they had been rewarded at the end of last month with the glorious news that, having failed to claim ascendancy over the brave RAF in the air, the Nazis were dismantling their invasion preparations in the Netherlands. Clementine and Winston had danced a foxtrot around the living room the night they'd heard that news from Bletchley Park, but Hitler had not given up his attacks on Britain and every night the sirens rang out, sending fear reverberating through her veins. It was horrible to find themselves right on the front line, with little means of defence, and it made her hate Hitler with increasing fervour. Plus, Winston regarded it his duty as prime minister to visit the displaced immediately, and would brook no arguments about his safety.

'If our people are having to take the flak, then, as their leader, I should too,' he would insist.

'But your loss, sir, would be rather more impactful than that of the average man,' Jock Colville, his principle private secretary would argue, to which Winston would simply humph and look for his hat.

Jock had appealed to Clementine for help. The civil service were rapidly discovering that she was a fast conduit to the prime minister, and she was starting to feel the pressure of keeping him alive, even in the face of his stubborn pride. She had tried pointing out that the king and queen only ever went visiting bomb sites the next day, and he had been swayed, but only momentarily.

'The king and queen are anointed monarchs so deserve protection. I am a mere common leader.'

She knew he didn't think of himself as 'common' in any way. It was simply that he was drawn to danger and loved heading out into the raids. She had tried bribing and cajoling, but he was oblivious to any words bar his own. She had tried hiding the car, but he just walked. She had tried replacing it with an armoured one, but he got out whenever he saw anything of interest. Tonight, she had just one idea left...

'I'm sure you're right,' she said, sending Diana a glance to warn her not to interrupt. 'I shall come with you.'

'You?' Winston looked horror-struck.

'Yes, me. I'm your wife, after all, so should be there to comfort the women of the city who are far more numerous than the men.'

'I would not want you in such danger,' Winston said.

'I don't mind. Other women are taking the flak, so why not me?'

'Because you're *my* woman.' She lifted an eyebrow and he gave a rueful smile. 'Point taken, my dear, though I am a public figure now, you know.'

'I know,' she groaned and then, as if mocking them, an air-raid siren blared out.

'Oh no!' Diana wailed. 'Mrs Landermare promised me coffee mousseline for dessert.'

Clementine looked at her in disbelief. 'I'm sure it will keep,' she said tartly.

'Of course it will keep, but that's hardly the point of a pudding!'

'Nor is it to explode out of your stomach when a bomb hits you.'

'Mummy!'

'Sorry, but really...'

She'd been getting on better with her eldest daughter since Diana had become a recruiting officer for the navy. The uniform suited her and so did the regular work and the grown-up company. The siren, unfortunately, seemed to have reverted her to nervy type, but there was little time to fight, for a bomb landed nearby and they all flinched.

'They're coming close,' Duncan said. 'I think perhaps we should get home to the children.'

'Quite right.' Diana was up, all thoughts of pudding instantly forgotten. 'They hate the noise.'

'Very sensible of them,' Clementine said, then grabbed Diana's arm. 'Your shelter is decent? You're all safe there?'

'As safe as any of us can be. Don't worry, Mummy.' Diana gave her a rare hug as they heard another bomb landing, even closer.

'Had you not better stay here?' Clementine asked anxiously.

'It's not far,' Diana said and then, again, 'Don't worry, Mummy.'

It was a nonsense, of course, for they were all constantly worried now the nights brought hellfire from above, but it had to be said. Chins had to be kept up. If Hitler thought he'd break British morale with a few bombs, he had another think coming. Mary said the underground nightclubs of Soho were fuller than ever with people determined to live in defiance of Nazi hatred and they must learn from that and not be cowed – though not be foolish either.

Another bomb fell, surely less than a hundred feet away. Winston strode to the window.

'Pray God they don't hit the House,' he said, craning to stare into the skies as if he could will the planes, gorgon-like, to miss his treasured Parliament buildings.

'Pray God they don't hit *here*,' Clementine said, joining him. She looked across the gardens to the perpendicular kitchens, where, through the vast, arched window, they could see Mrs Landermare working away, presumably putting the finishing touches to Diana's treasured mousseline. 'We should get to the shelters. The staff too.'

'Quite right. I don't know what I'd do if Mrs Landermare was taken from us. Did I mention how superb that stew was?'

'You did, but I'm sure she'd like to hear it herself.'

'Quite so.' Winston kissed Diana goodbye, shook Duncan's hand and strode from the room.

Clementine saw the pair out for their ten-minute walk home, then returned to watch the kitchen window. She saw the staff start at her husband's intervention and crowd around.

There was some gesticulating – almost certainly Mrs Lander-mare favouring food preparation over safety – and then the side door opened and they trooped out obediently. They were heading for the War Rooms, a vast maze of offices and sleeping quarters laid out two years ago in the Treasury basement by some far-sighted civil servants, clearly as unimpressed by Chamberlain's policy of appeasement as Winston. Clementine reached for her cardigan to follow when Winston returned, but he insisted on delving into his well-stocked cocktail cabinet for a particular brandy he was keen to try.

'Really, Winston, this is not the advice we give to the ordinary people.'

'I am not the ordinary people,' he said grandly.

'Only when it suits you, Winston. I don't think—'

Her words were splintered by a bomb, the closest yet. Winston's arms went round her and he pulled her to the ground, the brandy flung aside with a tinkle that was nothing compared to the shattering of glass elsewhere. She felt the building shake and clung to her husband. Was this it? Were they going to die in Number Ten, like some hubristic punishment for pride?

'Stay down, my darling,' Winston murmured into her hair. 'I'm here. All will be well.'

They lay together, their whole world shaking, and for a strange, time-out-of-mind moment she recalled their honeymoon, lying wrapped up together day after day. That, though, had been in the grand hotels of Europe's capitals, now all in Nazi hands, with theirs, surely, to follow if this brutal bombardment continued. The building settled. Another bomb sounded, but further away, breaking up other lives.

Winston drew back and dropped a kiss on her lips. 'You still feel good in my arms, wife.'

She smiled and let him help her up and brush the dust from her dress. She felt for her earrings, found them boldly dangling from her ears. The dining room seemed largely intact, only the brandy bottle and a small ornament broken – though where, then, had she heard glass breaking?

'I think we escaped the worst of it,' she told Winston cautiously, but then a flash of light caught her eye and, running to the window, she saw the Downing Street warden shining his red torch onto a million shards of glass on the lawn below. 'Winston – the kitchens!'

She pointed in horror at the vast kitchen window through which, barely ten minutes earlier, she'd watched him talking to her staff. She started to shake and was grateful when, yet again, his reassuring arms went around her. The window was utterly blown out and Mrs Landermare's precious ovens and store cupboards were in smithereens.

'That could have been them,' she gasped. 'That could have been *you*!'

The front door flew open and they heard Diana's panicked voice: 'Mummy? Papa? Are you all right?'

'We're all right,' they called, running to her. 'And you? You're all right?'

'We're all right.'

Was it true? They were whole, perhaps, but far from all right. This was the closest they'd come to losing anyone and suddenly the war, until now a military game that had catapulted Winston into this historic building at the heart of London, felt very, very personal. The Nazis were coming for them and Winston was about the only thing holding them back.

Clementine looked around the wreckage of their home and knew, with stark certainty, that she had to make sure Winston stayed safe and well to keep doing so – not just for her family but for Great Britain, for the Allies and for the future of the world.

ELEVEN

BBC BROADCASTING HOUSE, 15 OCTOBER 1940

JENNY

'This... is London.'

Ned's voice came out of the speaker, low and confident with the now-trademark pause after 'this' to grab the attention of his audience thousands of miles across the Atlantic. Jenny gripped the sides of her seat in the basement of Broadcasting House and looked up at the rough concrete ceiling, struggling to believe her husband was recording from seven storeys above.

'I am speaking to you from the rooftops of the city as the Luftwaffe roar in on us, surging up from the utter darkness of the blackout, only the glint of the moon on the tips of their wings to issue any warning that they are preying on the men, women and children below. There!'

A roar of an engine crackled out of the speaker and then the crump of a bomb and the ack-ack of machine-gun fire. Jenny ducked instinctively and clamped a hand to her mouth to stopper her screams. What on earth was Ned doing up there, exposed to Nazi fire? Why had she ever let him?

The answer, of course, was that once Ned's mind was made

up there was no stopping him. He'd broadcast the Blitz from the streets of London several times, but had been desperate to get onto the roofs for a 'bird's-eye view'. BBC bosses had repeatedly refused to allow the foolhardy broadcast, but Ned had gone to Winston Churchill, who'd approved it with a hearty 'Good show, Mr Miller,' and issued orders accordingly. The result was a breathtaking programme – especially if you were the broadcaster's wife.

Jenny cringed at the sound of more bombs, trying to focus on the technicians frantically twiddling knobs and dials to control the amplification down the wires. It must sound bad enough over in America, but here she could feel the bombs shaking the ground as they exploded through the radio, accompanied by Ned's calm, vivid descriptions.

'This bomb has ripped through the side of a house below me. I can see straight into a little girl's bedroom where, thank the Lord, a dolly tucked up in her bed is the only casualty. Others have not been so lucky. Earlier today the very building from which I am speaking to you was sideswiped by a bomb and I climbed to the roof this evening past stretchers bearing my colleagues to hospital and firefighters battling to kill the flames consuming thousands of transcripts and recordings in the BBC library. The smell of burning and iodine lingers on my clothes, as do the cries of my wounded friends in my ears. Here, in London, this war spares no one.'

Another chatter of gunfire broke across his words and Jenny screwed her eyes up tight and prayed to the God she'd been brought up to trust implicitly to keep her husband safe. The heavenly airwaves above London must be jam-packed with prayers and she could only hope hers got through. The problem was, she could not, in all honesty, see why God would save a man who was recklessly standing as close to the Luftwaffe as possible, while allowing innocent souls down below to be blown apart, but there seemed no rhyme or reason to who got hit and who escaped, so she prayed anyway.

They were over a month into what people were calling 'the Blitz' and it was hell on earth. The very first night the Luftwaffe had flown in, Jenny had been alone in the apartment and had gone up to the roof, keen to see what was going on. The bombs had been far away in the docklands to the east but many of the planes had flown on over London before circling back to Germany, firing their guns all the way. That, combined with the shells from the anti-aircraft guns around the city, had filled the air with shrapnel like deadly rain.

Jenny had turned to head back into the safety of the building and found that the door had locked on her from the inside. It had taken ten terrifying minutes of shouting for help, ducking falling spikes of metal, before a kind young man in the street below had spotted her plight and raced up to release her. She'd been so weak with relief she'd burst into tears and he'd had to half-carry her to her door. By then the all-clear had been sounding and she'd agonised over whether it was more improper to invite him in or impolite not to. In the end she'd simply thanked him and he'd gone on his way.

Ned had roared with laughter when she'd told him. 'The poor lad saved your life and you weren't sure whether it was appropriate to offer him a thank-you beer? Heavens, Jen, you're getting more English by the minute!'

It had been a hard way to learn the value of protection, though Ned didn't like the cramped public shelter down the road, and they usually chose to hide beneath his sturdy oak desk. It was foolish, for it offered little protection, but it felt like theirs and these last nights they'd slept under it as the raids had been relentless. The bombed CBS offices had moved twice and last night a bomb had struck so close to Downing Street it had blown out many of its windows. Thankfully the Churchills and their staff were safe but the reports said it had been a close call and Jenny had sent Clementine a note to offer any help needed.

'A cry rends the air,' Ned said down the wireless and, sure enough, a thin wail echoed behind him. It sounded like an actress standing at a mic, but this was a real woman, wounded and in pain, and Jenny felt sorrow pierce her heart. The broadcast was dramatic but this was not theatre; this was life – raw, immediate life.

'People have to feel it,' Ned always said. 'They have to jump at the bombs and flinch at the guns. They have to weep as the people here weep. Only then will they dip their hands into their pockets to send help and, more importantly, start to see this war as theirs too. No one will try to save people dying five thousand miles away, but they might try to save someone dying in their living room.'

He had a point. Jenny just wished no one had to die anywhere.

'That was a close one.' Ned's voice shook slightly down the microphone. 'I don't mind telling you that made me gasp. The plane was so close I could almost see the Nazi's trigger finger.'

Jenny screwed her eyes even tighter shut. Was this the night she heard her husband killed live on air? Why did he have to do this to her?

'Why did you have to do that to me?!' Jenny ran to Ned when he finally came down to the basement, grabbing his lapels and pulling him in to crush a kiss onto his lips.

'All in the name of broadcasting,' he said cheerfully when she let him surface. 'Was it good?'

'It was terrifying.'

'Excellent! Perfect.' He clapped his hands. 'That's exactly what I wanted. Come on, if we're quick, we can celebrate at the Announcer's Arms.'

'It's gone midnight, Ned.'

'I know, but there's a door at the back they've started keeping open if they know you.'

He was ebullient, wired, high on the thrill of his rooftop broadcast, and Jenny knew there was little point in taking him home. Besides, a small drink might calm her shredded nerves.

'Fine, but don't put me through that again, please,' she begged.

'No one makes you listen, honey.'

She groaned and took his arm as others crowded round to sing his praises. They all spilled down the street to a backstreet pub called the Devonshire Arms, so packed with BBC, CBS and NBC reporters that it had become known as the Announcer's Arms.

'That Mr Churchill was swell to swing it for me, wasn't he?' Ned said, as they traced their way carefully down the blacked-out street. The Luftwaffe, at least, seemed to be taking a break.

'He's not as priggish as some of these Brits,' Jenny agreed. 'Mrs Churchill is surprising, too, and she does so much for him. He wouldn't have gotten where he has without her at his side.'

'Behind every great man...' Ned said.

But he wasn't really listening.

She stopped, forcing him to do so too. 'Do you think *you* would have gotten where you have without me at your side?'

'Course not,' he said glibly.

'You do!'

He squeezed her hand. 'I think it's a spurious point. You weren't at my side in Vienna when I did that first big broadcast but I managed it all the same.'

'That's not what I mean.'

'Fine. Having you has made me happy, secure, more able to go out and attack the world. Is that what you want me to say?'

'Is that what you *mean*?'

'Jenny...' He sighed in the darkness. 'I love you and you me, isn't that enough? Besides, your job isn't to make me great but to have your own life, lived in partnership with mine, right?'

Jenny fought to consider this. It was a valid point and one she should perhaps have thought of herself.

'Luftwaffe!' someone called up ahead and she caught the faint drone of a plane engine on the still night air before the sirens shrilled out.

She cringed against Ned, who hastened her towards the pub. A hum of chatter suggested the landlord was playing fast and loose with licensing laws and the lure of happy company was strong, but she felt unsettled.

'Let's go home, Ned,' Jenny pleaded.

'Home? Why? They won't hit us here.'

'You don't know that.' The others were ducking down an alleyway to the side door and he tugged her after them, but she dug her heels in. 'We'll be safer under your desk. Or maybe in the shelter?' She indicated the stream of people emerging from houses and making for the gaping entrance to the public shelter.

Ned shivered dramatically. 'Not the shelter. I don't like it underground.'

She shook her head at him. 'You'll stand on the rooftops waving at the Luftwaffe, but not go underground to avoid them?'

'I don't like the thought of getting trapped.'

'Don't you think it would make a good broadcast, though, live from the shelter...?'

He paused, watching the people. An old couple went past, supporting each other, a quilt draped over their hunched shoulders. Behind them, a mother shepherded three sleepy children, helped by two women in party clothes and sky-high heels.

'It would,' he agreed. 'I still don't like it though. It worries me that once I got the cave-dwelling bug I'd lose my ability to go out into the streets.'

'Good,' Jenny said.

But he wasn't having that.

'You do it,' he suggested.

'Me?'

'Why not? You're a great reporter.' He kissed her nose. 'And even greater with me behind you, right?'

'Right,' she agreed with a smile but then a wave of planes came in, dropping bombs barely three streets away, and she shrank back. 'I'm frightened, Ned.'

'Really? We can't have that. Let's get you inside, hey? Look – Allan's on duty so we'll be fine!'

He pointed to where their friends Allan and Moira Wells were standing beneath the sign, sand buckets and extinguishers at the ready. A call had gone out across London for fire watchers and Allan and his wife had volunteered. They waved cheerily and Ned called a hello but it was drowned by a wave of Messerschmitts, passing so low Jenny could swear the whole pub shook. Bombs fell on streets scarily nearby and suddenly the neighbourhood was alight with hellish colour.

'I don't like it, Ned. *Please*, can we go home?'

'Fine,' he agreed, though his voice was tight and he marched her in silence towards Hallam Street. As they got to the junction, he said, 'You know it won't be any safer in the apartment than—'

More planes cut off his words and then a bomb dropped. She saw it, silver and flame-orange as it spun, seemingly straight towards them, then smashed into the Announcer's Arms. It exploded right where Allan and Moira had been standing, taking out a portion of the wall and exposing the shocked revellers to the night.

Ned pulled Jenny close and she clutched him, staring, aghast, at the building. Almost the whole front wall had fallen away and cries filled the air as people stumbled out of the jagged gap, bleeding and begging for help. Jenny and Ned ran over. Allan and Moira were gone, crushed beneath the wall, but

Jenny couldn't think about that now. There were others they needed to help – so many of their friends, so many strangers, were sitting on the pavement, cut and dazed. Someone scrabbled at the rubble, wailing as they tried to dig down to a loved one, and an ambulance screamed up, disgorging a medical team. A nurse handed Jenny a sponge and bandages and she moved to clean up where she could, while the planes still came and the bombs still fell and safety felt like something you only found in a dream.

'That could have been us,' Ned gasped when, finally, they'd rescued everyone they could and sent them off to hospital – or the morgue. 'We could have been in there.'

'We weren't,' she said, tears streaming down her face as she surveyed the wreckage. 'We're here, we're safe.'

'Thanks to you.' He put a hand under her chin and lifted it to kiss her tenderly. 'All that stuff about whether we make each other great or not doesn't matter, Jen. But love – you and me, together – that *does* and we mustn't ever forget it.'

He was right, but it was hard and getting harder every vicious night. They had come to London chasing a story and now, it seemed, the story was chasing them.

TWELVE

THE ANNEXE, TREASURY BUILDINGS, NOVEMBER 1940

CLEMENTINE

'Come in, Jenny, come in.' Clementine waved her American friend past the guards, closing the door on the freezing night. 'Excuse the chaos, we're still getting settled.'

She waved her guest into a small armchair in the hallway of her new living quarters and clambered over boxes to get to the coat cupboard. Moving yet again from Downing Street to the Treasury building had been hard work but she'd put her foot down after the night of the bombing and insisted Winston follow his aides' entreaties and move into what they were calling the Annexe – the ground floor of the Treasury, directly above the War Rooms. They should probably have moved into the War Rooms themselves but Winston hated being below ground, so being close enough to dart down if the bombs got worrying was the compromise.

It felt hard to be moving again, but she was trying to focus on decorating their new rooms to keep herself sane, an art she'd learned from her mother. Lady Blanche had not been good at many things – certainly not at keeping husbands, or staying out of casinos – but she'd been able to make any room a haven of light and space. Her rampant lack of concern for economy had helped, mind you, and that Clementine had most definitely not inherited. Growing up with money for roulette but none for bread had given her a horror of overspending and Winston's expensive tastes had been a bone of contention throughout their marriage.

'Silk underwear,' she muttered.

'Pardon, Clementine?'

She flushed, pulled back into the present, and grabbed the nearest coat. It was her favourite leopard-skin one. Was it too glamorous for today's visit? Probably, but why should people not have a little glamour?

Jenny Miller, perched daintily on the edge of the chair, was still looking at her curiously.

'My husband wears silk underwear,' she explained. 'I was horrified when I first found out but he insists he has delicate skin and that it is not an indulgence but a necessity. He is not a man who can bear discomfort.'

'How lucky then,' Jenny said, 'that he has you to look after him so well.'

Clementine felt a flush of pleasure. 'Thank you. He needs it, for he is ever careless of his safety.'

'It's good you're there for him, though I hope he looks after you too?'

Clementine frowned. 'He's far too busy looking after the country, my dear. Now, where's Jock?' She looked around for Winston's private secretary.

Jock was trying to avoid this trip, considering it below his manly dignity, but it was too important to shirk. Mrs Miller had come to her the other day, shocked at the state of a shelter she'd visited for a broadcast and asking if she might be able to help. Clementine had cursed herself for not doing so already and agreed immediately. Had she not worked in the Great War setting up hostels for young women workers coming to London for the first time? So was she not perfectly placed to do it again?

As far as she could see, men took a certain perverse pleasure in living like Spartans, but women were not so foolish, especially if there were children involved. And quite right too. The conditions Jenny had described in Southwark underground station sounded appalling and Clementine was keen to help. It would do Winston no good to be seen as a prime minister careless of his people's well-being, but he was far too busy fretting over battlefields to give it his full attention. She was happy to pick up the task, but had to get government funding to complete it and for that she needed a civil servant. Jock was the obvious choice, but he quite clearly did not agree for he had been objecting and stalling all week. Now, at the point of departure, he had simply disappeared. It was so childish!

'Excuse me, Jenny,' she said, embarrassed at keeping the earnest young American waiting. Laying down her coat, she slipped through to Grace's office.

'Have you seen Jock, Grace?'

'He's hiding,' her forthright secretary said. 'Scared he'll melt in the dirty air of real life.'

Clementine laughed. 'It'll do him good. I'll dig him out.'

She plunged into the offices behind her new living area. They were full of women typing assiduously and men talking pompously but Jock Colville was not amongst them.

'Where's Jock?' she asked repeatedly but no one seemed to know. 'Fine, where's Winston?'

'In his office, ma'am, but he said he wasn't to be disturbed by anybody.'

'I,' she said imperiously, 'am not "anybody".' It was bad enough having to share her living space with lackeys, but being obstructed by them was a leap too far. She took hold of the door to Winston's office and stepped inside to find Jock cowering behind a notebook.

'There you are, Jock! Have you seen the time?'

'Sorry, Mrs Churchill, we've been very busy.'

'No doubt, but surely your mother didn't bring you up to keep ladies waiting?'

He flushed. 'Of course not but this is wartime.'

'This is wartime because we are fighting for a just, fair, polite society. It is not an excuse for becoming as boorish as the enemy.'

Jock looked to Winston for help but Winston was chuckling merrily.

'She has you there, Jock. Off you go. I'll manage fine while you're out.'

'But, sir, we have the agenda for PM's questions to go through.'

He looked pained, desperate to stay safe in his paperwork, but Clementine wasn't having it.

'Governments have to stay in touch, Jock, or what is the point of them?'

'Quite right, my dear,' Winston said, thrusting his hands into the pockets of his romper – today a sturdy navy cotton – and giving her a conspiratorial wink. 'My wife has my reputation in her hands, Jock, and you must help her keep it up. Off you go.'

Clementine glanced at her hands, hoping they were strong enough for this precious charge, but standing around worrying would get them nowhere. Sending her husband a smile of thanks, she took Jock's arm and propelled him through to the hallway where Jenny was waiting patiently. She rose and held out Clementine's coat.

Jock baulked. 'You're going to visit a shelter in that?'

'In my coat, yes. It's November, Jock. It's cold.'

'Of course but surely you have something… plainer? You don't want the people to think you're lording it over them, do you?'

It was Clementine's turn to flush. She most certainly did not want that; it would not help Winston's reputation one bit.

Jenny, however, tutted audibly. 'Neither, sir, does she want the people to think she does not deem them worthy of her finest clothes.'

Jock blinked. 'There is that I suppose.'

Clementine nervously fingered her earrings – her pearl studs, as she had misplaced the drops that had so boldly escaped the near-bombing. Perhaps it was a good job if she was already looking too flashy? She glanced uncertainly to Jenny but the younger woman gave her a smile and stared Jock down once more.

'I heard the queen said that the people would wear their best clothes for her, so why should she not wear hers for them.'

'Did she?' Clementine asked, feeling instantly better. 'I admire Elizabeth Bowes-Lyon more and more every day. Let's go!' Grateful for such a forthright ally, she took her young friend's arm and they headed out to the car, leaving Jock to trail forlornly behind.

The shelter was as bad as Jenny had reported. Hundreds were crammed onto the platforms, some even sleeping between the rails. An attempt at erecting bunks had been made along the sides but the project had clearly stalled halfway and whole families were cramming into spaces barely fit for one person. She saw a young mother frantically rocking a youngster whose cheeks were bright with fever and her heart wrenched. She knew that feeling all too well and the memory of it turned her legs to jelly. She put a hand to the clammy tiles to steady herself.

'Are you all right, Clementine?' Jenny asked anxiously.

She felt guilty for indulging her past concerns when these

poor people were going through hell. 'Quite well,' she said. 'Where are these latrines?'

Jenny guided her to a curtain at the far end of the platform, from which an unholy stench was emanating.

'May I see?' Clementine asked a woman waiting in the queue.

'If you can bear it, ma'am,' she said, dropping into a sharp curtsy.

'Good gracious, I'm not the queen,' she said. 'I'm just one of you.'

'Hardly, ma'am, but it's lovely of you to say so. Lovely of you to take an interest. And what a fine coat. Nice to see a touch of glamour in this shithole, pardoning my French.'

Clementine felt Jock bristle at her side but she'd heard far worse in her time and this lively young woman was right – this place *was* a shithole.

'Thank you,' she said. 'What's your name?'

'Elsie, ma'am, Elsie Farthing.'

'I like your headwear.' She gestured to the exotically coloured scarf Elsie wore wrapped around her hair and curled up at the front, like a material version of a fine French chignon.

Elsie touched a hand to it. 'This, ma'am? It's just a silly thing to keep my hair free of the dust of poor old London. The factory girls are all wearing them.'

She gestured to a few others crowding round and Clementine noticed that they, too, had their hair wrapped up in a form of turban, each one in their choice of colour or pattern.

'What an excellent idea,' she said. 'I might try it myself. Now, Elsie, let's have a look at these latrines, shall we?' Sliding between the curtains, she clapped a hand to her mouth as she took in the three paltry buckets, rusted and already overflowing at just 10 p.m. 'This will not do,' she said. 'You wouldn't keep prisoners in these conditions! Jock, take a look.'

'I'll take your word for it, Mrs Churchill.'

She narrowed her eyes. 'Take. A. Look.'

He sidled miserably in beside her then gasped, fumbling for a silk handkerchief and pressing it to his mouth. And he'd scoffed at her coat, she thought with a bitter smile.

'Would you like your wife using this, Jock?'

'Good Lord, no.'

'So why should anyone else's? We are spending a fortune on munitions – as we must – but the price of just one bomb would buy these poor folk a set of decent latrines, and bunks for their children. It would be money very well spent and we must see to it that my husband allocates it.'

A cheer arose but she put a hand up to stop it.

'This is not a gift, but your God-given right in a civilised society. You are bravely withstanding the wrath of the Luftwaffe and deserve comfort while doing so. I am most grateful to Mrs Miller for bringing this to my attention and will be fighting for urgent improvements.'

'Thank you, ma'am,' Elsie said, almost bowing again, and a chorus of voices joined hers.

Clementine felt ashamed at the lowness of their expectations.

'We will do a memorandum to Winston,' she told Jock. She'd learned early in their marriage that her husband responded best to the written word and that had become doubly so since taking on the leadership of the country. Their 'house post' of cosy notes and pet cartoons had turned into a conduit for matters of both domestic and national importance. 'We should get in touch with the Red Cross,' she went on, looking to Jenny.

'I can do that.'

'I don't doubt it,' Clementine agreed, casting an eye to Jock who, for all his skills as an administrator, had been at a loss amongst real people.

'It's excellent to have women here to do women's work,' he muttered.

'What a shame then,' Clementine told him, infuriated, 'that women are not authorised to fund it.'

He swallowed. 'I will make sure your requests are... expedited.'

'Good. And arrange a series of ministers to come on my next visits.'

'*Next* visits?'

'Of course. Someone has to check that things are improving. We cannot simply throw money at the problem and hope it sorts itself out, can we?'

'No,' Jock agreed morosely.

She took pity on him. 'Don't worry, Jock. If you get me a juicy set of ministers, I won't make you come along.'

His eyes lit up. 'I shall get onto it straight away. What are MPs for, after all, if not to serve the people who elected them?'

'Precisely. Now, is there anywhere to get a cup of tea down here, Elsie?'

''Fraid not, ma'am,' Elsie said. 'We was meant to get a canteen but the urns had to go somewhere else.'

'To the troops,' another woman provided.

'Which is fair enough, Lord love 'em. My two lads are down in a camp near Dover waiting for their chance to get at Fritz again and I most certainly don't begrudge 'em a cuppa. It's just...'

'That you'd like a cuppa too, as is most understandable. Make a note, Jock.'

Jock fumbled for a pen, though Jenny, she spotted, had already written it down. She must remember to consult her before finalising her memo to Winston, she thought, relieved to have something active to do to help him, rather than simply fussing around.

'I have a flask here, Mrs Churchill ma'am, if you'd like to share with me?' Elsie offered.

'She would not,' Jock snapped.

Clementine felt anger flare at his insensitivity. 'I most certainly would,' she retorted, finding a space on the steps alongside Elsie and accepting a plastic mug of tea from a battered tartan flask.

Jenny sat on the other side and Jock leaned awkwardly against the wall and refused tea, though accepted a tot of something stronger from an elderly gent in a flat cap.

'Bit more crowded than you're used to I bet, ma'am,' Elsie observed.

Clementine looked around, reminded, for the second time that day, of a period long gone. 'Actually, it reminds me of when I was young, in Dieppe. I shared an apartment with my mother and two sisters in the centre, very near to the Café des Tribunaux, where everyone who was anyone went to drink and chat. Not the rich people – they were in their fancy villas along the front – but the arty lot, the musicians and writers and artists. Every evening around six o'clock they'd gather in the café to drink pastis and play pétanque and talk the world stupid. I was only about ten but I loved it. My sister Kitty and I would sit on the steps at the side, like we're doing here, and watch everyone going about the mysterious business of being adults.'

Elsie laughed. 'Me and my big sister used to do that down Southwark market. Where is she now, your sister?'

Clementine gulped at her tea. 'She died, I'm afraid. Typhoid. I've found my memories of Dieppe rather tarnished ever since.'

'There now, Mrs Churchill, I'm so sorry. Jim! Jim, over here! Mrs Churchill needs a bit of your magic brew in her tea, so she does.'

'No, I...' Clementine started to object but Jim was already bustling over.

He solicitously added some home-brewed spirit to her plastic cup, while Elsie patted her on the back, and it was rather nice to be so disarmingly looked after. Jock stood looking at her curiously and then someone struck up a tune on a penny whistle and all around them voices rose to 'It's a Long Way to Tipperary'. Clementine looked awkwardly around, but the notes echoed back off the curved roof so jauntily that it seemed the most natural thing in the world to open her mouth and sing along.

The stench of the latrines still stung the back of her throat and the press of the people weighed against her as heavily as the need to help them. The Nazis might not be launching their ships at Britain right now, but their air attacks were relentless and, with the rest of Europe under their cosh, it was far too easy to feel helplessly alone. There was so much to do and so little time to do it in, but for now, for tonight, it was enough just to sit with the brave folk of London and to sing.

THIRTEEN

DEAN'S YARD, WESTMINSTER, DECEMBER 1940

JENNY

Bundles for Britain! Jenny stared at the jauntily written notice on the ancient oak door, tucked into a corner of Dean's Yard behind the beguilingly beautiful Westminster Abbey. She'd thought it was some sort of joke when Ned had come home from CBS the other day saying that Sue White, the chief executive's wife, was organising a charity to provide supplies to the people of Britain with some New York socialite, but it seemed 'Bundles for Britain' was real enough, and Jenny was to head up the London office!

She'd been able to inform Sue that what was needed most was knitted goods – jumpers and blankets and socks. The winter had turned bitterly cold and so many people who'd been bombed out of their homes were without winter clothing. The forces, too, were short on 'woollies' as the Brits called them, especially the poor sailors patrolling the bitterly cold North Sea and, as Jenny had been rather proud of putting it, they needed 'all hands to the needles'.

Sue had reported that back to her contact in New York, a

high-society girl called Natalie Wales Latham, who'd promptly borrowed a Park Avenue store, purchased a box of wool and invited all her fancy friends in to knit for Britain. The press had been all over it and now half of America was knitting away, even Eleanor Roosevelt, the president's wife. The first shipment would be arriving within a fortnight and someone needed to organise distribution. That someone was, apparently, Jenny.

'Hello?'

She opened the door and found herself in a small, low-ceilinged room. A large desk sat in the centre, with a smaller one to the side behind which a young woman in a stylish green suit, with pale collars, cuffs and belt, was staring at a pile of papers. Seeing Jenny, she jumped up and rushed over.

'Mrs Miller?'

'That's me.'

'Thank the Lord you're here! Dora.' She offered a hearty handshake. 'I'm Lord Carlisle's daughter. I told Daddy I wanted to do war work and he said I'd be perfect for this but I don't know if he's right. I mean, I'm not stupid, I've got my higher cert in maths, and I've organised a few balls and dinners, but this is different. There's so much information!' Dora picked up the nearest sheaf. 'This says there are a hundred and twenty cartons arriving next Monday and I have no idea where we'll put them. They won't fit in here!'

Jenny looked around the small space. 'They certainly won't,' she agreed. 'We'll need depots.'

'Depots, yes!' Dora beamed. 'As I said, thank the Lord you're here.'

'I'm sure organising pullovers is far easier than organising debutantes, so you'll be fine.'

'Golly, yes,' Dora agreed with a giggle. 'They won't get drunk and run off with someone else's chap for a start.'

Jenny laughed. 'Very true.'

Dora looked at Jenny, her immaculate head cocked to one side like a well-groomed sparrow. 'You're American?'

'I am.'

'What does that feel like?'

Jenny blinked. 'I've no idea. Much the same as you?'

'I don't think so. Americans are so new, aren't they? So untrammelled by rules and traditions and history.'

'I suppose that's true. We're certainly brought up to believe that anyone can do anything. Any man can get to the White House if he tries hard enough.'

'But not any woman?'

'Not yet...'

Dora clapped her hands delighted. 'I like you, Mrs Miller,' she said.

'Call me Jenny, Dora, and I like you too. Now, shall we make a start on all this?'

It wasn't easy. Jenny soon had the numbers wrestled into some sort of sense and Dora putting them onto a card system, but finding out who to contact in ports and transport hubs was harder. She was very relieved, therefore, when Mrs Churchill knocked at the door. She'd seen her a few times recently, for the prime minister's wife had been true to her word about securing action on the shelters and Jenny had gone on several more visits with her. Even with Christmas approaching, the Luftwaffe attacks showed no sign of abating, but at least now most of the shelters were habitable.

Mrs Churchill had been relentless in her 'tours of inspection' and taken, Jenny was certain, a wicked delight in forcing MPs out of the hallowed confines of the Houses of Parliament and into the stink of life underground. Ronald Tree had done an excellent job, going round kissing the hands of the Southwark housewives like a true gent, but others had found it harder going. She and Jenny had had to avert their eyes while an MP well-known for braying about 'the man in the street' had vomited onto that very street after a trip to a shelter with blocked sewers.

'I'll try and get a few peers as well,' Clementine had said gleefully. 'They're harder because they have no obligation to the electorate, but I can be very persuasive.'

That, Jenny did not doubt. Clementine Churchill had the ability to cut through excuses and delays and get to the heart of what needed to be done. Jenny admired her hugely but was desperate to know more about the woman who'd sat and sung on Southwark steps, who'd run around Dieppe as a girl, and who'd lost her big sister tragically young. That Clementine, however, was kept firmly locked away and she suspected even her family rarely saw her. Besides, it was none of her business.

'Clementine, come in,' she said, leaping up to shake her hand. 'It's good to see you. I like your headwear.'

Clementine was wearing a turban similar to many of the factory girls, although hers was in dark blue silk to match her two-piece suit. She touched a hand to it.

'Good morning, Jenny, and thank you. It seemed such a practical idea that I thought I'd give it a go.' She gave Jenny a sudden wink. 'Stops one having to wash one's hair quite as often – marvellous!'

Jenny, taken aback, laughed. 'I suppose it does.'

'I know these days I have hot baths and luxurious lotions, but I still have an inherent hatred of bathing from cold tubs by the fire when I was younger.'

'In Dieppe?'

'That's right. Mother always went first and then Kitty and by the time I got to the water, it was tepid at best. But, heavens, that's hardly the point right now.' She shook herself and looked determinedly around the office. 'What a relief to see things so calm in here. I feared you'd be drowning in knitwear.'

Jenny sighed and looked at the paperwork before her. 'We

might be yet if we can't get logistics sorted. I don't suppose you know anyone in transport?'

Clementine thought about it. 'Not personally but the transport secretary has been to Chartwell on many an occasion so owes me a favour. I'll ask him for a list of companies you can rely on.'

'You will?'

'Of course. The government must be active in the assistance of her brave people. I shall tell him to make sure he secures you charitable rates. In fact, why don't you come to Downing Street with me now and see if he can be tracked down. No time like the present!'

'Perfect, thank you.'

As was so often the case with Clementine Churchill, Jenny found herself swept into action. She soon tracked down the transport minister in his office in the depths of Whitehall and, trapped by two determined women, he agreed to phone around companies willing to offer lorries for the transport of Natalie Latham's 'Bundles'.

'Mrs Miller knows where you are,' Clementine warned him. 'And she has my permission to check on progress whenever she sees fit. Our people are cold, my man, and we three can warm them up!' She strode from the offices, beckoning Jenny after her.

'Thank you so much,' Jenny said. 'This will make a big difference to the success of the Bundles for Britain project.'

'And therefore the success of the war, which is what it is all about. We must win, Mrs Miller. Winston must win.'

Jenny flinched. 'You mean the Allies must?'

'The Allies?' Clementine gave a squeaky laugh. 'At the moment, my dear, Winston *is* the Allies. We must give him every support we can.'

'It sounds exhausting,' Jenny said lightly.

'It is vital,' Clementine retorted, then caught herself and turned on a careful smile. 'Tea?'

Jenny nodded and followed her through a maze of offices to a guarded door, behind which was the Annexe, the PM's new living quarters. Clementine showed Jenny into what she called the 'parlour' while Grace fetched tea. The smell of the pretty duck-egg blue paint still hung in the air, and soft furnishings stood around a walnut occasional table on a pale blue rug. Creamy linen flapped at the windows, and the whole effect brought delicious light into the room.

'I love your drapes,' Jenny said, fingering the filmy fabric.

'Drapes? Ah, curtains! Though drapes is perhaps more appropriate for these. Most people think them rather déclassé but I love the softness they bring to a room. It's a trick my mother taught me.'

Jenny seized on this. 'In Dieppe?'

'Oui. The French love drifty fabrics.'

'Did you like it there?'

'Sometimes.'

'When you were with your sister?'

Clementine took the tea tray Grace had brought in and eyed her sharply. 'If you'd like to know about Kitty, Jenny, you only have to ask. I know, by now, that you're no idle gossip.'

Jenny felt disproportionately flattered. 'Thank you and, yes, I would like to know. It sounds so sad.'

'It was dreadful. We think she caught typhoid from the water at our convent school. That, too, was déclassé! The "noble" children were meant to go to the fancy private school in town but, although Mother had the grand name of Lady Blanche, she had no funds, for she frittered them away in the casinos. I've hated gambling ever since.'

'I don't blame you. Your father was...?'

'Absent. They were poorly suited. After three years and no heir, I'm told my mother took matters into her own hands. My father is probably Bertram Mitford, her brother-in-law, though there are other possible contenders.'

Jenny fought to take this in. 'That's why you don't look like Nellie?'

'Possibly. Though Mother's affair with Bertram lasted longer than her marriage so he may be Nellie's father too. I think dalliances suited Blanche's temperament better than the grind of fidelity.'

'It sounds very... Bohemian.'

Clementine grimaced. 'It was rather. I'm sorry if I've shocked you, Jenny. I know we English have a reputation for prudishness but the aristocracy are far from well-behaved. Almost all my mother's friends were divorced, or might as well have been.'

'So your father... That is, the man...'

'The man whose name I bore – Henry Hozier – decided he did not like society knowing his children were not his and cast us loose. Or, at least, he cast the twins loose.'

'Twins?'

Jenny glanced at her tea, wondering if it was spiked. As was so often the case with Clementine, she felt as if she were missing parts of the conversation.

'Nellie was a twin with Bill but we lost him some years ago. At the time, however, it was apparent they were not Father's as there was no history of twins in the Hozier family. My parents lived apart for a while but then Henry decided he would like Kitty and me back, so Mother put Bill into prep school and whipped us girls off to Dieppe to avoid him.'

'He didn't follow?' Jenny asked, gripped.

'Not at first. A year or so later he came to visit and took Kitty and me out to eat – separately. Kitty managed with aplomb but when I went the next day, he dismissed the maid and began plying me with questions about where in England I would like to go to school. I was terrified, convinced he was going to bundle me onto the ferry before Mother could find me.'

'What did you do?'

'Luckily, he went to the bar to choose himself a cigar and I made a run for it. Found the maid hovering outside, unsure what to do for the best, and we hotfooted it back to Mama together. He gave up after that and we stayed in Dieppe. Until Kitty...' She gave a deep sigh. 'There's little to tell about Kitty that you cannot imagine for yourself. Typhoid is a cruel disease. If unchecked, it works its evil slowly, dragging the victim into a steady, unyielding decline.'

'You had to watch that happen to your sister?'

'Worse – I did not get to watch it. Nellie and I were sent to my grandmother in Scotland so Mother could nurse Kitty to full health. We thought she'd succeeded when we got a telegram saying she was bringing her to Batsford and we should join them there. We got ready with such joy, until a second telegram, sent before the first but delayed, told us the tragic news that Kitty had gone. It was her body, no more, that was being brought home to England for burial.'

'Oh, Clementine, that's so sad.'

'It was,' she agreed simply. 'It was my first true loss, though sadly not my last. It wrecked my mother. Kitty was her favourite, you see. She was the vivacious, pretty, outgoing one. And the loss of a child, you know, is a terrible, terrible thing.'

She looked lost suddenly, but Jenny felt the sting under her skin.

'I don't know,' she said quietly. 'But I know how it feels to lose the possibility of one.'

Clementine simply reached out and took her hand and they sat there, together, as the drapes blew mournfully in the last of the December light and, somewhere down the street, a warden called the order for blackout.

FOURTEEN

CHEQUERS, BUCKINGHAMSHIRE, 22
JUNE 1941

CLEMENTINE

Clementine brought her spoon down again and again – and
again.

Take that, she caught herself thinking, then, looking at the
battered boiled egg, realised she'd been subconsciously
pretending it was Hitler's miserable head. She gave it one more
bash for good measure and glanced around, ashamed. Eggs were
rationed and Chequers only had a supply thanks to the local
hens; she had no right to misuse this treasure so. Thankfully she
was the only one in the dining room. It was early and the party
last night had been, from what she'd heard from her bedroom,
raucous and late. Thank heavens young Pamela was here and,
with Baby Winston now eight months old and very happily
ensconced here at Chequers with a nanny, had resumed her
social life with gusto. She'd happily hosted dinner last night,
leaving Clementine to gratefully slip away to supper in her
bedroom.

She'd be breakfasting there, as she usually did, if Mr
Harriman had not mentioned how much he enjoyed the first

meal of the day and she'd felt obliged to be in the morning room to keep him company. He was the 'Lend-Lease negotiator' over from the States as Mr Roosevelt's personal envoy to arrange the 'lending' of American equipment and supplies to Great Britain and Winston was anxious he should enjoy all comfort.

'We need the Americans, Clemmie,' was his endless refrain these days. 'It's the only way to beat the Nazis.'

Her husband looked so tired, so bowed down with the weight of a world that was relying more and more heavily on him, and Clementine hated to see it. If getting the Americans onside would help, then she, as his loving wife, must do all she could to secure them. The news was relentlessly bad. The Luftwaffe had continued to hit London throughout the first half of this long year, and targeted many of England's other cities too. The industrial Midlands had been badly hit, with Coventry and Birmingham suffering terribly, and many cities of the north had also taken sustained attacks. Every night had been a battle for survival. Clementine, along with many others not in 'active service', had signed up as a fire warden and done her turns of duty, sitting on the rooftops with sand and water to quash any fires before they took hold. It was very effective against the small incendiaries that took about a minute from impact to release their charge, but useless before the larger bombs that ripped homes apart immediately.

The public weren't happy, and understandably so, though the fall of every other European country beneath the onslaught of Nazi Blitzkrieg had shown them how well they were doing to hold out. In the last few weeks Yugoslavia and Greece had been occupied, completing the ravaging of the continent. Any country not declared neutral was now either allied to the Nazis or occupied by them and how long Britain could hold out was anyone's guess.

The Luftwaffe had ripped London apart last month and both St Paul's cathedral and Winston's treasured House of

Commons had taken a hit, but they had been coming only sporadically since. The let-up had brought some relief to people's nights but it felt like the calm before the storm – like the point when you realise a toddler has gone quiet and must go and find the carnage that is bound to have ensued.

Bletchley Park were frantically monitoring Nazi messages and were certain Hitler was planning something big. Spies and reconnaissance analysts were tracking all enemy movements on the continent and Winston was full of it. After the comms nightmares of Dunkirk, he'd had a map room set up in the War Rooms, kept as up to date as possible by an army of ATS workers. He spent hours in it with the chiefs of staff, striding around in his romper, marking out positions like a boy with tin soldiers. But then, he had been that boy. Many of his favourite models were kept in a cabinet in his study and some of his most popular books had been about military strategists like his ancestor, Lord Marlborough.

'Information is the key,' he would tell her regularly.

She supposed he was right, but for her, less able to conceive the movement of battalions and battleships, it felt like a brutally clear lens into the future – a future full of pain and fear and, ultimately, occupation. Hitler had retreated last autumn but that did not mean he would not try again and however brilliant Bletchley Park were proving, surely Hitler could keep some secrets? Would our boys be able to resist if he mounted a full-scale attack? Clementine had no idea. Poor Chartwell would be the first thing to go, of course. Hitler would snatch it as his personal command centre, and the thought of the Wehrmacht swimming in the children's pool and trampling all over her rose garden churned her up inside. Chartwell might be a money pit, but it was *their* money pit and Hitler couldn't have it!

She told herself to calm down. There was no intelligence suggesting Hitler was heading for the Channel and even if he did, the sheer process of having to land on the south coast would hamper the attackers. Men in the War Rooms spent hours trying to decide which beaches the Nazis might target and posting those troops not yet shipped to North Africa to cover them. Clementine hated thinking of the young men who'd escaped from Dunkirk having to face the onslaught again. But of course, if the Nazis hit British shores they would *all* have to face it.

A sudden, absurd image of herself and Winston poking machine guns out of the windows of Number Ten in a desperate last stand sprang into her mind. She pictured herself in tea-dress and turban wielding her gun alongside Winston in a velvet romper, and a dark laugh escaped from her. Would that be where Winston's treasured job of prime minister ended?

'Enjoying yourself there, Clemmie?'

She looked round to see Pamela in the doorway, staring at her with unconcealed amusement, and flushed.

'Quite the reverse, I'm afraid; I was imagining how an invasion might look.'

Pam's smile faded and she came over and gave her a warm hug. 'It's just too horrible to think about, isn't it? I met a Dutch chap in a bar the other day and he was telling me how hideous it was when the Nazis marched into the Netherlands. He says Blitzkrieg is impossible to resist – the tanks roll in, blasting everything in their path, and behind them come thousands of soldiers, armed to the teeth and trained like automatons. The Nazis, he said, believe that the only lives worth bothering about are their own, so they have no compunction about taking anyone else out – women, children, pensioners. They're not people to them, not really, they're just—'

'Yes, thank you, Pamela.' Clementine put her hands to her ears, then felt childish. Every other nation had had to face this horror, so why not them? 'Sorry. I can't bear it.'

'I know. It's vile.' Pamela pulled a face, then bounced over to the breakfast buffet, her appetite apparently undiminished by the fear of imminent annihilation.

'Did you sleep well?' Clementine asked, taking refuge in comfortable civilities.

'Like a dream, thank you.' Plate piled high, she all but skipped to the table.

Clementine eyed her suspiciously. 'You're very bright this morning. It was a late one, wasn't it?'

'Terribly,' she agreed cheerfully. 'And I drank far too much. Your husband is a devil with the brandies.'

'I know! You were up with the men?'

'Why not? Times are changing, Clemmie. We women are proving our worth. Look at all those girls in the factories and tilling the land, and even training to be pilots. I've heard they're damned good at it too, like those fancy American aviators, Amelia Earhart and Jacqueline Cochran. And why the hell not?'

'Pamela!'

'Sorry. The Americans are rubbing off on me.' She giggled and hurriedly picked up a spoon to bash her egg.

Clementine looked at her ruined one and then back to her daughter-in-law, suspicious once more. Pamela was not usually up before ten o'clock and not usually this talkative before midday. Plus, she was dressed to the nines, complete with dangly golden earrings that were surely too flashy for morning? Clementine might be an old married woman but she'd been through the debutante circuit for several years and recognised the sparkle in Pamela's eyes. Her heart sank.

'How was Mr Harriman?' she hazarded.

Pamela jumped a mile, confirmation that Clementine had, sadly, hit her mark.

'Sorry?'

'Mr Harriman, Averell – did he enjoy the dinner, do you think?'

'Oh, oh I see.'

Pamela had gone bright red and Clementine's stomach churned. Her fingers went to her ears to feel the reassuring firmness of the modest amethyst studs Winston had bought her for their last anniversary. No one else's marriages seemed to have quite the same solidity these days. Mr Harriman had a wife back in America and of course Pamela was married to Clementine's son. She'd recently discovered where Randolph had been while Pamela had laboured to produce the heir he'd been so desperate for – in the arms of another woman. He was off in Egypt now, having left the Hussars under the suspicion that Winston had ordered them kept out of active duty (quite possibly true though Winston wouldn't admit it, even to her) and signed on with a parachute unit of the new Special Air Services. She'd been impressed until she'd heard that he'd gambled away so much money on the boat to Egypt that poor Pamela had had to sell almost all their wedding presents and give up their nice house for a tiny apartment.

Why, she supposed, if she was putting up with so much, should Pamela not have some fun? Women, as her daughter-in-law had just said, were proving their worth and maybe that meant husbands had to step up and deserve them. It was a headily modern thought and, feeling rather giddy, Clementine rose to fetch more coffee.

'I believe Averell thoroughly enjoyed himself,' Pamela said, composed once more. 'He says he has the utmost admiration for the British, so that's good, isn't it?'

That *was* good. Winston needed the Americans to help him fight the Nazi menace, but did that mean they should – what was the vile word the children used? – pimp out their family in the cause?

'He'll tell Roosevelt we're worth supporting?' she asked Pamela cautiously.

'He will. He'll keep up the Lend-Lease supplies and he'll push for more active involvement.'

'I see.' She swallowed. 'Good work.'

Pamela looked at her sideways but Clementine ducked her gaze. She was no prude – the chance would be a fine thing with a mother who'd only loved casinos more than men – but she couldn't help feeling there were standards to maintain, especially from Number Ten. She could not be seen to condone any shenanigans, however good the cause. Besides, here was Averell Harriman himself, strolling into the room with a determinedly nonchalant whistle, and Pamela instantly smiley as she made overly formal conversation. It might have been amusing, if it wasn't so very painful.

Clementine forced herself to turn again to her egg. Peeling away the remaining shell, she took a small bite. She had to eat, Dr Moran – Winston's physician – had said so when she'd complained of tiredness. Stifling a laugh and placing a warm hand on her shoulder, he'd told her, 'Mrs Churchill, you are running a country at war, of course you are tired.'

'*I'm* not running it,' she'd protested.

He'd simply raised an eyebrow and said, 'But you are running Winston and that is even harder.'

It had reminded her of Nellie's comments when she'd had to escape poor Bertram's wake to join Winston for his entrance into Number Ten. 'The world needs you, Clemmie. Or rather, Winston needs you and that, in the end, amounts to much the same thing.'

Did it really? Clementine suspected others held her in falsely high regard but nonetheless Winston was her husband and it was her job – and her joy – to support him in everything. If Winston had to defend Number Ten with a machine gun, she would most certainly be at his side.

She tutted at herself and lifted the last of her maligned egg into her mouth. But as it touched her lips, the door was flung open and Winston himself entered at a trot, his silk dressing gown flying behind him. The sight was terrifying, for Clementine had not seen him leave his bedroom before mid-morning in twenty years, nor travel at more than a sedate walk. That was nothing, however, to the wild look in his eyes.

She leaped up. 'What's happened?'

'They've invaded!'

Her heart stopped at her worst fears realised. Bletchley Park had been wrong, their spies had been wrong, their reconnaissance had been wrong. Somehow the Nazis had snuck past them all and this was the moment that sunbathed England faced the Nazi hell.

'Where?'

'All along the border.'

Clementine's mind went into overdrive. Where were the children? Pam and Baby Winston were here, and Randolph off in Egypt so they were safe for now. Sarah was working for the WAAF at Medenham, not far from Chequers, but Diana was in the heart of London and Mary had stayed with her to go to a friend's twenty-first birthday party. Why had she allowed that? How could they get them back? Ever since last autumn there had been a ship readied somewhere near Liverpool to evacuate the royal family and the government to Canada in the event of the invasion, all the Churchills included. The various exiled European royals and governments would also go, to attempt to continue a semblance of non-Nazi rule from overseas, but it was very much a last resort. Clementine had been part of planning it, but had not, she realised, truly imagined them having to leave all they knew and loved to the Nazis' doubtful mercies.

'Three and a half million forces, they're saying,' Winston went on.

Three and a half million?! For this little island? That would be impossible to resist.

'All along from the Arctic Ocean to the Black Sea.'

Clementine stared at him. 'Where?'

'The whole Russian border, Clemmie. And bombing raids on Leningrad, Kronstadt, Sebastopol and who knows where else.'

'The Russian border?' she repeated stupidly.

'Yes, Clemmie, aren't you listening? We knew something big was on the way and here it is – the Nazis have invaded Russia!'

She fell against him, weak with relief. 'I thought you meant here, Winston!'

'Here?' He grabbed her shoulders. 'Britain? No, my dear. No, we're still safe – for now.'

She battled to take this in. 'If Hitler is invading Russia, does that mean he's given up on us?'

'Perhaps,' Winston agreed uncertainly. 'Or perhaps he's just looking to gain more troops before he heads our way.'

Averell came over, his handsome face creased with concern. 'If Hitler takes Russia, he could link up with Japan. Roosevelt won't like this.'

'If Hitler takes Russia,' Winston said, 'he could link up with anyone he chooses. We will be next, Averell, and after us, the States. Roosevelt won't like that either.' He grabbed the handsome American's shoulders, his eyes bright with desperation. 'Tell him, man, tell him we need him or we'll all be saluting the swastika by Christmas.'

FIFTEEN

THE TREASURY, AUGUST 1941

JENNY

Jenny felt her way up the narrow staircase behind the dapper soldier, wondering if this was an elaborate joke against her as an American.

'You lot should be here in the fight,' he'd said when he'd caught her accent down in the lobby of the magnificent Treasury building.

'*I* am,' she'd pointed out, and he'd conceded that with a gruff, 'fair point' and asked if she could convince a few of her buddies to join her.

'We're working on it,' she'd assured him, and they were.

Ned was broadcasting to the States every day and she'd recently done a long feature on rationing, explaining to American housewives the strictures their English cousins were facing in the simple daily task of feeding their family. She wrote regularly to her parents for an update on the American mood but most people were still, her mother said, resolutely isolationist.

'They don't see it as their war,' she'd written. 'And they don't want to send their sons into someone else's fight.'

'Hitler won't stop though,' Jenny had written back. 'If he takes Russia he's in a position to rule the world. All they're doing by delaying is moving the front line onto their doorsteps.'

It was a line she, Ned, and everyone at CBS, repeated regularly, but it wasn't what the folks back home wanted to hear. The invasion of Russia had shaken them, being a country of a size and standing they recognised as similar to their own, but even with Blitzkrieg pointed straight at Moscow, your average American preferred to hug the Atlantic and Pacific like a safety blanket and pretend the war wasn't anything to do with them.

'Is it much further?' Jenny panted to the soldier as they hit a tiny landing and pushed on upwards. Her very bones seemed to ache; she must be getting unfit with living in the city.

'One more floor, ma'am. Look, there's the door out.'

Sure enough, just above him, a metal fire door stood ajar. It looked scarily like the one that had locked Jenny out of her building on the first night of the Blitz and she stepped uncertainly out, but then gasped, any personal safety forgotten in the stunning view of the city. Whitehall's roofs, silver in the moonlight, were a collection of turrets and tessellations set around the graciously open, circular court at the centre of the Treasury. For now, the skies were clear of everything but stars and Jenny felt as if she had stepped into a fairytale not a night of fire duty.

Until she saw her.

Clementine Churchill was alone in the darkness at the edge of the nearest roof. She was, most unusually, in slacks, her right foot resting against a metal bucket of sand, while she cradled an extinguisher like a baby in her arms. Her shoulders beneath her light jacket were tight as she looked across the capital like the sole guardian of the government of this brave little nation.

'Clementine?'

Jenny edged over and Clementine turned and gave her a weary smile.

'You came.'

'Of course.'

Clementine had invited her to join her fire-watching stint earlier in the day when Jenny had been reporting on a hostel inspection. With the shelters much improved, Clementine had taken on the presidency of the YWCA Wartime Appeal and was transforming the many hostels housing girls pouring into the cities to work in factories and sign up to the forces. Clementine said the government were debating conscripting single women. Winston thought it an 'abomination', if, 'perhaps, a necessary one'. Their daughter-in-law, Pamela, had apparently told him he needed to 'open his eyes and see how capable women truly are'.

'She told him,' Clementine had laughed, 'that he was married to a woman with far more talent than he ever gave her credit for, and said he was wasting me on making sure his tea was served on time. I clapped.'

Jenny had felt like clapping too; her new friend always underestimated herself. Look at her here, up on the roofs at midnight having spent a whole day touring hostels with astounding rigour. She'd had beds unmade to check the quality of the mattresses, eaten the food with the girls to be sure it was up to standard, and looked in every single latrine. Jenny thought Clementine the best role model available for any woman adjusting to work outside the home, but she did worry about her. She was well into her fifties and sitting atop the city bomb-watching after a long day on the road was surely overdoing it. Jenny joined her and together they sat, looking out over London.

'Thank you for coming,' Clementine said. 'One can feel rather alone up here at night.'

'I can imagine! I brought tea.' Jenny took the flask from her bag. 'And cake. I've been experimenting with Mr Wootton's wartime recipes. This is apple cake made with powdered egg and honey. It's not the nicest, I'm afraid, but it fills a hole in the stomach.'

'It looks splendid.' Clementine took a slice and bit into it with admirable gusto, given its crispy edges and soggy middle. 'Delicious.'

'You're not a very good liar.' Jenny laughed and had the pleasure of hearing Clementine laugh with her.

'It needs work,' she allowed. 'But none of us should be turning down food, and the apple is yummy.'

They ate in companionable silence, but then a siren wailed on the far edges of the city and beams shot into the air, waving like medieval swords. There had been no major raids for weeks, but that did not mean they would not come at any time. Clementine sat up straighter, her hand literally to the pump, and Jenny, her heart tightening, edged closer to her friend.

'How do you bear it?' she asked.

'What choice do I have? At least they're high above us and not marching over our doorsteps – yet.'

She gave her sudden laugh, the one that always made Jenny jump and then instantly want to laugh too.

'What is it?' she asked.

'A few weeks ago I had a ludicrous picture of myself and Winston holding the fort in Downing Street.'

'Like in a Western?'

'Precisely. Winston loves a Western. But he's no Roy Rogers and I'm certainly no Linda Darnell.' She chuckled self-depre-catingly at the reference to the luscious young starlet.

'And wouldn't want to be,' Jenny told her stoutly. 'You're far more elegant. More beautiful too.'

Clementine looked strangely shy and Jenny felt a curious urge to cry. Clearly the endless days of bombing were getting to her more than she'd thought.

'I got called a "beauty" when Winston and I were courting,' Clementine admitted, 'but I don't think it was true. I was tall and reasonably athletic, so striking amongst a crowd of simpering saps, but any "beauty" was merely the lustre of celebrity. I was terribly gauche as a child, you know. Kitty was the pretty one.'

'I'm so sorry you lost her.'

'As am I, my dear, but we all stand to lose people now.'

As if hearing her, two planes flashed across the beams and swooped overhead. Jenny ducked instinctively and remembered the fear of Ned reporting from the roof of Broadcasting House. He'd been delighted she was fire watching with Mrs Churchill but would not be so happy if she were wounded. Or worse. The planes dropped their bombs somewhere to the west and Jenny felt a rush of relief, then guilt for whoever had been hit in her place.

'There are far fewer planes nowadays,' she commented.

'Yes. The poor Russians are taking the attacks instead.'

'At least they're our allies now.'

'And are still standing up to the Nazis, although the depravations their poor people are suffering sound terrible.'

Jenny nodded grimly. She'd seen newsreels showing horrible scenes of devasted towns and villages across all three lines of Nazi attack, on Leningrad in the north, Moscow in the centre and the Crimean peninsula in the south. The Red Army were fighting hard but how much longer could they resist?

'Stalin is spitting at us for help,' Clementine said, 'but we don't have much to offer – without the Americans at least.'

'I'm sorry.'

Clementine looked at her and laughed. 'It's not your fault, my dear. And maybe, if I was on the other side of the Atlantic, I'd want to stay out of it too but that leaves poor Winston trying to fight the Nazis all alone.'

'He's doing a wonderful job of it,' Jenny offered.

'He is.' Clementine grabbed her arm. 'He really is. I'm so

proud. But he can't do it alone. I have to help him. I have to do all I can.'

Her eyes were manic as she scanned the roofs of Whitehall for trouble, as if she might personally manhandle it away – which, Jenny thought, she just might.

'Winston has many people around him,' she said gently. 'His secretaries, his cabinet, the chiefs of staff—'

'Yes, yes. They're all marvellous. But do they know Winston like I know him?'

'Do they need to?'

Clementine looked confused, then shook herself. 'Quite right, Jenny. Of course they do not. I'm sure they are all very good at their jobs, so I must trust them to do them. I just feel... responsible.'

'And you're doing all you can, really.'

It tore at Jenny's heart to see this bold, brave woman doubting herself. Winston was a heavy charge and she longed to lift a little of the weight, but it seemed Clementine was not inclined to share it.

'Listen to me whining about myself,' she said. 'Boring old woman that I am.'

'You're not—'

'Let's think about you, my dear. Let's think about your safety. What's your evacuation plan?'

'Evacuation plan?'

'If Hitler takes Russia and turns his guns on us. You must have one, you know. Surely your husband has thought of it?'

Jenny shook her head. 'Ned prefers to head into danger.'

'Well, then, you must simply come with us.'

'Sorry?'

'If there's an invasion. We're all booked onto a ship to Canada. It's been ready since Hitler was gathering troops in the Netherlands last autumn and the plans are still in place, just in case. It's us Churchills, the cabinet, the royal family, many of the civil service, quite a few of the staff at the, er, government buildings at Bletchley Park.'

'The intelligence group?'

Clementine squinted at her. 'You know about that?'

'Winston told Ned when he came to call for me after that Bundles meeting the other day. He didn't even get down the corridor before Winston put his head out his office door and asked him in for "several whiskies".'

'That sounds like Winston,' Clementine said drily. 'And over these whiskies he divulged all our secrets?'

'On the strict understanding we would not broadcast them. Winston told Ned he was "padlock", whatever that means?'

Clementine smiled. 'That's our term for the people we can trust. There are not many of them, I'm afraid. I've even had to let some of my best friends go. Not for being traitors, you under-stand, just for being rather... loose-lipped.'

'Let them go?'

'Not see them. It's easier than having to endlessly think about what I'm allowed to say.'

'I'm so sorry.'

No wonder Clementine looked so bowed down if she didn't even have friends to rely on. Jenny felt another tear prick and told herself not to be so stupidly sentimental.

'The perils of leadership, my dear, but if Winston says your Ned is padlock then you must be too, so you should definitely come on the ship.'

'With you? Surely that wouldn't be allowed. We're not nearly important enough.'

'But you're family.'

'What?' Jenny stared at her, her heart swelling. 'We're not family.'

Clementine patted her knee. 'You feel like it to me, dear. I'd be delighted to have the pair of you along.'

Jenny felt a rush of emotion and could do nothing to stop

the foolish tears spurting out of her eyes. She wiped at them, horrified, but Clementine simply produced a handkerchief and put a gentle arm around her shoulders.

'Time of the month?' she suggested.

Jenny froze. She thought about it, then thought again. She'd been far too busy to notice but she hadn't bled since... Before the Russian invasion. She looked at Clementine who looked back at her and, as if in slow motion, put a hand to her mouth. Above them another plane swept in, dropped a bomb on some poor innocents, and arced off into the night, without either of them even noticing.

'I'm late!' Jenny cried and this time she couldn't stop herself hugging Clementine Churchill who, without hesitation, hugged her firmly back.

'Now,' she said, 'you are definitely on the boat out of here.'

'If needed.'

They both sobered.

'If needed,' Clementine echoed.

Jenny looked out over London, kissed with moonlight, and prayed that the great city would stay secure. If God had finally granted her greatest wish and sent her and Ned a child, she wanted it born here, in Europe's last bastion of freedom. Only time, however, would tell if either the baby or the city would hold.

'I told you it would happen, Jenny,' Ned said proudly. 'You and me, we were meant to be parents. You're so clever, honey, so precious.' He fussed around, bringing her tea (they were proper Brits now) and producing a mouth-watering cake from a brown paper bag.

'Where on earth did you get that, Ned?'

'Never you mind, honey. You need your strength and anything I can do to help, I will.'

She smiled at him and tried her best to eat the delicious bundle of cream and sugar, but her stomach rebelled and, in the end, she had to hand most of it over.

'You're sweet enough already,' he said, grinning at her and wolfing it down.

Briefly, Jenny wondered if the entire nine months would be padded out with such trite platitudes, then felt ungrateful. She was having a baby, at last! The doctor had confirmed it this morning and Ned, hovering anxiously in the waiting room, had swept her into his arms with a cry of delight that had made all the other patients leap in alarm.

'So sorry,' Jenny had said to a woman sitting with a toddler on her lap, blood leaking through a makeshift bandage wrapped around his head.

'Don't you be, love,' she'd said with a kindly smile. 'There's enough sadness around; any good news should be celebrated.'

'Quite right,' Ned had agreed, adding, 'Isn't she wonderful, my wife? Isn't she clever?!'

'It's not clever, Ned,' she'd admonished him, tugging him out of the surgery. 'Getting my degree was clever, this is just biology.'

'Well, I think it's clever,' he'd insisted.

She hadn't been sure whether to be glad of that, or sad. And as the weeks passed and he continued to treat her like royalty, she became increasingly unsure. She thought of Clementine, doing so many bold, worthwhile things with her life, while supporting her genius but frankly impossible husband in even bolder things, and still beating herself up for being a 'bad mother'. It felt wrong.

'How come you never mollycoddled me like this before?' she asked Ned one evening.

'I did,' he protested. 'That's to say, I looked after you, watched out for you, fancied you...'

'And you don't now?'

'I sure do, as much as ever. But you're something more now. You're a vessel, a sacred vessel.'

She laughed; this was getting ridiculous. 'There's nothing sacred about me, Ned. I'm just a woman, doing what women were made to do.'

'And it's marvellous.'

There was no real arguing with that and why should she, when her happiness matched his? Ned told everyone at CBS and when she went into the studios, people rushed over to congratulate her.

'Make sure you give young Ned a son,' Paul White, Head of CBS, said heartily, as if Jenny were a chef cooking up dishes on demand.

'I guess it will depend what he put in there,' she shot back.

Paul looked rather startled.

'Jenny,' Ned hissed, 'don't be so coarse.'

'I thought you liked me coarse,' she teased, but apparently that wasn't true any more.

Not that it mattered when her baby was growing inside her. Every morning she woke and put her hand to her belly, whispering hello to the dot of Miller life within. She couldn't wait for the time when her womb began to push outwards, when she could feel their baby moving and know, for sure, that the two of them would become three. She couldn't wait to buy maternity clothes and to fit out a nursery in their apartment and – impossibly delicious to imagine – actually hold their son or daughter in her arms.

'You must have your baby in Fulmer Chase,' Clementine insisted when she called her to confirm the good news.

Jenny pictured the cosy maternity hospital, imagined herself sitting in one of those beds, just like Maisie Proctor, and wept for joy.

'What is it?' Ned asked anxiously.

'It's happiness,' she blubbed.

He looked confused but gamely held her while she cried, stroking her back and presumably marvelling at what their baby was doing to his sacred vessel. It was lovely to be cherished like that, annoying but lovely.

And then, one night, she woke up with cramps tearing through her belly.

She ran to the lavatory, clutching her hands around herself, trying to hold the precious baby safe inside, but the blood across the linoleum traced a warning line. When she sat down, she felt as if her insides were tearing apart and there, in the thin light of a September dawn, their dream dropped down the pan.

'No!' she wailed over and over, as Ned came running, bleary-eyed and frightened.

He stood in the doorway looking helplessly down on her. Suddenly she didn't feel clever or precious, just useless and sad. Very sad.

'It's only a miscarriage,' the doctor told her later that morning. 'They happen all the time, I'm afraid. It doesn't mean you won't have another child.'

'Another child.' Ned seized on this. 'That's what will make you feel better, honey. We'll have another child.'

It had been kindly meant, but it had taken five years to make one scrap of lost humanity and Jenny wasn't sure she could bear to wait five more. Not that she had much choice. Her womb, it seemed, was an incendiary bomb within her and she could only wait, emotional sand bucket and stirrup pump in hand, to see if it caught fire once more.

SIXTEEN

TEN DOWNING STREET, OCTOBER 1941

CLEMENTINE

Clementine put the picnic basket on the oak table and unloaded the scant remains of Mrs Landermare's feast. Her cook had insisted on returning to Number Ten's patched-up kitchens, saying they were far superior to the set-up in the Annexe, and only ever took to the safer quarters if the sirens went, rushing the kitchen maids over with armfuls of pots and pans. She wasn't alone. Winston worked in Downing Street whenever he could and Clementine usually drifted over there in the day too. It felt right, somehow, to operate from the ancient heart of power.

'How were the Scotch eggs?' her cook asked anxiously.

'Delicious.'

'Really? I was worried because that sausage meat was offal, what with it not being rationed, so I thought it might be a bit overpowering.'

'It was wonderful.' Clementine couldn't actually remember eating a Scotch egg but it was bound to have been wonderful, all Mrs Landermare's cooking was.

'And the tart? At least apples are plentiful now – a great heap came up from Chartwell on Monday. Honey too. That'll be the last of it but I've got plenty stored in the pantry. It's a bit stronger-tasting than sugar but I don't think that's necessarily a bad thing, do you?'

'Hmm? Oh yes, the tart was wonderful.'

'Wonderful?' Mrs Landermare put her hands on her capacious hips. 'Did you actually eat any of the picnic at all, Mrs Churchill?'

Clementine grimaced apologetically. 'I did, really, I just don't think I was paying much attention to the food. I'm sorry.'

Mrs Landermare softened. 'It's no wonder, with your Mary there to talk to. An apple tart was the least of your concerns.'

That much had been true. Mary had joined the ATS last month and been posted off to Aldermaston for initial training. She wrote enthusiastic letters about what she was up to, but it wasn't the same as having her at home and Clementine missed her dreadfully. Today Mary had had a day off and Clementine had motored out to see her. It had been a little chilly for a picnic, but they'd taken blankets and flasks of coffee, determined to do something jolly. Hitler was marching deeper into Russia every day and if he took Moscow, Britain would stand alone against the Nazis. Would they have to surrender? It was a debate she knew Cabinet had held several times, to Winston's fury.

'It's strategy, Winston,' she'd said when she'd caught him fuming over it in his bath the other day.

'It's not a strategy I like.'

'That is irrelevant. If the Nazis take Russia, we will surely be their next target?'

He'd harrumphed dramatically. 'And if we are, we will simply have to defend.'

'Or surrender.'

'We discussed that at Dunkirk and rejected the notion. Nothing has changed.'

'But it will if they take Moscow...'

He'd ducked under the water at that, refusing to listen, and Clementine supposed she didn't blame him, though she still worried. The lives of all this country's citizens were in his hands and she longed to do something to assist.

'Mrs Churchill?'

Clementine snapped out of her reverie and looked at her cook. 'Sorry. Again. What were you saying?'

'I was asking if you're happy with herring for the king of Norway this evening. They like fish, don't they, the Norwegians? I was hoping for cod but there was none to be had anywhere.'

'The king of Norway?'

'He's coming to dinner, remember? He's a brave man, Mr Churchill says, much loved by the king and queen, and we're to treat him well. I'm not sure herring counts as treating anyone well but I can do it in a dill sauce and we've still got plenty of Chartwell potatoes and greens. Will it do?'

The last thing Clementine wanted was to entertain King Haakon. He was indeed a brave and principled man, elected to the throne by the Norwegian parliament at his insistence, and deeply invested in democracy. When the Germans had demanded he recognise Vidkun Quisling, leader of the Norwegian fascist party, as prime minister, he'd refused. Under threat of his life, he'd fled with his true government over the mountains before finally escaping to Britain aboard a naval ship. He'd taken refuge in Buckingham Palace, alongside Queen Wilhelmina of the Netherlands, who'd also narrowly evaded Nazi capture. Clementine admired all these gutsy European royals but tonight she just wanted to curl up with Winston and tell him about Mary.

As if that would ever have happened!

'Herring will be good,' she told her cook. 'And perhaps the rest of the apple tart for pudding? Winston is right that Haakon deserves a few treats after all he's been through.'

She had to stop being so selfish and think of others. After all, if Hitler came, she'd be an exile herself.

'Is Mary well?' Mrs Landermare asked.

Clementine snatched at the subject. 'She's very well. She looks so smart in her uniform and she was so bouncy. Even having to scrub floors and clean latrines doesn't seem to have put her off. I should have got her at it years ago!'

'Mary told me she had to clean her bedroom every Saturday morning,' Mrs Landermare said.

'Did she? That would explain it then.'

It explained, too, why Mary was so much more grounded and stable than her older sisters. Cousin Maryott had brought Mary up from the cottage at Chartwell where she'd gone to the local school and, it seemed, done domestic chores like other, less privileged children. And, indeed, like the royal princesses. She and Winston had been invited to dine at Windsor Castle the other day and the queen had told her that her daughters had to make their own beds, tend the royal allotments, and even muck out the stables.

'The poor dears have enough people telling them they're special,' Queen Elizabeth had said. 'They need reminding that they're ordinary human beings too.'

Clementine was sure she was right. Dinner had been a cosy, down-to-earth affair, the royal couple exuding warmth and talking of their family like any other parents, with affection, pride and not a little humour. The princesses had joined them for drinks beforehand and they were lovely girls, with Lilibet, at fifteen, growing into an earnest, dutiful young woman. In contrast, Diana and Sarah under the control – or lack of it – of Clementine and a succession of nannies, had never known a steady life.

She sighed. If she could have her time over, she'd do things differently with her children, but that was easy to say. No doubt if the country could have its time over, they'd attack Hitler back when he first made demands on other people's land. The man would be dead and buried and everyone would be enjoying a peace they didn't even know was such a blessing. But you couldn't look back; only deal with what was in front of you.

'Mary's off to Oswestry next week for her anti-aircraft training,' she told her cook sadly. Oswestry was in Shropshire so there would be no picnics and little chance of seeing her youngest until Christmas. It felt impossibly far away.

'She's doing a good thing,' Mrs Landermare consoled her.

'I know, but it's a dangerous job. The Luftwaffe target the batteries, you know. What if she gets hit?'

Mrs Landermare put an arm around her. At five foot five she had to reach a long way up to get close to Clementine's shoulders, but Clementine appreciated it all the same. This woman had become more than a servant; she had become a friend, tight in the padlock.

'I blame Winston,' she told her. 'He insisted on having General Pile for dinner and then when the general was complaining about how few men they had for the anti-aircraft batteries, Winston only went and suggested using women.'

'Which you must approve of, Mrs Churchill, seeing as you've been pushing for more females to join the forces.'

Clementine bit her lip. 'That's true, blast you. I did approve. I didn't, however, expect Mary to dash off and join the very next day.'

'She's a good girl, that one.'

'A good girl,' Clementine agreed on another sigh.

'As is Diana, nursing her poor husband.'

That was also true. Duncan had had a horrible accident in the blackout a few weeks ago, his feet crushed by a speeding car. Doctors had battled hard to save them from amputation, but it would be a long road back to walking. Diana had had to give up her naval post to care for him but was proving a most devoted nurse.

'And your Sarah, working all the hours at Medenham.'

Vic had taken a role in America and Sarah had got a job as a reconnaissance analyst, perusing the photographs brought back from planes for clues to enemy plans. She was clearly happy in her work and doing well. Maybe Clementine hadn't done such a bad job with those girls after all?

'That Pamela though...' Mrs Landermare said. 'She's *not* a good girl!'

It was said with a certain glee. Mrs Landermare had been married to a Frenchman and had few scruples about the game of love. Also, she clashed with Randolph, who was always demanding snacks or trying to change her menus – a crime indeed. That said, she was right about Pam. Baby Winston, just turned one, was permanently in the country with his nanny while Pamela shared an apartment with twenty-three-year-old Kathleen Harriman, Averell's daughter, and did nominal war work at the Ministry of Information. Pam's hours were not long and left plenty of time for socialising with Harriman and his fellow Americans, though that, as Winston repeatedly told her, was the most precious of work. It made Clementine squirm allowing this affair to continue, often under the Chequers roof, but Britain could not stand alone, especially if Russia fell.

'We need the American onside,' Clementine said to Mrs Landermare.

She was rewarded with a loud belly laugh. 'Well, your Pamela has got that one on his side, on his back and no doubt all sorts of other positions besides.'

'Mrs Landermare!'

'Come now, we're women of the world and Harriman is a fine figure of a man. If I were a younger woman...'

Clementine shook her head at her cook, but she was irrepressible.

'As for that Mr Miller, he's a dapper chap, isn't he? And with a voice like Chartwell's best honey. I could listen to him all day. His wife's good too. She did a clever piece on rationing last week. Included my tip about using beetroot in cake. Did you hear it? Mentioned me by name and everything. Said I was "working wonders" with war rations.'

'Which you are.' Clementine looked fondly at her ageing cook, flushed with pride at her moment in the spotlight, and reminded herself to tell Jenny the next time she saw her.

The poor girl had been terribly down since she'd lost her baby. Clementine had accompanied her to do her broadcast and been very impressed with her professionalism. Really, this war was bringing out the best in the young women, but that didn't mean they weren't still vulnerable to the usual hurts. Ned Miller had booked Jenny a passage back to her family in America in a few days' time. It was for the best. A girl needed her mother after a hurt like that and Clementine was a poor substitute, but she would miss her and worried that, once safe over the Atlantic, she would not return. But that was just her being selfish again. She'd got used to confiding in the young woman and, with true friends so hard to come by, the loss was keen.

She needed more to do to distract herself. She had her domestic tasks and they were vital, but the shelters were more or less sorted and, with the Luftwaffe hiding over the Channel, little used. The hostels, too, were running smoothly and her inspections were becoming an intrusion. Fulmer Chase was operating like a dream and there was little she could do with Fircroft until the builders finished the necessary renovations. That left her with entertaining exiled kings which was important but felt so... insubstantial. They would all be off over the Atlantic at the whiff of an invasion, as would she. Was that sensible? Or cowardly? And what was the point of fretting about it whilst the Nazis were still tearing up poor Russia?

'Herring,' she said determinedly. 'Thank you.' She touched a finger to the picnic basket, as if it could transport her back to Mary, but of course it could not and there was little to do but head to the Annexe and be sure the dining room was fit for a king.

To her surprise, however, Jock Colville came rushing eagerly towards her the instant she stepped upstairs.

'Mrs Churchill, I've been looking for you everywhere!'

'I was in the kitchens.'

'Of course!'

She cursed herself for confirming all his prejudices about women but for once he was too preoccupied to comment further.

'You have a visitor.'

'I do?'

'Field Marshal Sir Philip Chetwode.'

That explained his eagerness – a field marshal *and* a sir.

Clementine smiled. 'Philip? How lovely. I do hope he's come for a game of croquet. I beat him down in Chartwell before the war and he's been champing at the bit for revenge.' It was mean of her to tease Jock like that but he was such a snob.

'I don't think so. That is... we don't have a croquet lawn. Do we?'

'No. Shame. Ah well, perhaps just tea then. Do ask Mrs Landermare to send some over.'

'Me?'

'I can hardly keep Sir Philip waiting any longer, can I?'

'No. Of course not. I'll, er, ask Grace to sort it. This way.'

He ushered her into the drawing room where her old friend, Philip Chetwode, was standing admiring her paintings. He turned as she entered and came over to kiss her.

'Clemmie! You've got the place looking beautiful.'

'Thank you, Philip. Let's hope it stays that way. Tea?'

'Thank you, but I'm not here on a social visit. I have a job for you.'

Clementine looked at him in surprise. 'You do?'

'As you know, I'm in charge of Red Cross war ops.'

'Yes.'

'And we've been picking up a swell of public sympathy for the poor Soviets facing the German onslaught. They're putting up an astonishing resistance.'

'They are,' Clementine agreed eagerly. 'The greatest of any country Hitler has attacked so far. Winston's very impressed with them. Says they're doing a damn fine job for—'

She cut herself off but Sir Philip knew her husband well.

'For commies?' he finished.

She nodded and he smiled.

'It's true. But the Wehrmacht are taking towns and cities with brutal force. They've surrounded Leningrad and are getting dangerously close to Moscow.'

'I know,' Clementine agreed. 'And treating the civilians appallingly.'

Philip nodded grimly. 'We're hearing atrocious stories of their suffering, especially the women and children. The women, in particular, are not being treated well by the Nazis. They see them as... prizes of war.'

Clementine shuddered. 'Why must men be so barbarous?'

'I'm not sure and I apologise on their behalf. Possession appears to be a strong male motivator – of power, of land, of goods and—'

'Of women. Pathetic.'

Philip swallowed. 'But all too real. The women are being so brave. We hear that in Moscow twenty-five thousand have volunteered, along with their teenage children, to dig defences by hand.'

'Women are really proving themselves in this war,' Clementine said proudly, though what was she doing, other than watching for rare incendiaries and turning over a few hostel mattresses? Keeping Winston safe, she reminded herself, but he was wilfully resisting most of her efforts and it felt like an uphill struggle.

'They certainly are,' Sir Philip agreed. 'We're receiving many voluntary donations from the British people, moved by accounts of Soviet bravery and suffering, and we think it pertinent to set up an independent purse to keep things focused. An Aid to Russia fund.'

That sounded interesting. Worthwhile too.

'And you want me to run it?' she asked eagerly.

'Good heavens, no.' Her heart sank. 'I wouldn't presume so much,' he hurried on. 'I was hoping you might be my vice-chair, a figurehead for the fund to lend it elegance and charm. It would require merely a few events and photographs.'

A figurehead? What sort of use was that to anyone? She shook her head. 'No, thank you.'

'Oh. Oh, dear. I know Winston has never been all that keen on the Soviets, but—'

'I mean, I don't want to be just a figurehead.' She folded her arms. On this she was certain. She didn't want to be the one taking a picnic to her soldier daughter, the one choosing fish for an exiled king, the one making sure the prime minister's bath water was the right temperature. She wanted to do something of her own. She wanted to stand up and man a battery like Mary, or analyse photos like Sarah, or broadcast like Jenny Miller. She wanted to *do* something to counter the Nazi threat and not just plan the menu for when they arrived.

'Then...?'

'Then I will run it, if you think I'm up to the job.'

'Up to it? Goodness, Clemmie, of course I think you're up to it. I simply assumed you'd be too busy.'

'Well, I'm not. Those poor women and children are facing

the brutality of the Nazi front line and the least I can do is step up and coordinate help. Plus, of course, any assistance from us might help sustain their defence that little bit longer.'

'Quite right. The Russians are putting up a heroic resistance that's draining the invading troops. Plus, the Russian winter is a powerful force. Even Nazi tanks can't roll over that one.'

'I shall ask God for the most terrible of snows.'

'And I shall thank Him for sending me to you. We—'

His words were cut off by the bang of the door and a gruff shout of, 'Clemmie?'

Clementine leapt up. 'That's Winston.' She ran to the door. 'In here, dear. Sir Philip is with me.'

'Sir...?' Winston strode in. 'Ah, Philip. What brings you here, my man?'

'Your wife,' Philip said.

'Hands off, she's mine.'

'Your wife's brilliance,' Philip corrected with a smile. 'I'm delighted to say that she's agreed to be the executive chair of our Aid to Russia fund.'

'Has she indeed? Splendid! With my Clemmie on their side, the Russians will soon see Herr Hitler off.'

'Winston!' Clementine flushed. 'Don't be ridiculous.'

'Nothing ridiculous about it. You've got the very best woman for the job, Philip.'

'We're honoured,' Philip agreed, flustering Clementine further, and she was grateful when her very welcome guest excused himself for another meeting.

As they were seeing him out, Grace appeared with the tea tray.

'Sorry I'm late,' she apologised.

'On the contrary,' Clementine reassured her. 'You're in perfect time for Winston's return.'

Grace, looking relieved, placed the tray on the table, but Winston was having none of it.

'We don't need tea. Champagne, that's what's required.'

'But Winston—'

'We must celebrate your new role, Clemmie. And Grace, break out that piece of beef we've been saving, will you?'

He was all pride and it was lovely, but this was hardly the time for such indulgence.

'The herring, Winston,' Clementine protested.

'Herring?' He wrinkled up his nose.

'For King Haakon, remember?'

'Ah yes. About that...' Winston took her hands. 'I had word before I left the House that Haakon is unwell and cannot join us. Sad for the poor chap, but champagne, beef and the pair of us alone together for once... how does that sound?'

'It sounds marvellous,' Clementine admitted, her heart swelling at the prospect of such a blissful evening. It was naughty, really, but sometimes one had to be naughty to stay sane. Tomorrow, she would go to the Red Cross offices and get started on her new role, but tonight, for a few precious hours, she would have her husband to herself, and the war – the endless, bloody war – could stay back and wait.

SEVENTEEN

JENNY

Jenny paced her hotel room feeling cross. And then cross with herself for feeling cross. She was in one of Washington's finest hotels, a crisp winter sun was streaming through the window, and tonight she was going for supper at the White House. OK, so it was only an invite to a 'scrambled egg supper' but she'd been assured by friends in the know that this was the finest meal in the White House. Eleanor Roosevelt kept a frugal (some even said unpalatable) kitchen and the cosy family supper every Sunday was a treat. Plus – cosy family supper! At the White House! How on earth could she be cross?

It was all down to Ned, of course. He'd been welcomed home to the States like a star. The night of his arrival, there'd been a gala dinner attended by over a thousand top people, including movie stars like Cary Grant. Ned, weary from his journey, had looked stunned and Jenny, desperate to have her husband to herself after nearly two months apart, had probably looked disgruntled. Still, it had all been very exciting with speeches in his praise and snippets of his broadcasts played on speakers, one even set dramatically to a slide show of photographs.

America couldn't get enough of Ned Miller and it was heady stuff. Back in London, he'd been simply one of a group of dedicated hacks putting themselves in danger to report the losses and perils of war that everyone was experiencing on a day-to-day basis. Over here in America, Ned's reports *were* the war. The American people were living it through him and had welcomed him like a hero. It had felt in some way distasteful to Jenny; perhaps she'd been in England for too long. Ned, however, had loved it. His parents, when they'd come to visit, had been wide-eyed with pride and Jenny's parents much the same.

'You picked a good one there!' her dad had said to her with glee, as if choosing a husband was like finding the ripest watermelon on the stall.

'As did he,' her mother had said staunchly, but, after a month of them nursing her over her miscarriage, the clear flaw had hung in the air and they'd all hastened back to praising Ned.

It had been good to be home for a few weeks though. Her father had hugged her tight and her mother had gathered her under her wing, insisting she lie in late, making her chicken broth and bringing her iron supplements. After the shock of losing the baby, it had been the balm she'd needed.

'You must rest,' her mother had told her. 'It sounds appalling over there in London with all those bombs. No wonder your body is weary.' As if war impacted fertility in some way. As if the foetus, cocking an ear to the womb-lining, had heard the flare of an incendiary and decided it wasn't worth the effort.

It was, as far as Jenny had been able to see walking around London in the painful aftermath of her loss, quite the reverse. Men came home on leave and left babies behind everywhere.

Half weren't even born in wedlock. Soldiers weren't shy in seeking 'comfort' on their few precious days back home and there were plenty of girls happy to oblige. Living in everyday reach of death made moral scruples less important than basic human warmth and many a girl, grown unfeasibly plump on rationing, was slipping away to the country for mysterious war work. Some weren't even bothering with that and it drove Jenny insane to see them swelling with an unwanted child when she, with five years of loving marriage under her belt, could only re-tighten it across her aching womb.

'I really thought it was happening this time,' she'd wept to her mother, when an excess of kindness had finally loosened the tears she'd been keeping tight inside.

'I know, angel, I know. But it will.' She'd stroked her hair and then, unfathomably, added, 'We never should have let you go to university.'

'What on earth...?' Jenny had pulled back and stared at her, horrified. 'You wanted me to study, Mom.'

'I know!' her mother had wailed. 'I'm so sorry.'

It had made Jenny want to scream, though it had, at least, dried her tears. She'd raged for days about her mother assuming that growing her brain had in some way shrivelled her womb.

But that wasn't why she was cross today. Ned had been invited out to play golf with two senators and had suggested she come along to make up the foursome. She'd snatched at the rare chance to spend a day with him amidst his celebrity activities but then they'd found out the game was to be at Burning Tree Golf Club – a fine course, for sure, but one that was closed to women. Totally and utterly closed. She wasn't even allowed in the bar afterwards.

'It's ridiculous,' she'd raged when Ned had apologetically broken the news. 'I bet I play as well as that pair of old duffers.'

'I bet you do, honey, but it's not allowed.'

'So, say you want to play somewhere else.'

'That's their club.'

'It's a bad one.'

'I know. I'm sorry.'

He hadn't been sorry enough to turn the invite down, mind you, so he was off on that beautiful course in that beautiful sunshine and she was here, pacing a hotel room and feeling bored and let down and pining, strangely, for London. Sure, it had bombs (though a lot less these days with the war mainly taking place over Russia and Africa); sure, it had rationing and blackouts and boys with black-edged telegrams; but it also had women running the factories and manning the buses and working with the wounded and bereaved. London teemed with women going about their lives with courage and tenacity, not sitting around having their hair set and their nails done while their husbands played golf in men-only clubs.

It just all felt so... decadent. So cruelly self-indulgent. A few days into her return to the States, Jenny had gone past a hair salon and seen women flicking through magazines, comparing Thanksgiving table decorations, and boggled at the mind-numbing unimportance of it. She'd wanted to run into the salon and scream, 'Do you know there are people dying over there?' But what would have been the point? She'd have got herself arrested as insane and they would have flicked onto the next article on winter flowers as if there weren't soldiers killing each other in deserts, or Russian women being raped by German troops, or mothers weeping on their doorsteps at the arrival of the worst of news.

Jenny forced herself to stop pacing. This was getting her nowhere. She glanced at her watch: 4 p.m. She was frittering her day away getting angry and it wasn't good for her.

'You need to try and be calmer,' her mother had told her, as if having a passion for the important things in life somehow made her unable to carry a child.

'Come on, Jen,' she told herself sternly, 'you're going to the

White House tonight. Most Americans would kill for that opportunity.'

Not that they'd kill for basic human freedoms, or to defend the right of persecuted minorities, or...

She stopped herself. She would go shopping. That's what women were meant to do, right? She would go and buy a nice frock for supper at the White House and that would make everything feel fine and dandy. She grimaced at herself in the mirror but picked up her purse and was heading for the door when the phone rang, making her jump out of her skin. This was the first hotel she'd stayed in that was fancy enough to have in-room telephones and she stared at it, vibrating on the sideboard like an alien creature, before she came to her senses and ran to pick it up.

'Hello?'

'Jen? It's me.' Ned's voice trembled.

'Ned? Are you all right? Why aren't you on the golf course?'

'It's happened, Jen. It's happened right here in America.'

'What has?'

'Well, in Hawaii, but that's a state, right, even if it's a thousand miles out in the Pacific? The Japanese have bombed it. I found out on the fourth hole.'

Jenny struggled to take this in. 'The fourth hole?'

'Yes. I was about to chip for the green and a messenger came running saying they'd bombed Pearl Harbor. I couldn't believe it at first. Even took my chip, though it was rotten, but you could see people all over the course stopping and heading in so we did too. And it's true! Roosevelt will have no choice but to declare war on Japan. Can you come and fetch me, Jen?'

'From Burning Tree? Am I allowed in?' She couldn't resist the snipe.

'You are today,' Ned said, his voice so strained she felt instantly ashamed of her pettiness. 'Everything's changed today. This is war, Jen. Finally, this is America's war.'

· · ·

The mood in the White House was charged. Jenny couldn't quite believe she was there but when she'd rung to ask if they should cancel, Mrs Roosevelt herself had come to the phone and insisted not.

'We all still need to eat, right? Come on over. I can't promise Franklin will be around, but I'd sure welcome the company.'

So Jenny and Ned were sitting in a drawing room in the West Wing with a handful of Roosevelt friends and family, drinking martinis and watching the first lady expertly scramble eggs in a smart cruet in the centre of the table while men hurried endlessly along the corridor to join the president in his office.

'I usually hold these suppers in the East Wing,' Eleanor told Jenny with an easy smile. 'That's my lair, you know. But I thought tonight our best chance of getting any food into Franklin was to come over to his side.'

It was all rather bewildering. It turned out that the oval office, seen in so many newspaper pictures and newsreels, was not in the elegant main house, but tucked onto the side of the sprawling west wing, accessed by a long corridor from the central residence. The White House had, understandably, been crawling with security when they'd arrived, but Eleanor had come out and swept Jenny and Ned inside with a smiling, 'They're with me.' And now, in this cosy room full of cushions and family photos, it was almost like any family Sunday.

Almost.

'It's a tragedy,' a grey-haired woman, apparently called Tommy, said, laying out copies of every newspaper in the land.

They had tomorrow's date on them, Jenny noticed, and she felt curiously ahead of history, as if these tragic events hadn't yet happened and there was still something that could be done to stop the Japanese fighter planes coming out of the blue skies over the Pacific and wreaking carnage on the naval installation at Pearl Harbor. Although it was six in the evening here in Washington, it was still midday in Hawaii and the fight for survivors would be ongoing beneath a burning Pacific sun.

Most of the papers had only screaming headlines and witness reports, wired in from the tiny island in the Pacific, but a few rich enough to carry the technology to wire full pictures were displaying them in all their Dantesque glory. Jenny stared at the grainy image of a giant battleship sinking amidst plumes of black smoke, men frantically waving for help from the burning waters, and shuddered. Was this her fault? Had she somehow, with her crazed anger at American housewives, brought war upon them? Her rational mind told her that was nonsense, but she couldn't help feeling guilty all the same. War was horrible, she knew that more than most people here. The sensible thing had been to want to stay out of it. But there were evil forces in the world and staying out wasn't an option, not even for America.

'Will they strike again?' asked a young man called Joe Lash. He was in uniform so would presumably be one of those sent to fight, and Trude, who'd been enigmatically introduced as his 'partner', was sat tight in at his side.

'We can only assume so,' Eleanor said, stirring eggs. 'Mayor La Guardia and I will be travelling to the west coast to check their defences tomorrow.'

Jenny gasped. 'You think they'll attack the mainland?'

'I think we have to be prepared for it. If they can get to Hawaii, what stops them reaching San Francisco?'

Jenny swallowed. 'Would they dare?'

'It seems so.'

'And you're going to travel towards that?'

Eleanor laughed. 'I'm co-director of the Office of Civilian Defense, dear. It's my job. Now, how do you like your eggs?'

'They look perfect,' Jenny stuttered, adding, 'You seem very calm.'

Eleanor turned off the gas flame under the cruet. 'As you know, Franklin and I have been saying for some time – like both of you – that this is not a war America can ignore. Now, perhaps, the people will see the truth of it.'

'But it's an appalling way for that to happen.'

She nodded sadly. 'It was always going to be. There are men out there who want to impose themselves and their hateful brand of elitism on the world and we have to stand up and stop them. That's always hard. Bullies are notoriously unpleasant and these ones come with guns and tanks and fighter planes.' She put a hand on the hellish newspaper pictures. 'They still have to be stopped, though.'

There was a clatter in the corridor and Jenny looked to the door to see a clutch of men in heavily beribboned uniforms march into the president's office, jostling for position as they went.

'The problem is,' she said, 'if those trying to stop them are bullies too.'

'Jenny!' Ned protested.

But Eleanor put up a hand. 'Quite right, my dear. Power is an intoxicating liquor and we must be very sure to temper our desire for it. America will enter this war as defenders of freedom, not as a counterforce to the Nazis or the Japanese, and we must be sure to keep it that way.'

'Is that possible?'

'I truly hope so. A genuine League of Nations would help but even without that working fully I believe, perhaps naively, that most people are inherently decent.'

'Even Nazis?'

Eleanor seemed to think about this as she dished out scrambled egg onto slices of toast Tommy was distributing. 'Not real Nazis, no. Anyone who thinks they have the right to call other human beings lesser is functioning on a fundamentally skewed world view and must be stopped. But they will drag many impressionable people in their all-encompassing wake and we must stand up and show them the errors of their leaders.'

Jenny sighed. 'It sounds like we must stand up and do a lot.'

Eleanor nodded solemnly. 'That's true. Eat your eggs, dear. You'll need the strength.'

Jenny picked up her fork and tried to do as asked. The eggs were good, soft and rich with butter, in a way eggs had not been in England for over a year, but they tasted like sawdust in her mouth. She edged closer to Ned but he was eating eagerly, his eyes on the president's office door and the important manly conversations humming through it.

Then suddenly that door burst open and there was the president, propelling himself into the room in his wheelchair and smiling round. 'Smells like the eggs are ready?'

'They sure are,' his wife agreed, jumping up and making space, as if this were any old Sunday.

Jenny glanced to Ned, who squeezed her hand under the table. He'd met President Roosevelt at a couple of his fancy events but sitting at his supper table was another thing altogether.

'Delighted to meet you, sir,' he said, shaking his hand. 'I'm only sorry it has to be on such a sad day.'

'Me too, son,' Franklin Roosevelt agreed. 'It will be war now.'

'You'll declare it?'

'With the senate's blessing, I will do so tomorrow.'

'Against Japan?' Jenny asked.

'For now. I don't doubt that Hitler will weigh in soon enough.'

Jenny watched him tucking into his eggs, a silver-haired man in a wheelchair, preparing to take a nation into a vast, distant war, and wished with all her heart she was not here to see this. She wanted America to help Britain fight, but that didn't mean she wanted Her attacked. All over the country, mothers and fathers with sons stationed in Pearl Harbor would be crouched by the phone waiting to hear if their boy was one of the corpses in the petrol-coated waters of the Pacific. It was a dark day for America.

'Right.' Roosevelt finished his supper and, with a polite dab of his napkin, looked apologetically around the table. 'I'd better get back to business.'

'Of course, sir.'

Ned jumped to his feet, Jenny with him, but Roosevelt waved them back down.

'Stay. Enjoy your supper. I shall be late, I expect but, Mr Miller, if you care to wait I can fill you in more fully when these meetings are over.'

'Of course, sir,' Ned agreed again. 'I'll be here.'

'Thank you. I think I'd better go and call Mr Churchill.'

'He'll be glad to hear from you,' Jenny said.

The president turned his warm, intelligent eyes to her. 'I believe he will. You know him?'

'I know his wife better, sir, but, yes, I know him and he will be *very* glad to hear from you.'

Roosevelt nodded. 'He's a good man. Eccentric, but good. I'm only sorry, as you said, Mr Miller, that it must be on such a sad day. This is a friendship that will have to be forged of the strongest – and darkest – steel.'

'But a friendship all the same,' Jenny suggested.

Roosevelt smiled suddenly. 'A friendship all the same.' And then he was gone, patting his wife's hand and wheeling from the room, leaving scraps of scrambled egg behind as the door to his office opened and the noise of a country in crisis roared in on their supposedly cosy supper. 'Get me London on the phone,' she heard Roosevelt demand.

She closed her eyes and imagined the call ringing out a

thousand miles across the Atlantic where Winston and Clementine would be dining in muted British elegance. She remembered her friend, tense and wild-eyed on the roofs of Whitehall last summer, taking all the weight of supporting her husband in keeping Britain free of the Nazi menace, and thanked God that at last someone else could help shoulder it.

EIGHTEEN

CHEQUERS, 7 DECEMBER 1941

CLEMENTINE

Clementine stretched out her aching back, watched Pamela laughing with Kathy Harriman, and wondered if she'd ever been that carefree. She thought she had. If she looked in her wardrobe the stunning evening gowns told of parties and balls and coming home with the dawn, but she couldn't recall how it had felt to have that much joie de vivre. Most of the dresses still fitted her but it was Mary who wore them now, while she stuck to staider designs and fabrics for the endless dinner parties that made up her prime ministerial social life. They said content-ment came to you in middle age and she supposed that was nice, but it didn't beat outright giddy joy. And, besides, content-ment was hard to find in wartime.

A cake was being brought in, alight with candles, and everyone was singing happy birthday to Kathy, who'd turned twenty-four last week, so Clementine told herself to buck up and sing. It was hard to feel grumpy while warbling the silly ditty and the girls' laughter as Kathy attempted to blow out all twenty-four candles was infectious. Clementine rubbed her earrings – emerald clusters to match her dark green dress – and counted her blessings. Not many people had jewels like these, or big houses or smart friends, though friends, these days, were more people to be courted than true loved ones.

'Happy birthday, darling,' Averell said, getting up from Pamela's side to kiss his daughter, who, Clementine couldn't help noting, was only two years older than Pamela, now Averell's undisputed lover. They were all over London together and it was only the fact that there were a hundred and one not-so-illicit love affairs going on under cover of blackout that kept it from being bigger gossip. Clementine still felt awkward having them under her roof together, but Winston said it was his job as PM to entertain Harriman and it was up to Harriman who he chose to accompany him. It was a very Winstonian fudge and at least saved her the decision.

'Nearly nine o'clock,' Winston announced, stretching out in his romper (a plush red velvet tonight to mark Kathleen's special day) and ringing for the butler to bring in a wireless for the news.

Nothing, not even birthday celebrations, got in the way of world affairs. A surprising amount of even the prime minister's information came from the BBC and its hotwires into every news agency around the world. Winston monitored this and all the papers for news that might have escaped the governmental net, as well as to take the mood of the public. It was rarely good and Clementine wished that, for once, they could leave the wireless off. But that's precisely why she wasn't prime minister.

The set was duly carried in on a silver tray. It was a tiny thing, a gift from President Roosevelt when Winston had been to visit him in Canada under a veil of secrecy back in the summer, and was testament to American ingenuity, if not American commitment. Winston set it in front of him and turned it on. A burst of static filled the room and he twiddled at the dial but found it too small for his chubby fingers and tutted in frustration. It was the same every evening and Clementine was grateful when Pam jumped up with a, 'Let me, Papa.' He submitted obediently and Pam swiftly found the BBC as the dongs of Big Ben sounded out the news, the only time anyone heard them these days as the bells themselves had been silenced since the start of the war.

Dong – Reports from America of a bombing at Pearl Harbor.

They all looked at each other, even the girls' giggles instantly quietened.

Dong – Thousands reported dead in air strike on naval base by Japanese fighter planes.

Winston jumped to his feet.

Dong – This is surely an Axis declaration of war on America.

'It's a miracle!' Winston grabbed the hands of the nearest man, the quiet American ambassador Gil Winant, and danced him around the table.

Gil detached himself. 'Thousands of US forces murdered?' he asked.

Winston sobered. 'Yes, sorry. Terrible. Tragic. Headline-hittingly tragic.'

'Winston!' Clementine reprimanded.

'I'm sorry, my dear. It's awful, truly it is, but we're losing thousands every week in Africa and will continue to lose thousands more. America is the only country with the firepower to defeat the Nazis.'

'*And* the Japanese,' Averell Harriman pointed out.

'The Axis forces of evil gather,' Winston agreed. 'I must speak to the president.'

The party was over. World affairs had stolen it from them. Clementine kissed Winston and took herself off to bed.

. . .

He came to her later, sometime after she'd heard midnight strike on the grandfather clock in the Chequers hallway. Sleep, despite her weary bones, had refused to come and he found her lying in her bed, trying to imagine young American sailors blown out of their own waters on a sunny Sunday morning. She wondered if Ned Miller would broadcast about it and then if, by the time she woke tomorrow, there would have been further strikes to report.

She remembered the sickening feeling of having enemy invaders so close to your doorstep you could smell them and pitied America. Then she remembered that every country in Europe had Nazis not just on their doorstep, but over it, and understood Winston's unseemly jubilation.

'Did you speak to Roosevelt?' she asked, moving over to make room beneath the covers.

Winston rarely slept a full night in her bed, both of them preferring their own space, and his more amorous visits had ceased some time ago. But tonight it was cold – both literally and metaphorically – and she was glad to snuggle into his arms.

'I spoke to him. He is grim but resolute. He will go before both the Senate and the House of Representatives tomorrow and, with their approval, will declare war.'

'And they will give it?'

'They must. Their shores have been attacked and their people are afraid. The Axis feels close to them now. They will doubtless have forgotten that they ever opposed rearmament and expect instant defences. Production will be upped immediately.'

'It's as you wanted then.'

He held her so tight she could barely breathe.

'None of this is as I wanted, Clemmie. If they had only listened to me back in 1933 when Hitler came to power in the most dastardly of ways, or in 1935 when he introduced laws deciding what class people fell into, or in 1938 when he asked for Sudetenland and really meant all of Europe. If they had listened to me then, we – Europe – could have struck together and none of us would be in this bloody mess and having to pray for American casualties to bring us hope. It is a messy world, my dear.'

'And ours to try and tidy.'

He gave a low chuckle and kissed her. 'Tidy. I like that. It sounds manageable. And, Clemmie...' He pulled away to look into her eyes. 'I believe that, with America on our side, we can win this. Roosevelt has invited me to go over for talks and I must do so immediately.'

'But Christmas...'

'Must wait. I'm sorry. It's too important. For the first time since you and I stepped into Number Ten, I honestly, truly believe we can win. It will take a lot of hard work and a lot of cooperation but this, my dear, is the key to beating Hitler.'

She put her hands to his face and kissed him. Christmas would be miserable without him here, but the war had to come first.

'Funny the shapes salvation comes in,' she said softly.

'Grim. But they look less so with you at my side. You are at my side, aren't you, Clemmie?'

'Of course, Winston, I—'

'I know I'm a demanding, stubborn, bullish pain in the whatsit, but there's just so much to do.'

She clasped his hands. 'I know, Winston. I do know. But you have help now.'

'You're right. I've been working hard on this alliance, Clemmie. Many people don't like the Americans, don't want them dragged into "our war", but we cannot win it without them. I can see that, and Franklin can see that. We can make it work together.'

'I don't doubt it,' she assured him, though her ever-foolish heart quailed. Winston was right – he was the link; the pivot in making this grand alliance work. It was more important than ever that he stayed alive and well to lead the world against Hitler.

'The Axis bullies have got above themselves,' he was saying gleefully. 'The Nazis were foolish to attack Russia and the Japanese foolish to attack America. Now all we need to do is hold those two victims together as our allies and we can triumph.'

'All...?' Clementine said faintly. From where she was sitting, triumph looked like very hard work and she just prayed that she could stay strong enough to keep Winston alive and well to reach it.

PART TWO

NINETEEN

THE ANNEXE, APRIL 1942

JENNY

'Mr Miller, the conquering hero! Come in, come in.' Ned beamed as Mr Churchill ushered him into the Annexe with a hearty handshake. 'And the lovely Mrs Miller. Charmed you could both make it.'

The prime minister kissed Jenny's hand with a flourish then ushered Ned over to the drinks cabinet, plying him with questions about his time in America. They made an odd pair, Ned tall and dapper in his Savile Row suit and Winston, short and stocky in a romper of incongruous khaki silk, but they laughed easily together.

Jenny had last seen the British prime minister at a White House Christmas reception, held in a hurry when he'd rushed over to meet Roosevelt after the tragedy of Pearl Harbor had catapulted America into the Allied forces. Winston had been an unusual festive guest for the presidential couple and Jenny had gathered that Eleanor had not been given much notice of his arrival.

'First thing I knew was when I was told to stock up on

champagne and cognac,' she'd confided as they'd stood to one side watching the eccentric British prime minister holding centre stage amongst the befuddled Americans.

But then Winston had spotted Jenny and come over, greeting her like an old friend, which had upped her stakes in Washington society no end.

'It must be hard, being away from the family at Christmas,' she'd said, earning a glisten of ready tears in Winston's blue eyes.

'It's *very* hard. Clemmie always makes Christmas special for us. And our cook is top-hole. Unlike the one here!'

Then he'd winked and been gone again, swept into crowds of curious well-wishers. He'd spoken on the White House lawns on Boxing Day too but he'd been far more formal then and looked tired. A rumour had circulated that he'd had a minor heart attack and to Jenny's concerned eyes he'd certainly looked unwell.

Now, four months later, he still appeared exhausted but was thankfully in good health. She turned to Clementine, who took both her hands, kissing her warmly on her cheek. 'You look divine, my dear.'

Jenny knew her simple off-the-peg dress wasn't a patch on Clementine's rich, taffeta gown, but appreciated her friend's praise. 'It feels good to be back.'

'I'm so glad you returned.'

Jenny was surprised. 'Of course I returned, Clementine.'

The older woman shrugged. 'It must have been tempting to stay safely over the Atlantic.'

'It didn't feel so safe last December.'

'No. Terrible business. Were you scared?'

'That they'd invade? I was a bit. Thirty Japanese planes were picked up over San Francisco on December eighth, you know. They didn't actually make land, or drop any bombs, but it was enough to put everyone on high alert. Mrs

Roosevelt went to the west coast to shore up defences and the—'

'Mrs Roosevelt did?' Clementine interrupted.

'Yes. She's co-director of the Office of Civilian Defence.'

'Is she indeed? The president's wife sounds a formidable woman.'

There was something guarded in Clementine's tone and, looking at her more closely, Jenny saw that beneath the perfectly coiffed hair and immaculate make-up, she, like Winston, looked grey and tired.

'The president's wife does not have to look after the president. He has all sorts of other people for that.'

'Staff, you mean?'

Jenny shook her head. 'He has staff, yes, but he has an... entourage, as well. So does she. They operate out of two wings of the White House, together but, well... not.'

'Oh.' Clementine glanced over to Winston, who was laughing heartily with Ned over some shared joke. She gave a small smile. 'That's sad for her.'

'For them both. But I suppose marriage works differently for everyone.'

'That, my dear, is very true. Now, come, I'm being a most remiss host. What will you drink? Champagne?'

'Are we celebrating?'

'No, no. It's just Winston's favourite aperitif.'

Winston turned at his name and gave Jenny a bow. 'We are celebrating still being alive to enjoy this divine drink and that, for now, is enough. It has to be,' he added darkly.

Jenny felt suddenly desperately sad. She pictured her parents, much the same age as the Churchills, but content to spend their time gardening and reading. For them, a trip to the shops was a day out, while the Churchills, she at fifty-seven and he at sixty-seven, were running not just Great Britain, but the entire Allied war effort. No wonder they looked tired.

'How's Fulmer Chase going?' she asked Clementine as Winston poured her champagne.

'Very well,' Clementine said, lighting up. 'We've had over four hundred babies born and not one lost. And Fircroft is up and running too. You remember Fircroft?'

'Of course.'

'Jenny came to inspect it with me,' Clementine told Winston.

'Inspect what?'

'Fircroft, Winston!' He looked confused. 'Our post-natal home.'

'Of course! For the officer's wives. Good thing that.' He looked to Ned. 'Stops the chaps worrying about their wives and babies when they're off at the front, you know. Do you have children?'

There was an awkward pause that only Winston failed to notice.

'Not yet,' Ned said quietly.

'Well you should, man, you should. Jolly little things. I made mine a treehouse at Chartwell, and a swimming pool. We had great fun there. Got grandkids now, several of the buggers. Baby Winston is coming up to one and a half, and he's quite a chip off the old block. Does a man good to have kiddies. A woman too, obviously. You don't fancy it, Mrs Miller?'

'I'm very busy,' Jenny squeaked.

'Jenny runs Bundles for Britain,' Clementine supplied hastily. 'And broadcasts for CBS.'

'Ah, a husband-wife team, hey?'

'I wouldn't say team,' Ned said, then caught himself and added lamely, 'as such.'

Jenny felt stung. Obviously, she wasn't as famous a broadcaster as he was, but he didn't have to get defensive about it. She was no challenger to his precious new title of America's favourite newsman.

The celebrity status had continued on Ned's lecture tour around the States in the new year. Jenny had completed her set of fifteen talks about Bundles and the importance of aiding Great Britain, and had been pleasantly surprised at the size of the audiences she'd attracted. In several places two thousand people had been packed into the halls, eager to hear her speak. It had been most flattering, but nothing to the thousands desperate to hear Ned. The organisers had had to find bigger venues and, even then, there had been people standing in the aisles.

She'd worried it might be intimidating for him but he'd taken to a live audience like a duck to water, bantering with the crowd and answering questions with wit and charm. And he'd looked amazing in his Savile Row tweeds, his hair slicked back and his dark eyes sparkling, speaking to the people in the rich voice they knew from their bedrooms. If he'd been a celebrity when he'd arrived, he'd been a superstar by the time they'd left. A number of important people had asked him to stay in the States but Ned wasn't stupid.

'They like me because I'm exotic,' he'd said to Jenny. She'd laughed and he'd flushed. 'You know what I mean. I'm reporting on faraway unknowns, like fiction but with the added lustre of the truth. If we stayed here, what would I talk about – knitting and digging shelters?'

'Like me,' Jenny had pointed out.

'You talk about it in London, honey. You're exotic too.'

They'd both laughed at that, but he'd been right. Despite a few days' scare, for Americans the war was still resolutely far off in Europe and the Pacific and they needed reporters to bring it into their front rooms. Neither of them had hesitated to book their passage back across the Atlantic and people had lined the docks to wave them off. Or, rather, to wave Ned off. There had been crowds of doting women wafting their handkerchiefs at him as if he were their personal sweetheart, and Jenny had felt quite the gooseberry, especially when one audacious young woman had shouted out, 'Let me have your babies, Ned!' She'd been mortified.

As she was now.

'Perhaps I can do a broadcast about Fircroft?' she managed, directing herself at Clementine.

'That would be good,' she agreed. 'We must get a date. The Duchess of Gloucester came to visit, you know, and—'

'What we need,' Winston cut across her, 'is broadcasts about Africa. Do you fancy Africa, Mr Miller?'

'I surely do, sir. I hear it's not going so well out there.'

'Shocking, my boy. Rommel is driving us back every day. I fear for Tobruk, truly I do. I'm talking to Roosevelt about an Allied invasion but he's not sure. Some live broadcasting from the desert would be just the ticket. Ah, dinner!'

He beamed at the appearing butler and led the way through to the dining room. It bore all the hallmarks of what Jenny was learning was Clementine's style of pastel shades and soft fabrics, and felt like a haven in the middle of Whitehall.

'You've made a fine home here in the Annexe, Clementine,' she said.

'She has,' Winston answered. 'Clemmie is a marvel with decorations. Not like me. I'm a simple soldier at heart, you know, happy with a sturdy bed and a washbasin.'

Jenny looked at the silken khaki of his peculiar all-in-one suit and thought there was nothing simple about this Englishman.

'And yet you're a painter,' she pointed out.

He considered this, head on one side. 'So I am. Maybe, then, we all use our artistry in different ways. Mr Miller's is his voice, mine is my painting, and Clemmie's is soft furnishings.'

Jenny frowned. 'I think she does more than that. How are the hostels, Clementine?'

'Excellent,' Clementine said as they sat at the long table,

laid at one end for greater intimacy. 'The YWCA is doing amazing work and all sorts of people are donating. So many of us have children serving away from home that the need for good accommodation for these brave young people has really hit. With that and Aid to Russia, I'm invited to all sorts of fundraising dos. I went to a football match a few weeks ago – England versus Wales, great fun – and the other day, I had to do an appeal at the stock exchange. Imagine! All those important, shouty men. Ronald escorted me, which helped, but I was still terrified when I went in. They were very kind, though. Gave lots of money.'

'They *have* lots of money,' Winston said. 'Fat cats! I hope you talked to them about the Home Guard, Clemmie. We may not need them to defend against the Wehrmacht directly but there's all sorts of jobs still required – wardens and fire watchers and—'

'Like Clementine,' Jenny said.

'Sorry, my dear?'

'Clementine is a fire watcher.'

'Is she?' Winston peered at his wife. 'Are you?'

'You know I am, Winston. You admired my armband the other day.'

'So I did. Jolly good.'

'It's hard work,' Jenny said. 'And scary.'

'Is it? I mean, of course it is. Clemmie's a marvel, truly.' He blew her a kiss and turned to Ned. 'What about the Far East, Mr Miller? Would you go there? Appalling, what's going on. We were devastated to lose Singapore, devastated.'

'That was a terrible loss, sir.'

'British territory for over a hundred years, Mr Miller. Vital to our trade. And such a valuable garrison.'

'Though poorly defended,' Clementine put in, 'as I said when I visited on Walter's yacht in '38.'

'Was that when you went dragon hunting?' Jenny asked eagerly.

Even Ned, whose attention had all been on Winston, turned to Clementine.

'Dragon hunting?'

'Poor Clemmie twisted her ankle and nearly got eaten by one of the buggers,' Winston said. 'I could have lost her.'

'*That*,' Jenny said firmly, 'would have been a terrible loss.'

'Greater than Singapore,' Winston agreed, leaping up to kiss his wife's hand.

Jenny watched him, fascinated. He clearly loved his wife, was, indeed, in love with her, but he saw little of her achievements.

She tried again as a fragrant clear soup was served. 'How is the Aid to Russia fund doing, Clementine?'

'Amazingly, thank you. We've raised over a million pounds! The suffering of the women and children of the borderlands has touched everyone's hearts. Thousands of schoolchildren bring in a penny every week for their Russian counterparts, despite having so little themselves. It's very moving.'

'If they weren't communists, they wouldn't have been so poorly off in the first place,' Winston muttered.

'The women and children didn't choose to be communists, Winston,' Clementine said sharply. 'As well you know. And I don't think even being rampant capitalists would have stopped the German soldiers from raping and murdering them.'

Winston bit his lip. 'Quite right, my dear. I'm sorry. The Nazis are beasts and your fund is helping alleviate much suffering. Forgive me, I'm a grumpy sod at the moment. I thought having America on board would be our salvation, but salvation takes time to build and the weight of it lies heavy on me.'

'Of course it does, sir,' Ned said. 'But you're a great leader.'

'You think so?' Winston looked at him closely.

Jenny had to stop herself laughing at this demand for ego-stroking but then, studying the man as Ned offered an obsequious answer, she thought perhaps he was genuine. It must be tough, running the country at the heart of the war effort, but it surely wasn't all about him?

'And with a great wife behind you,' she offered lightly, when the platitudes had run out.

Winston nodded earnestly. 'As I have often told her, Clementine is the light that lets my star shine.'

'That's beautiful, sir,' Ned said.

'Beautiful,' Jenny agreed, looking to Clementine, who was blushing sweetly. 'But who, sir, lets Clementine's star shine?'

Winston Churchill gaped. Beneath the table Ned kicked Jenny furiously but it felt like a fair question and she mulishly moved out of his way.

'More soup, anyone?' Clementine said, rushing to fill the awkward silence.

Both men leaped to accept. Jenny declined. The soup was excellent but her appetite was gone. She found herself almost envying those women whose menfolk were at the front, leaving them free to step up and work without comparison or constriction, but then she felt ashamed. They must wake up every day wondering if their husband was alive. At least she had hers to hold close in bed, when he finally came to it. It was just that sometimes it felt as if anything she did would always be overshadowed by him and that was sure as hell true for Clementine Churchill. She bust a gut to support her husband in so many ways and he didn't even seem to realise what it cost her.

All was fair in love and war, perhaps – but sadly not so in the everyday ins and outs of marriage.

TWENTY

CLEMENTINE

'Oh, Clemmie, it's so good to be back. Is it not? Is it not good to be back?'

Clementine watched Winston standing on the terrace at Chartwell, staring out across 'his view' of the Kentish Weald, his arms held wide to the summer skies, and her heart swelled with love.

'It is,' she agreed, putting an arm around his waist. 'It truly is.'

Chartwell was looking very fine on this glorious day, as if she'd put on her best dress specially for them coming. For once Clementine could feel nothing but affection for the big old house that had been the scene of so many happy family times. Winston had always been better at them than her, more able to throw himself into the children's games, dropping out of trees as a 'gorilla', or running boisterous piggy-back games in a way Clementine had never quite managed. For her, games were better with rules and definitions, courts and fairways. She'd had a tennis court and a croquet lawn at

Chartwell and the children had played, up to a point, but they'd all preferred Winston's more haphazard, ebullient form of play.

Still, they'd loved having her watch and had always brought her back the finds from their treasure hunts, or flowers from the wild meadows. Winston called her the Queen of Chartwell and although she'd never been sure of the formality of that role, it had been nice to be looked up to. Right now, though, standing high above southern England, she was reminded of the flighty joy of the house the first time she'd seen it, before she'd done the sums and buried that joy in practicalities. Impetuously, she undid her turban – a dark grey one to match her mood – and let the wind ruffle her hair. It felt wonderful.

'I thought I was flying the first time we came here,' she said to Winston.

'I remember. You liked flying back then.'

She shuddered, not enjoying the rush of memories. 'That was before you insisted on learning and I spent every day convinced you would fall out of the skies to your death.'

'I never did.'

'No, though we lost plenty so it wasn't an unreasonable worry.'

'And where there's a worry to be found, you'll find it, my dear.'

She looked at him, surprised. 'Do you think so?'

'I do. It's in your nature. In all women's natures, perhaps. You feminine creatures seem to have more imagination for the possibilities inherent in any action. Us simple men just look for what we might achieve.'

She gave a rueful chuckle. 'You might be right. I was forever fretting about the children getting injured, whereas you would simply leap up and play.'

'I'm sure you stopped a lot of accidents with your care.'

'And a lot of fun too?'

He looked at her. 'Are you all right, Clemmie? Is it all getting to you a bit?'

She laughed again, more darkly this time. 'If by "all this" you mean the war then, yes, I suppose it is. I hate that Mary is on live anti-aircraft batteries now.'

'And doing a damn fine job of it.'

'A damn dangerous one. She might get killed, Pug. Look at poor Randolph.'

Randolph was convalescing in a private hospital in London, having been invalided home from the desert after a nasty truck accident on the way back from a night raid on Benghazi.

'Randolph is mending well,' Winston said stoutly.

Which was true. He was very keen to rejoin his regiment in Egypt and fight again and she was proud of him for that, but it also put him back in the line of fire.

'He'll be at risk again, Winston, as we all are. Hitler might not have invaded last autumn, but he's storming through Russia. I get briefings on it all the time, and a hundred letters every day besides. The Red Cross people have made it public that I'm running Aid to Russia and many of their civilians write to me direct. It's heartbreaking.'

'Is it?'

'Oh yes. I have to keep a spare handkerchief in the drawer these days.'

'Clemmie!' Winston looked at her, his eyes welling up. 'That's so sad. I didn't know you were suffering like that.'

'*They* are the ones suffering, Winston. My meagre sensibilities are nothing. There's a town called Rostov-on-Don, miles down in the south-west, which the Germans took last November, though only for a week before the Soviets threw them out. Now they've gone for it again and with such brutality. They've all but destroyed both their main hospital and their children's one. Imagine! They're such brutes. I've had so many letters from doctors and nurses begging for help.'

'The Russians are suffering,' Winston agreed, 'but they're fighting hard. They threw the Germans out of Moscow last winter, did they not?'

'For now...' Clementine conceded, 'but the bombing continues. And they still have Leningrad under siege. It's been nearly a year and those poor people are starving. I can't imagine what it's like. We send all the food parcels we can but they have to be taken by brave couriers tracing hugely dangerous passages under the German's noses. Many of them are killed, and the supplies lost. Children are dying, hundreds of them every day. We know what that feels like, don't we?'

He looked at her, his eyes misting again. 'We know what that feels like,' he agreed sadly. 'I forget, sometimes, when the statistics come in, that every one of those incomprehensible thousands is a personal loss to someone.'

Clementine sighed. 'I don't. And I don't forget that it will be all *our* children if Hitler wins out in Russia and turns his new might on us.'

'Which is precisely why I'm flying there to shore up Stalin.'

'And precisely what is "getting to me".' She hadn't put her finger on it before, but there it was. With the Allied forces now constituting Britain, America and Russia, vital diplomacy must be done either by crackly phone line or by flying thousands of miles to sit around a table. Winston was the lynchpin and as he very much favoured personal diplomacy, that meant flying. Maybe the aviation industry had improved since he'd frightened her to death learning to pilot tiny biplanes in the early years of their marriage, but there were still enough incidents to catch at her heart, not to mention the presence of enemy planes behind every cloud. And the fact that he was well into his sixties and his heart was paying the price for all those cigars and whiskies.

He was due to leave from RAF Lyneham later this evening but they'd come via Chartwell to check all was well. The house was shut up for the war, only Cousin Maryott's cottage and the skeleton staff running, but she looked magnificent in her repose and Clementine wished they could stay here all day. All week. All damned year.

'You don't think I'm up to it?' Winston asked.

'Flying at altitude in freezing cold temperatures with nothing more than a padded suit to keep you warm? Not many people are up to it.' She took his hands. 'I know your mind is very, very willing, my darling, but what about your body?'

He bristled. 'The RAF did the tests at Farnborough, and all was well. The old ticker can take it, Kat, I promise you.'

Clementine was not comforted. She'd watched the tests herself, peering into the pressurised chamber through a tiny porthole, like looking in on a coffin. So many people were invested in Winston making this trip to Moscow that there must have been pressure on the medics to skew the results. It may only have been a little, but how much did it take to tip a man's heart over the edge? These things were all, surely, in the fine margins? And there was another thing...

'Dr Moran says you may have had a small coronary on Boxing Day.'

'Dr Moran exaggerates.'

'How can you exaggerate a heart attack?!'

'It was a flutter, no more. Probably indigestion brought on by the damned awful White House cooking. You should have tasted it. I'm not sure I'd even wish it on Hitler.'

'Oh, you would.'

He nodded grimly. 'I would. D'you know, Clemmie, if I could walk into a meeting with that man and shoot him through the heart, I'd take the consequences. I wouldn't mind.'

Clementine wrapped her arms around him. 'Well I would, so don't you dare.'

He chuckled. 'Fine. Just for you, my dear.'

Somewhere around the front of the house, Clementine heard the sound of a car – the driver, come to take them to

Lyneham for Winston's flight. She gazed across their land, so quintessentially English, and wanted to stop it all – stop the globe turning if that's what it took – and just be here, quietly, forever on the brink of something but not having to know what that something was. Defeat or victory; they were stark choices.

'Do you think this war will kill us, Winston?'

His sigh was long. 'I think it might. But if it must, then please God let us save Britain first. Let us go down in history for that.'

'Us, Winston? It won't be us, just you.'

He turned to her. 'I'm nothing without you.'

'That's not the way the world will see it.'

'Does that matter?'

Did it? Clementine had sworn to support Winston in his political career on the day she'd agreed to marry him and she'd stuck to that through thick and thin. Now he was at the top, precisely where he'd always wanted to be. She had to be there for him, but so many letters came seeking her direct help that it was hard not to start wanting to make a difference herself. Not that it was important now.

'Only a very little,' she said. 'What really matters is that you are not history *yet*. I want to survive the war, Pug. I want to win it of course, but I want to survive it too. I want to travel with you into old age. I want to see our children grow into full adulthood and indulge our grandchildren. I want to be grumpy and quarrelsome and irritable together.'

He chuckled again. 'That sounds fun, my Kat. I want that too.'

'So don't get killed on an aeroplane!'

'I'll try my very best.'

It was all she was going to get. The sound of feet on gravel and a discreet cough told her the driver was there and their time was up. Planting a soft kiss on her husband's lips, she retied the grey turban over her wind-ruffled hair and turned heavily back towards duty.

Three endless weeks later, Clementine stood at RAF Norton, watching for the dot in the sky that would signal Winston's safe return. He had survived the fifteen hundred miles to Moscow and soon she would know if he had made it safely back. She stared at the clouds, willing them to deliver her husband. The big Liberator plane had to trace a path right over Nazi Germany, occupied Poland and war-torn Belarus. It would fly at altitudes high enough to, hopefully, evade Luftwaffe attacks, but also to put pressure on an old man's heart.

'I'm not old,' Winston had assured her as he'd kissed her goodbye on the runway. 'And my heart is filled up with love for you so will be resilient to all onslaughts.'

It had been a classic piece of Winstonian flourish, but comforting all the same. She was aware, however, that she often got impatient with her bullish husband and, as she waited desperately for his return, she prayed she'd been a loving enough wife to keep the armour strong around his all-important heart.

He had sent her telegrams and the odd letter from Russia but, subject to the prying eyes of Moscow censors, they'd been stiff and formal and had left far too much to her imagination. It had been peculiar thinking of him in the country for which she was working so hard and she had to admit to having felt envious at times. One day, she would like to be the one flying into the skies, not the one waiting agonisingly at home.

'There it is!'

Randolph was at her side, released from hospital and keen to see his father. He pointed into the wispy clouds and Clementine's heart leaped into her mouth as she saw the tiny shape form into a plane, wobbling precariously as it drew close to the runway. She closed her eyes against the scary sight of it landing but could not stop the roar of the engines filling her ears, or the vibration of the runway shuddering up through her legs. This was the most dangerous part, someone had told her once, and she dreaded seeing him explode before her eyes.

Finally, however, the engines whined to a stop and she drew in a deep breath and prised her eyelids open. There was the plane, vast and solid, a ladder being rushed up to it and the door already opening to reveal a tubby silhouette in a jaunty homburg hat.

'Winston!' She was running. Her heels click-clacked idiotically over the tarmac but she didn't care because he was half-tumbling down the ladder into her arms. 'You made it.'

'Of course I did. How could I not come back to my beautiful wife?'

'Engine failure,' she countered. 'Pilot error, enemy fire—'

'Oh, my Kat, ever the pessimist.'

He kissed her protests from her lips and she succumbed gladly. But then Randolph came up and Winston pulled away to hug his son and lead them both to the car. He waved merrily to a journalist who'd somehow got a tip-off of his landing and lit up a cigar.

'Excellent trip,' he said, as if he'd simply been to Brighton for the day.

Clementine sat back in the soft leather, free to be exhausted at last.

'How was Stalin?' she heard Randolph ask eagerly.

'Steely,' Winston said. 'And wily. He may be our ally for now, but he's in this war for himself and we'll have to keep a very careful eye on him.'

Clementine shuddered and slotted an arm through his. 'I hope you won't have to do that yourself again, Pug?'

'Oh, I think I will,' he said cheerily.

'There'll be more flights?'

'Many, my dear. You'd better get used to it.'

He patted her hand and turned back to tell Randolph more of the Soviets. Clementine tried to listen, but all she could really focus on was the solid, beating reality of him at her side. She feared that, however many times he had to fly to see this war to its end, she would never, ever get used to it. But fly he would and, however hard it was, she would be here, waiting.

TWENTY-ONE

BUCKINGHAM PALACE, OCTOBER 1942

JENNY

Jenny stood, her back to the elegantly patterned wall, and wondered what on earth she was going to do. She was in a stunning hall in Buckingham Palace for a reception of the most influential charitable ladies of London and should be loving it. It was being held in honour of Eleanor Roosevelt, visiting to see how Britain was running the domestic war effort, and the president's wife had personally asked for Jenny. Clementine had kindly said that the queen would have invited her anyway and she'd been delighted to attend, but now she was too embarrassed to move.

She'd been so happy earlier. It had been fun to put her golden dress on again for this smart party and Ned had been most complimentary, which was sadly unusual these days as he dashed from one dangerous assignment to another, lured by the siren call of war – and the even louder one of broadcasting fame. She'd neglected to tell him it was an all-female do which had perhaps been a cheap trick but had worked because he'd assured her he'd be eagerly waiting for her return. Thank heavens! Dangerous assignments did not babies make and she hadn't yet given up hope.

She'd taken a rare cab to the palace, feeling a million dollars, but then, halfway up a grand staircase, had caught her damned heel in the back of her skirt and pulled the stitching. Now her hem was dangling, threads loose, like some street-girl. All sorts of women were arriving in designer gowns, dragged eagerly out of pre-war wardrobes, and the queen herself would be here any moment. Jenny couldn't bear to be presented to royalty like an American hick who couldn't even hold a hem, so, here she was, backed up against the wallpaper, nursing a glass of wine and trying to look relaxed.

She knew a lot of the women from her work with Bundles, though she'd thankfully handed the day-to-day running over to an increasingly competent Dora. The BBC had asked her to do a series of features on American history that were absorbing her time and were more interesting than directing knitwear around Great Britain. It also fed into her other new role, working on the Special Relations Committee, to integrate the GI troops arriving in Britain. Winston was keen to ease their welcome with information for their curious hosts and Jenny's BBC broadcasts, with their combination of potted history and cultural context, were part of that. She was loving the challenge.

The challenge of her hem, however, was no fun at all. She looked around and spotted Nellie Romilly chatting away to Dora, who was looking stunning in a silver gown with a daringly low back and a perfect hem. Remembering how kind Mrs Churchill's sister had been to her at Ditchley, Jenny wondered if she might be able to help her out. She headed their way but then trumpets sounded and all heads turned as the king and queen walked into the room.

Everyone swept into a curtsy and Jenny followed, keeping her lowered eyes on the ravishing royal couple. The king was slim and surprisingly handsome and did not seem at all fazed at being the only man present. The queen was petite but her eyes sparkled, lighting up the room as naturally as the sun coming out. Behind them were the two princesses, twelve-year-old Margaret and sixteen-year-old Elizabeth, fresh in matching tea-dresses and very composed as they began, like their parents, to talk to those nearest them. Jenny's throat closed up and she tugged awkwardly at her dress in a vain effort to hide the frayed hem. This was horrible.

Behind the royal family came Eleanor Roosevelt, creating her own flurry of excitement, though she barely seemed to notice. She was with Clementine, and Jenny was struck by how similar the two women were. Both stood above the crowd at around six feet and carried their height with dignity. They were about the same age and both had greying hair, though Clementine's, carefully permed every four months, was swept into an elegant bun and Eleanor's seemingly yanked into a clip. Clementine was undeniably the more beautiful woman, with her high cheekbones and wide eyes, but Eleanor's smile, as she looked around the people gathered to meet her, was wide enough to illuminate the entire room.

The first lady spotted Jenny and made a beeline in her direction. There was nothing for it but to move forward and shake her hand.

'Jenny! Lovely to see you. You look so well. Rosy.'

Jenny tried to smile. 'It's warm in here.'

'Isn't it?' Eleanor looked to a hovering servant. 'Can we have some windows open?'

He looked horrified. 'No, ma'am, sorry. It would break blackout regulations.'

Eleanor's hand flew to her mouth. 'Of course it would. How terribly stupid of me. Thank you for reminding me, young man.'

She reached out and shook his hand, to his obvious mortifi-cation and the astonishment of most of the women in the room, who would no more think of shaking a servant's hand than flying an aeroplane. Then again, Jenny reminded herself, women *were* flying planes these days. Living and working together in factories, offices and shops was breaking down class barriers all over the place, so maybe Eleanor was simply ahead of her time. It wouldn't surprise Jenny and she suspected that London was about to get a rush of fresh air from the first lady of America – or, more likely, a tornado.

'How's your visit going?' she asked, stalling for time.

'Very well,' Eleanor said. 'I've had a lovely weekend here in the palace.' She glanced over to the king and queen with a wide smile. 'You know, for royalty, Bertie and Elizabeth really are marvellously down to earth. The queen talked to me at length about how she'd helped fit cardboard to the windows when they were blown out by bombs. And they live most frugally. There's a line drawn on the bath to show where you're allowed to fill the water, even if you're the king of England himself!'

'The war affects us all,' Jenny said. 'The palace has been bombed several times.'

'It has,' Eleanor agreed. 'I've seen the holes myself – though it has to be said that there's still plenty of it left to live in. This place is huge!' She gave a hearty laugh and tucked an arm through Jenny's. 'Now, then, you must introduce me to some of these lovely ladies.'

'Of course,' Jenny agreed, but she could swear two women behind were sniggering at her dress and it was hard to concentrate.

Eleanor peered at her. 'Are you well, my dear? You look rather pink.'

Jenny coughed. 'I'm quite well, thank you, it's just...' There was nothing for it but honesty. 'I caught my hem on the way up the stairs and it's loose at the back.'

Eleanor burst out laughing. 'Is that all? Oh, Jen, it's only a dress. It doesn't matter in the slightest. People are what count.'

She was so right. There was a war on after all. Men were

fighting in sandy trenches in the deserts of North Africa without the right protective gear, women and children were living with relatives in borrowed dresses, Jews were fleeing Nazis with nothing more than the clothes they stood up in, and even the king and queen were having to take meagre baths. She had no right to fret about one silly hem.

She was still fretting though.

'I can't be presented to the queen in a frayed dress!'

'Queen Elizabeth won't mind. Those dresses the princesses are wearing are sewn from old curtains. She told me so at breakfast.'

'But still sewn perfectly!'

'She won't even notice.'

Jenny wasn't so sure but, gritting her teeth, she led Eleanor over to Dora and Nellie.

'This is Dora, executive officer of the Bundles for Britain charity.'

'Executive officer!' Dora gave a tinkling laugh. 'That still gets me every time you say it, Jen.' She shook Eleanor's hand heartily. 'Very pleased to meet you, ma'am. I'd so love to go to America. I nearly went to sixth form there, you know, but Daddy was afraid I'd learn "uncouth manners". How silly is that!'

'Very silly,' Eleanor agreed. 'Ironically, I did my sixth form here, in London.'

'No!'

'Yes, at a brilliantly progressive school led by a wonderful woman called Marie Souvestre. She took me all over Europe in the holidays. I loved it. Paris especially. I can't bear to think of that glorious city stomped on by Nazi thugs.'

Everyone rushed to agree, telling stories of their times in 'poor Paris' and Jenny stepped back, wondering if she could escape to the lavatory and try and fix her damned hem before the queen closed in.

'Jenny, dear, are you well?'

She felt a light hand on her shoulder and spun round to see Clementine looking at her with concern. Goodness, another great lady she was bothering with her nonsense.

'Very well, thank you.'

Her hostess wasn't fooled. 'Tell me what's wrong.'

Jenny gulped. 'It's silly really. It's just that I caught my hem on the stairs coming up and I'm embarrassed.'

She waited for the laugh; it did not come.

'I can imagine,' Clementine said. 'Let's see what we can do about it. Ah, Princess Elizabeth.'

Jenny thought she might die, for before her was the young princess, smiling and holding out a slim hand. She took it and bobbed a flame-faced curtsy.

'Honoured to meet you, ma'am,' Jenny said.

'Your royal highness,' Clementine whispered and she flushed even deeper red.

'I'm so sorry. I—'

'Please don't concern yourself,' the princess said, all smiles. 'And you are...?'

'Jenny Miller.'

'The broadcaster?'

Jenny felt her whole self thrill and suddenly her hem truly did feel insignificant. 'I make a few programmes, yes.'

'My sister and I listened to your one on the American civil war the other day. Fascinating.' She leaned in. 'I have history lessons from the vice-provost of Eton and he's very clever but he never makes anything seem as clear or as engaging as your programme did. Thank you.'

'No, thank you,' Jenny said, hastily adding, 'your royal highness.'

'Ma'am,' Clementine whispered.

Jenny looked at her, totally confused. 'But last time, I said—'

'It's your royal highness at first address and ma'am after that.'

'I see,' Jenny said, though she didn't.

'It's all rather stuffy I'm afraid,' the princess told her. 'I forget myself half the time.'

Jenny was certain that was not true, but liked the composed young woman for her kindness.

'Do you know, ma'am, where we might find a needle?' Clementine asked her. 'We have a hem issue.'

She discreetly indicated Jenny's skirt while Jenny wanted, once again, to die.

'Of course,' the princess said with an easy smile. 'I tear my skirts all the time. Crawfie will sort you out in a jiffy.' She indicated a soberly dressed woman sitting at one edge of the room, knitting.

'Thank you,' Clementine said.

With a bob of a curtsy, she escorted Jenny over, introducing her to Miss Crawford, the princesses' governess and, it seemed, all round carer. Calmly and with no fuss, Crawfie led them into a side room and produced a needle and perfectly matching golden thread from a pretty sewing box.

'If you'd like to sit down here,' she directed Jenny and within less than two minutes, the hem was mended so neatly it was impossible to tell there had ever been an issue.

'Thank you so much,' Jenny gasped.

'My pleasure.'

'Good work, Miss Crawford,' Clementine said. 'A lady doesn't like to look dishevelled, does she?'

It was such a Clementine thing to say that Jenny couldn't resist hugging her. She seemed surprised at first but then hugged her back.

'There now, what was that about?'

'Eleanor told me people were more important than clothes,' she admitted.

'And in that she was absolutely correct, but personally I find that people are so much easier to deal with when your clothes feel right. It is, perhaps, an English diffidence.'

'In which case,' Jenny said as they returned to the main room, 'I am becoming more English every day.'

Clementine looked at her and, to Jenny's huge surprise, threw her a broad wink.

'There's hope for you yet then, dear! Come on, let's sally forth and meet the queen.'

Jenny wasn't sure she was up to that, even with her hem intact, but Clementine was 'sallying forth' at pace and, with her arm tucked firmly through Jenny's, there was little choice but to sally along. Queen Elizabeth was talking to Eleanor, looking almost fairy-like against the statuesque first lady.

She turned to Jenny, saying, 'Thank heavens, someone my own height. I swear, you have to be Amazonian to support the rulers of the known earth these days.'

'Merely Amazonian of the heart, your royal highness,' Jenny said, and the queen clapped her hands delightedly.

'Amazonian of the heart! I like that. And you are?'

'Mrs Jenny Miller, ma'am.' No one flinched – perhaps she'd mastered the peculiarities of English address! 'I run Bundles for Britain here in London.'

'Wonderful. I'm quite jealous of some of those fabulous jumpers I've seen on our sailors. The palace can become so draughty, you know! Not that I'd dream of depriving the boys serving bravely in those horrible northern seas.'

'It must be very cold up there.'

'It is. The king was posted to Scapa Flow for a while in the Great War and said it took months to thaw out.'

'The king was in the navy?'

'He wasn't king then – nor ever meant to be.'

The queen's brow darkened and Clementine stepped in.

'But thank the Lord God that he is now, for your husband is the best possible monarch we could ever hope for.'

'And yours the best prime minister.'

Clementine smiled gratefully, then turned to Eleanor Roosevelt to add, 'And yours, of course, the best president.'

Eleanor looked lost for a reply to this rare outpouring of British sentiment and glanced to Jenny for help.

'What a dazzling set of men you have,' Jenny trilled. It sounded embarrassingly gauche but the three women caught in a triangle around her just looked thoughtful.

'And what a responsibility,' Clementine commented.

Silence fell. The palace party buzzed around them but here, at its centre, all was still.

The queen recovered first. 'What a good job, then,' she said stoutly, 'that we have Amazonian hearts.'

They all laughed gaily, but Jenny thought nothing had ever been more truly said and prayed that God kept these brave, strong, self-deprecating women alive, for the world needed them more than it would ever know.

TWENTY-TWO

WRVS CLOTHING STORE, CHEAPSIDE, OCTOBER 1942

CLEMENTINE

Clementine leaned surreptitiously against the wall as an excited Women's Royal Voluntary Service superintendent answered Eleanor Roosevelt's questions about the operation of her clothing store. She was exhausted. The American woman never stopped! In the last week, Eleanor had travelled all the way up to Glasgow docklands and all the way down to the cliffs of Dover, visiting a number of cities in between. Thankfully, Lady Stella Reading, Eleanor's friend from her schooldays in England, had accompanied her, but on her return, she'd asked to see as many of Clementine's projects as she could.

'That's very kind of you,' Clementine had said, 'but would you not like a rest?'

'I slept on the train,' Eleanor had replied breezily, as if the three hours from Sheffield were all she required this week. 'And I don't want to waste a second of my time here.'

She certainly hadn't done that. So far today they'd toured one of Clementine's new hostels, visited the fully kitted-out

Southwark shelter and taken refreshments at an Aid to Russia fundraising tea in a Red Cross club. Mrs Roosevelt (she kept insisting Clementine call her Eleanor, which felt most peculiar on so short an acquaintance) had been fascinated by all of it. At the hostel, Clementine had followed her usual practice of having one of the beds stripped to be sure the mattress and linen were of decent standard and Mrs Roosevelt had lain right down and tried it herself. She'd looked rather inelegant bouncing up and down in front of everyone, but Clementine had to admit there was a certain charm to her girlish openness.

'I stood on those white cliffs of yours, down in Dover,' she was telling the superintendent, Mrs Robinson, 'and I thought, damn, Hitler is *so* close.'

'Well he won't be getting any closer,' Mrs Robinson shot back.

'That's the spirit!'

'And he won't be stopping our kiddies having clothes on their backs if I have anything to do with it.'

Eleanor clapped. 'Excellent work. You collect donated clothes and distribute them to the needy, is that right? Like Bundles for Britain?'

'Exactly like,' Mrs Robinson confirmed eagerly. 'Only the clothes are second-hand, not knitted fresh.'

'Nothing wrong with hand-me-downs,' Mrs Roosevelt said crisply. 'And where do you store the goods, Mrs Robinson?'

'Upstairs. We have them laid out in categories so that if anyone comes in, they can have a good riffle through. Would you like to see?'

'I don't think Mrs Roosevelt needs to look at piles of jumble,' Clementine said hastily, but, sadly, Mrs Roosevelt did seem to need to and was already making for the stairs – the long, steep stairs. Clementine's knees ached just looking at them.

'Are you the prime minister's wife?' a small voice asked.

Clementine looked around to see a girl of about eight sitting, legs dangling, on a bench to one side.

'I am,' she said, moving over to her. 'Who are you?'

'I'm Daisy. Me mam's upstairs looking for clothes for me cos I've got "far too damned tall".'

Clementine laughed. 'Don't you want to look yourself?'

Daisy shook her head. 'Too many stairs.'

'Well, quite. May I join you?'

She pointed to the bench and Daisy nodded and shuffled over.

'You go on up,' Clementine called faintly after Mrs Roosevelt. 'I need to chat to Daisy here.'

'So, what's it like living in that posh house?' Daisy demanded.

'Number Ten? It's not too bad, I suppose, though we did get bombed you know?'

'Did you?' The girl's eyes widened. 'So did we. My bedroom fell right into the kitchen and all my toys got crushed, and so did my baby brother.'

Clementine's breath hitched with a familiar memory of loss. 'Your brother? I'm so sorry.'

Daisy nodded and kicked at the bench. 'He was sleeping in the kitchen, see, cos it were cold and Mam thought he'd be warmer down by the stove. Mam says he wouldn't have suffered, which is good, isn't it? But I reckon Mam's suffered enough for twenty babies. She cries all the time.'

Clementine felt like crying herself. 'At least she has you.'

'She does,' Daisy agreed, 'but I'm naughty sometimes and that makes her cry more. I try not to be, but then I forget. Last week I tore my dress playing with Bobby and Frank on the rubble heap and Mam said I was an "ungrateful little madam" but I wasn't, honest, I was just having fun.'

Clementine took her hand. 'I'm sure your mam knows that really. She'll just be tired.'

Daisy nodded again. 'She *is* tired. All the time. It's the crying, see – it stops her sleeping. And then being in the factory all day.'

'Factory?'

'Making bombs. It's turning her skin yellow but she says she doesn't care. She says she'll happily be as yellow as a bloody canary if just one of those bombs stops that bastard Hitler tearing up our lives.'

Clementine blinked. The girl's language was ripe, but she was engagingly earnest. She touched a hand to her turban, today in a deep orange silk, and felt a fraud. She might wear her hair like these women but her life was nothing like theirs. Nothing.

'Do you think,' she said to Daisy, 'that it would make your mam feel better to come to tea in Downing Street?'

Daisy's eyes lit up. 'With you? In the posh house?'

'Exactly.'

'I think it would make her feel like the least tired person in the whole wide world.'

Clementine severely doubted that, but now a young woman, shoulders bowed like someone three times her age, was coming down the stairs with a small bag of clothes and Daisy leaped up and ran to her, babbling about tea at Number Ten. The woman started to scold her and Clementine leaped up to intervene.

'Daisy is telling the truth, Mrs...?'

'Jones,' the woman supplied, staring up at her. 'Are you...? I mean, is she...?'

'I am Clementine Churchill, Mrs Jones, and I've been having a chat to your Daisy. She's a charming girl.'

'That she is,' Mrs Jones stuttered.

'So I invited her and your good self to tea. Would Friday suit?'

'Friday?' Mrs Jones looked flustered. 'Erm, I work earlies

Fridays so, er, yes, Friday would be good. That is... are you sure? Me? And Daisy? In Number Ten?'

'Very sure,' Clementine said, loving the light in the weary woman's eyes and feeling humbled that she had the power to make her so happy. 'Shall we say four p.m.?'

'Erm, yes, ma'am, thank you, ma'am.'

'And, Mrs Jones, please come as you are. No new clothes will be needed.'

Mrs Jones heaved a sigh of relief. 'That's very kind. Clothes is hard to come by these days.'

'And matter not one jot,' Clementine said. She looked up to see Mrs Roosevelt descending the stairs and said goodbye to Daisy and her mother, looking forward to seeing them again.

'You didn't make it to the store,' Mrs Roosevelt said.

'I was talking to a little girl. Clothes don't matter; people do.' She smiled at Eleanor. 'Jenny Miller tells me someone very wise taught her that.'

'Really? Who?'

Clementine laughed. 'You!'

Clementine was grateful to slide into the waiting car and relieved to see even the redoubtable Mrs Roosevelt sinking into the soft leather with a sigh of relief.

'The old bones aren't what they used to be,' Eleanor confided.

'It's good to see you're human,' Clementine commented.

Mrs Roosevelt blushed. 'Do I come across as a machine?'

'No! Heavens, no. I simply mean that you have unending stamina.'

Eleanor laughed. 'I expect it comes from being plain.'

'You're not—'

'I am, my dear. Always have been. I learned early on not to worry too much about what other people think of me and that is most liberating. Other people's opinions can be very draining.'

'That's certainly true, but really, you're a very striking woman, Mrs... Eleanor.'

'You're too kind, Clementine, though worrying about how you convey your opinions of others can be very draining too. You needn't worry with me. I'm not easily offended.'

'Well, I honestly think you're amazing to get so much done.'

Eleanor sighed. 'The problem is that there's so much *to* do, is there not? It nags away at me day and night and I simply cannot escape feeling responsible for it.'

That Clementine understood. For so many years she'd stood by Winston in his political goals but now, with the endless heartbreaking letters that arrived through her letter box and the endless people she met enduring suffering with such stoicism, she was feeling the weight of her responsibilities. It was not unwelcome, for at least with her chosen tasks she could get on and do something about them, but there were always so many more waiting.

'I invited that young girl, Daisy, and her mother for tea,' she told Eleanor, 'and they positively glowed. They've had a frightful time with the bombing and something as ridiculously easy as having a cup of tea with me can make them happy. If that's true, I should be having tea with people every single day, yet I would still leave far more out than I saw!'

'The power to effect change is a privilege, but a weight as well, and it's so hard to do at a micro level. We have to change the inherent way we run the world. We need a united nations group to create international cooperation and settle disputes in a civilised way long before they have to come to war. Maybe that's just a woman's way of looking at it, but if so, I'd say it's time women ran things.'

'Time you did, certainly.'

But at that Eleanor shook her head. 'I'd be useless. I've been butting my head against injustices in my country for decades. Franklin says I take it too much to heart. He's a consummate politician. He can balance what he wants to get done against what is practical for the time and situation. I cannot. If I were president, I'd go charging in trying to sort everything immediately and so many people would object that I'd be out on my ear before I could manage even one solid reform. That's what frustrates me.'

Clementine fiddled with her earring – her pearl studs again today; she still couldn't find the pretty drop ones anywhere – and thought about this. Over the last fortnight, she'd heard some details of Mrs Roosevelt's work with the youth movement in America, with the battle for racial integration, with civil defence and trying to help refugees fleeing Nazi territories. This woman had a true social conscience, not simply a desire to make a few people's lives more comfortable. Winston had that too, though in a rather more bullish way than this genteel American, and Clementine admired him greatly for it, especially at the moment. With Rommel still rampaging in Africa and no one ready, yet, to invade France, her husband had faced a vote of no confidence in Parliament. He'd won, of course, but he was like a bear with a sore head and she longed for them both to be able to escape into private life. What sort of coward was she?

'It seems to me, Eleanor,' she said, 'that you are a better politician than you think. I'd like to step away from public service and live my life with Winston and the children, as a family.'

'Ah,' Mrs Roosevelt said. 'Well, that's where you're lucky.'

Eleanor turned to the window, apparently gripped by the sight of Londoners going about their everyday business, but Clementine saw her hands clench in her lap and her throat work to swallow back what might be tears. She remembered Jenny saying something about her and Franklin Roosevelt living separate lives and felt desperately sad for the driven, inspirational woman at her side. She fought for the words to say that she understood loneliness, if not, perhaps, in the same way, but she was far too English to speak so personally. She contented herself with patting her new friend's hand and then sat quietly, counting her blessings for having a loving husband. Winston might be a bear with a sore head, but he was her bear and she was determined to keep him to the end.

TWENTY-THREE

HALLAM STREET, OCTOBER 1942

JENNY

Jenny stirred the eggs with care and tried to block out Ned's voice, though it was all but impossible as it was rising in decibels with every sip of his very strong martinis. What would Eleanor think? Jenny had invited her over for Sunday-night scrambled eggs, feeling she might appreciate some home comfort after her hectic three weeks charging around Great Britain, but Ned had got overexcited at having the first lady in his home and invited every American in London.

Their apartment was rammed and the second martini bottle was being opened before the eggs were even ready to serve. Plus, it meant there weren't nearly enough to go round, even with the extra dozen that Sue White had kindly brought, so it would be tiny helpings. Jenny set her jaw. She'd make sure Eleanor had a decent portion, even if Ned had to go without, though the way those martinis were going to his head, perhaps that was an unwise strategy.

'I'm working on the RAF to let me fly in one of their

bombers,' Ned boomed. 'Imagine that – broadcasting live as the hatches open to drop bombs on Berlin!'

There were noises of male appreciation, though Eleanor looked unimpressed. Jenny stirred the eggs harder and sought for something to distract her guest, but the first lady was not easily distracted.

'Will you broadcast them falling on innocent civilians, Mr Miller?' she asked.

'*German* civilians,' he retorted, waving his martini glass to cheers from his colleagues.

Eleanor stood up. 'You think all Germans are Nazis, do you?'

Ned froze.

'They voted Hitler in,' he said.

Eleanor nodded. 'That's true. Mainly on his promise of greater economic stability, rather than his remarkably under-stated policies on exterminating Jews or taking over the whole of Europe.'

'Well, yes, but that's clear now and he's still in power.'

'Because the elections of both 1936 and 1938 offered the electorate merely the chance to confirm the Nazi leadership, with no alternative option.'

Ned swallowed. 'Is that right?'

'And even if not, German democracy, at least nominally, is the same as ours – victory by majority. How many people in America do you think voted for my husband two years ago, Mr Miller?'

Ned looked desperately around for help but his colleagues had all melted to the edges of the apartment. It was really quite funny. Jenny switched off the eggs and watched.

'Around twenty-seven million. That's not quite 55 per cent, and it was considered a good victory – 55 per cent. That means that 45 per cent of Americans did *not* vote for the current president. Is it not safe, then, to assume that some similar number of people did not vote for Adolf Hitler in Germany?'

'I'd have to look at the numbers,' Ned stuttered.

'You won't find them. Goebbels is in charge of Nazi numbers so they will state that the Führer carried 99 per cent of the vote – that he is, against all possible logic, the most wanted leader in any country in all of history.'

'I see your point, ma'am.' Ned was looking cowed, clearly regretting inviting his buddies over to see what good friends he was with the presidential family.

'I'm told by the German resistance, for example—'

'German resistance?'

'Oh yes. There are brave youngsters out there trying to combat the worst of Hitler's many excesses in the back streets of their country. They send us reports when they can, and they estimate there may be some twenty thousand Jews hiding in private homes in Berlin. That's at least twenty thousand Germans prepared not only to dislike Hitler but to actively work against him, at huge danger to themselves. Some of your bombs may fall on them, Mr Miller.'

'I...' Ned floundered and finally fell back on an old stand-by. 'I'm merely there to record what's going on.'

'And I'm sure it will make excellent radio.' Eleanor smiled at him and turned to Jenny. 'Those eggs look wonderful, my dear. Shall we eat before they spoil?'

The evening recovered as the food was served. The first lady smoothly asked the gathered CBS staff about the difficulties of broadcasting from war zones and everyone was glad to retreat into talk of signals and amplification, studiously steering around who, or what might be amplified. The eggs went down well, the martinis were finished and someone, thankfully, produced a packet of excellent coffee. Conversation was lively and convivial and only Ned, still smarting from his history lesson, was unusually quiet, though he leaped up eagerly when Eleanor announced she should go.

'You must be weary, Mrs Roosevelt.'

'Weary? No, the excellent company has invigorated me, but I have an appointment to join a fire-watching team at eleven, so must take my leave. Thank you so much for having me.'

'It's been a pleasure,' Ned said, though that was patently untrue.

Eleanor patted him on the arm. 'You're a clever broadcaster, Mr Miller, and I'm sure you will find meaningful stories to bring to the world.'

'I shall look into the German resistance,' he said.

She beamed at him like a proud mother. 'That would be good.' She embraced Jenny warmly. 'Take care of yourself, my dear. You must miss your family.'

'I have Ned,' she said, looking to him.

He put his arm around her but it felt stiff and awkward and as soon as Eleanor disappeared into the night with her bodyguard, he dropped it and rushed back to his buddies.

'She had you there, Ned my boy!' Jenny heard someone laugh. She hovered in the corridor, unwilling to join them.

'Forty-five per cent of Germans aren't Nazis? What nonsense! Besides, Hitler's bombing our civilians so why shouldn't we bomb his? Women! They should stay out of the business of making war.'

'And into the business of making lurve,' someone added, to rowdy cheers.

Jenny leaned against the door and wished she had Eleanor's courage to stand up to them, but she did not and could only be grateful when someone pointed out that they should get to the station in time for America to wake up and want her first broadcasts. Coats were gathered and backs slapped. Jenny opened the door and let them all file past. All but one.

'I have to get going,' Ned said when she stopped him. 'I'm on air at midnight.'

'So I have to tidy this up on my own?' She indicated the mess of plates and glasses littering their apartment.

'Why not? It's your job.'

'It isn't. I'm a broadcaster too, Ned.'

'Your little history shows?'

'Little?!' She felt as if he'd punched her in the gut. 'You said they were good.'

He flushed. 'They *are* good, Jen. But they're only once a fortnight and they're features, you know, not news.'

'Not dropping bombs on civilians?'

His eyes narrowed. 'That's not fair. You know that's not what I meant. She twisted my meaning.'

'*She?* The first lady of America?'

'It doesn't matter what position she holds, she still twisted my meaning.'

'Then you didn't do a very good job of putting her straight. I thought you were the one who was good with words, Mr Silver-tongued broadcaster?'

'You don't think so?'

She felt tears prick. They rarely argued and she hated it, but this was important. 'I *do* think so. But we mustn't get lost in the drama of war and forget the cost in human life.'

'And you think that's what I'm doing?'

'No!'

'You think I'm becoming some sort of cold-hearted hack, chasing the story for its own sake not for its wider truth and importance?'

'No, Ned, I don't. I just think that maybe, tonight, you got slightly carried away.'

'Carried away?' His voice was dark with menace.

She shrank back. 'Please, Ned, this isn't you. This—'

'You think I was showing off? "Look at me, with the first lady in my home..."'

'Of course not,' she said, though that was exactly what she thought. 'Ned, please, let's forget this. Let's—'

But he was raging now, hands on hips and eyes wild. 'Perhaps, Jenny – wife – if we had a baby—'

Jenny gasped. She staggered back, desperate to get away from him, and caught her head on the living room doorframe. Pain spiked through her but she forced herself to keep her eyes open and made it through to sink onto the sofa.

Ned followed, instantly contrite. 'I'm sorry.'

She couldn't even look at him. 'You're right.'

'I'm not. I shouldn't have said that. It was mean.'

'It *was* mean, but it was true too.'

'It's not your fault.'

'You don't think that.'

'I do.'

They were both lying to each other now. Jenny felt the world spin and longed to be home in Connecticut, but she was in London, in the middle of a war, and the one thing that would make it OK would not stick in her womb. Maybe her mother had been right and university had killed her fertility. She tutted at herself. That was as illogical as assuming all Germans were Nazis. But she wouldn't go there again, not now. Ned was hovering over her and when she dared to look up she saw contrition in his eyes.

'We should talk about this, Jen.'

They should, but not here, not now. She was too bruised to make sense.

'You'd better go, Ned. You're on air soon.'

He glanced at his watch and tutted. 'It can wait,' he tried, but they both knew that wasn't true either. CBS was a demanding mistress.

'So can I,' Jenny said. 'Go, Ned, please.'

He bent and dropped a kiss on her forehead. 'I'm sorry,' he said again.

And then he was gone, leaving Jenny as neither, it seemed, a proper broadcaster nor a proper wife to 'do her job' and clean up the detritus of an evening gone terribly wrong. When, she wondered desperately, was this damned war ever going to end, and would it destroy everything she held dear before it did so?

TWENTY-FOUR

THE ANNEXE, JANUARY 1943

CLEMENTINE

Clementine jumped out of the car beneath icy blue skies and might have danced into the Annexe if it hadn't been for the presence of the officers on guard, stamping their frozen feet in her doorway. Did their opinions matter? Mrs Roosevelt would probably say not, but Mrs Roosevelt wasn't here and Clementine had only her hard-learned set of formalities to guide her. She glanced at the left-hand officer, a lad barely out of school, and wondered what he'd think if she grabbed his hands and asked him to waltz her into Horse Guards Parade. She smothered a childish giggle. He'd think her an insane old woman. He'd be wrong, though. She was just happy. It was a peculiar feeling in this, the fourth year of the war, and she almost felt guilty for it, but *that* really would be insane.

The war was, tentatively, going well at last. In November, the Allies had secured a major victory against Rommel at El Alamein in North Africa. Winston had been so over the moon at this first major triumph that he'd ordered all the church bells in England rung on the following Sunday. Clementine had feared it was precipitous but Montgomery's forces were driving the Nazis mercilessly back along the coast towards Tunisia so it seemed not.

Meanwhile, in Russia, the Red Army had encircled the Wehrmacht in Stalingrad and, against all the odds, were reversing the Nazi advances of the last two years. People across occupied Europe were hailing these successes with joy. The news was filled with Red Army advances and of particular pleasure to Clementine was the retaking of far-off Rostov-on-Don. The Russia Fund was poised to send help in to rebuild the hospitals as soon as it was safe, and raising enough money was consuming Clementine.

For perhaps the first time in her life she was doing work that was hers and hers alone and she had to admit she was loving it. Letters from grateful women in Russia reached her every day, travelling thousands of miles across the war-torn continent. They gladdened her heart but also made her determined to do more. She'd put out several radio appeals, written personal letters to the papers, and attended every event she possibly could, though those events then brought her into contact with British people also suffering hardships and losses. There too, however, she could act. Her afternoon tea with Daisy and her mother three months ago had gone well and she'd asked Grace to invite others. It felt good to help, in however small a way.

Today, she was back from Fulmer Chase where, in a joyous ceremony, she'd had the privilege of presenting a layette gifted by Queen Elizabeth to the mother of the thousandth baby born in the hospital. Diana had come along, full of the fact that Duncan had walked again and blooming with her third pregnancy. She'd bounced around Fulmer Chase and then asked to see Fircroft and been fulsome in her praise. It had been lovely.

Now Clementine was home and, if she was really lucky, Mary, whose leave started today, would have arrived and they could have lunch together. This evening there was to be a piano recital by Moiseiwitsch in aid of the Russia Fund, and she, Mary and Winston would attend with Jock, Nellie and Sarah. All in all, it was a fine family day to be seized amongst so many tough ones. Perhaps she *would* waltz the guard down to Horse Guards Parade – at least it would warm up the poor lad.

She was stopped by the door opening and Mary coming flying out. 'Mummy!'

She ran into Clementine's arms and Clementine drew in the exuberance of her youngest daughter like the finest summer sunshine.

'Mary!' She held her out before her, drinking her in. 'You look so well. Khaki suits you!'

Mary laughed. 'Khaki is a rotten colour, Mummy. I've no idea why I didn't join the Wrens – navy is so much more flattering.'

'Because you were determined to man an anti-aircraft gun,' Clementine reminded her.

'I was! And now I am! We had a direct hit on a Messer-schmitt the other day.' She sobered. 'We saw the pilot bail out and float down on his parachute. Called it in on the radio but I've no idea if the military police got to him. Some of the girls heard about a Luftwaffe pilot being beaten to death by a group of villagers. That's not right, is it?'

'That's not right,' Clementine agreed. 'It's against the Geneva Convention and it's against all common dignity. There is no need for us to descend to their levels of barbarity or else what is the point of the war at all?'

'Well said, Mummy.' Mary perked up immediately. 'I'll say exactly that if it comes up again. Now, let's get inside – it's freezing out here.'

'It is,' Clementine agreed, letting herself be guided past the soldiers and confiding, 'I nearly took one of those poor men off on a waltz a minute ago.'

'Oh, you should have. He would have loved it.'

Clementine laughed at her daughter's easy joy. 'He would have loved it with *you*, maybe.'

'And with you. You're a beautiful woman, and a very important one besides.'

Clementine laughed again but she had to admit that recently, making a tangible difference for people, she *had* been feeling a teensy bit important and it wasn't unpleasant.

'Let's have lunch,' she said, taking off her coat and unwinding the soft woollen turban from her hair. 'I can't wait to hear everything you've been up to.'

'Maybe not everything,' Mary giggled.

Clementine looked at her sharply. 'Do you have a young man on the go?'

'On the go! Mummy, you're so crass. I might be stepping out with a rather charming officer every so often but nothing serious. There's a war on, you know. I'm far too busy for romance.'

'Well, thank heavens for that,' Clementine said.

'You don't want me to fall in love?' Mary mock-pouted.

She was joking, Clementine knew, but it wasn't a joking matter.

'I *do* want you to fall in love, my darling, for it is the most wonderful thing in the world. But I want you to do it when you have time and space to be certain that it truly is love and not...'

'Lust?' Mary giggled.

Clementine rolled her eyes. 'I suppose so, though I wouldn't have put it that way. I'm not sure all this independence is doing women good.'

Mary stamped her foot. 'Now that, Mummy, is a *very* poor thing to say. This is our time. This is where we prove that us girls can do more than just pop out boys to rule the world. We can rule it ourselves!'

'And have babies?'

'Why not?'

'And support our husbands?'

'As much as they support us, yes. Equality, Mummy. You were a suffragette, weren't you?'

Clementine frowned. 'I most certainly was not. I was a suffra*gist*, yes, but I wasn't chaining myself to railings or blocking events. The cause was noble and deserved to be conducted in a noble way.'

'Noble?' Mary muttered scathingly. 'Noble would have been men admitting that half the population had a right to a voice.'

'As they did.'

'Eventually. Did you know Papa was against it at the start?'

Clementine burst out laughing. 'Of course I knew, Mary. We had long arguments about it when we were first married. Your father is chivalrous – overly so. He wants to wrap up women in silk and let them have the "easy life" he thinks they deserve for being such beautiful, fascinating creatures.'

'That's what he says. Papa's always been good with words. What he means is he wants to wrap them up in the home where they can't interfere with running all the businesses and events and governance.'

Clementine blinked at her daughter. 'You've clearly been having some very... robust discussions at the barracks, Mary.'

'Robust!' Mary laughed. 'We certainly have. The world is changing, Mummy, and when we win the war, we need to be sure it's changing in the way we want it to.'

'Oh. Right.' Clementine hadn't thought about this before. It was hard enough to see to the end of next week, let alone the end of the war, and certainly not the shape of the world after it. 'Is it not enough just to defeat Hitler?'

'No! How would you like your life post-war, Mummy?'

Clementine thought hard. She was enjoying her responsibilities, but trying to sort out so many things was so very exhausting. 'Peaceful?' she hazarded.

'Not the world, *you*.'

'Still peaceful.' Mary looked disappointed and she hugged her. 'I'm sorry, my dear, but I'm old. And tired. I know much needs to be done. Eleanor tells me we should have a united nations group and I believe she's correct, but it sounds a very, very hard thing to achieve. Now you tell me that we must have liberation for women, and that too sounds both excellent and exhausting. After the war I simply want to rest, though I'm very, very happy for you to forge a brave new world however you and your friends see fit.'

Mary looked as if she was about to protest again but then nodded. 'Fair enough.' She hugged her back. 'Your generation have opened the way for us, Mummy, and I'm sorry if it's so hard. Are you *very* tired?'

'A lot of the time, yes, but not today. Today we had our thousandth baby at Fulmer Chase.'

'Amazing!'

'Thank you. And you are home—'

'Which is obviously dreamy.'

'Mrs Landermare has made your favourite meat loaf for lunch.'

'Super!'

'And tonight we're going to a piano concert with Papa.'

'Even better!'

Mary's brief delve into politics was, thankfully, lost in a rush of youthful happiness and as they tucked into the meat loaf, Clementine was happy to sit back and listen to her chatter away about training and duties and parties and all sorts of high jinks her other girls would never have confided. Lunch went on well into the afternoon and was only stopped by Mary realising the concert was an early start and she had nothing to wear.

'Can I look through your wardrobe?' she asked, already up and heading for the corridor. 'And maybe your jewellery box? Do you still have those delicious diamond cluster earrings?'

Clementine laughed. 'It's a concert, Mary. It's not that fancy.'

'These days, Mummy, anything that doesn't involve uniform is fancy. Come on!'

Clementine went gladly, but in the corridor they were stopped by Dr Moran, looking grave.

'Charles, is something wrong? Is Winston ill?'

Her husband was preparing to fly to Casablanca to meet Roosevelt and plan the Allied strategy for the next phase of the war. With the tide possibly turning against the Axis in both Africa and Russia, Winston was keen to seize the initiative and even keener to persuade the Americans to do it his way – using North Africa to launch into Europe via Italy, rather than the direct but more heavily defended route through Northern France. He was all set, and Clementine had been enjoying how busy it kept him so she could focus on her projects, but if he was ill that would...

'He's not ill.'

'Then what?'

Charles Moran shifted from foot to foot like a schoolboy. 'Would you rather talk about this in private, Mrs Churchill?'

Clementine looked to Mary, but her daughter linked their arms resolutely. Clementine smiled gratefully.

'Mary can hear anything I can.'

'Very well.' He cleared his throat roughly. 'We did some routine tests on Winston's heart recently...'

Clementine's own heart pounded instantly and she was grateful for her daughter's firm arm. 'Right. And they said...?'

'They said that he's at risk of thrombosis.'

'Which is?' Mary asked.

'A blood clot within the veins that limits the flow of blood to the heart and may...'

'And may?' Clementine prompted anxiously.

'May lead to coronary arrest.'

'A heart attack?!'

'Yes.'

'Like he had in Washington last Christmas?' Clementine asked.

'He had a heart attack last Christmas?' Mary squealed.

'A minor one,' Clementine told her hastily.

'Very minor,' the doctor agreed, 'but it would have done some damage, created some scar tissue, such as you would get on a cut knee, say. Scar tissue is less flexible than normal tissue, so less responsive to attack.'

'And the risks of thrombosis are increased by, don't tell me, drinking and smoking?'

'Yes. Also... flying. Especially at high altitudes.'

Mary's hand crept into hers. 'High altitudes such as those needed to fly to Casablanca?'

Dr Moran nodded grimly.

Clementine stood there, in the blank corridors of the Annexe, all her earlier happiness draining rapidly away.

Was I not allowed one day? she felt like shouting to God, to Hitler, to the world – to anyone who was listening. But what would be the point? Was this her fault? She'd been stepping away from Winston, focusing on Fulmer Chase and Fircroft and the Aid to Russia fund, and this was a timely reminder that he must be her first concern.

'Should I stop him going?' she asked anxiously, though Lord only knew how she'd do that.

'It's only an increased risk,' Dr Moran said. 'It doesn't mean it will happen. It probably isn't even as high a risk as his plane being hit by enemy fire.'

'Thank you, Charles!'

He looked ashamed. 'Sorry. Stupid thing to say, but it's true. And that's very unlikely because his whereabouts are closely protected.'

'So, you're telling me this because...?'

'Because I don't know whether to tell Winston.'

'Ah. I see. You don't know whether to burden him with the knowledge in case it, in some way, exacerbates the risk?'

'Exactly.'

Clementine looked to Mary, who gave a resigned sigh.

'I don't think it will stop him going, Mummy.'

That much was true. No risk to his person had ever stopped Winston doing what he wanted. Despite being an overweight old man with poor health, he believed himself invincible. How Clementine envied that. She looked to Charles, feeling the weight of the decision heavy on her already weary shoulders, but it had to be made.

'We don't tell him.'

The doctor looked relieved. 'I agree. Totally. Very much for the best.'

Then why did you ask me? she wanted to demand. But what was the point? He was just the adviser. She was the one closest to the prime minister and, it seemed, the one holding his heart in her hands – in more ways than one.

She glanced out the window at the road up to Horse Guards Parade and wished she'd taken that young man's hands and waltzed him up there and on – far from the Annexe, far from Downing Street, far from the seat of the damned power which might cost her husband his life. The burden of the knowledge would be kept from Winston; but nothing, now, could keep it from her.

TWENTY-FIVE

HALLAM STREET, JANUARY 1943

JENNY

Jenny sat, hands curled around a mug of the ubiquitous British tea, and pulled the covers further up to her chin. It was freezing, the sort of dank, misty cold that seeped into your very bones and made you fear you might never be warm again. It would be warmer if Ned were here, she thought, but Ned was rarely here nowadays. He was working longer and longer hours and, since the Eleanor Roosevelt debacle, wasn't bringing people back to the apartment between broadcasts nearly as often. At first she'd been glad of the peace; now she was just lonely.

She was doing her history broadcasts and they were going well. Paul White was pleased with her and she'd even had a few fan letters. Not a patch on the number that poured in for Ned, of course, but enough to merit more programmes. Plus, she found the work very satisfying. It was like being back at university, doing the hard graft of the research and then pulling it together into a coherent point or story – increasingly a story.

History, she was coming to see, was all about narratives. There were a number of lines that could be traced through the myriad events of the past and it was the job, and privilege, of the teller to pick the one they wished to trace. In many ways the events of the past were more satisfying than those going on around you, because at least you knew where they led. The frustration of what people were starting to refer to as the Second World War was that it could still go any way. Jenny felt impatient not just for it to end, but to know the way in which it did so.

But there was a long time to go to that.

Her tea had gone cold and she set it on the side, knowing Ned would tease her about it in the morning. She looked at the clock. This evening he'd been meeting a refugee Jew who'd fled Poland last year and was now a leading member of the Polish resistance in Britain. Ned had been convinced he'd have a good story and it had clearly gone well because he wasn't back yet. If, of course, he was truly meeting a Jewish refugee and not...

She stopped herself. Ned was *not* having an affair. He wouldn't. It was just his job keeping him away from her, that was all – his job and the celebrity it had turned him into. That's what he was in love with. Though what was it Dora had said when she'd checked into the Bundles office with her the other day? 'Your Ned likes a party, doesn't he? Saw him in the Ritz when I was out for cocktails. Quite the life and soul he was!' Jenny had laughed and tried to look as if she knew all about the Ritz, but it had jarred. She and Ned used to mock the cocktail crowd with their airhead approach to life, so what had changed? She'd asked him about it, but he'd been evasive.

'Paul White insisted we went, honey. Some rich donor he wanted to schmooze. It was very dull.'

That's not the way Dora made it sound, she'd wanted to say, but that would have been shrewish, so she'd stopped herself. It didn't mean she wasn't worried though. He'd always had a bit of a sparkle, of course. She could still remember the women that used to follow him around the student congress and how delighted she'd been that he'd preferred her. She remembered that first ever breakfast together, when he'd ordered strawberries to impress her. The next time they'd had them had been at their wedding – a private joke that they'd laughed over in bed later.

Her body sang at the memory and suddenly tears were falling. She pulled the bedclothes over her head – all three heavy, scratchy layers of them – to try to block out what felt like a vast gap between then and now. A little voice had been telling her at times that she wasn't good enough for him, but she hadn't gone through all that education and hard work to be pathetically down on herself for things beyond her control. But there was no doubt the voice was getting louder. It felt like hearing a Messerschmitt closing in, knowing that at any minute the bomb doors would open and destruction would rain down. She was manning her anti-aircraft battery but she was running out of ammunition.

Jenny tutted at herself and got a mouthful of woollen blanket. Honestly, did these Brits not even know what a quilt was yet? She'd tried and tried to find one when they'd first moved over but London was wedded to wool. She was, in all honesty, beginning to wonder what she was doing here. Ned didn't need her, and the endless cold, tea and tinned spam would grind down any girl's resilience.

The door opened with a slam and she sat upright. 'Ned?'

'Hey.' His voice was low, subdued even.

She scrubbed at her eyes and tried to push her hair into some sort of order as he came into the bedroom. But as soon as she saw him she stopped worrying about her looks, for his were dreadful. His dark eyes were sunken into their sockets and his skin had gone a peculiar shade of grey. She leaped out of bed.

'Ned, what is it? Are you ill?'

'Sick, for sure.'

He pulled her tight in against him and she felt him shaking.

'You're frozen.'

'I've been wandering around, lost track of time.'

'Why?'

He didn't seem to have an answer, so she decided to at least help him warm up and, pulling off his coat and shoes, dragged him into bed with her. Again, he held her tight and laid his head against hers. She felt a tear against her cheek.

'Ned, please, you're scaring me. What's wrong? Did you have your meeting?'

'I did. God, Jen, I did and I've heard the most awful thing.' His hands went to her hair, stroking it over and over.

'Can you tell me?'

'I can. I will. I mean, I have to. But this isn't just news, Jen, this is... This is a horror story. This is something the world must know and I have to find a way to tell it.'

She took his hands, holding them tight in hers. 'Start with me then, honey. I don't need fancy words or convoluted phrases. Just talk to me, tell me what you've heard.'

He nodded. 'Thank you. Yes. Yes, I can tell you.' But even then he hesitated.

Jenny sat in silence, willing him on, and eventually he started.

'The man I met this evening, Vladej, he's a Jew.'

'You said.'

'And you know the Nazis have been segregating the Jews, pushing them into ghettos and... and camps.'

'Yes. It's appalling.'

He shook his head violently. 'It's far, far worse than that. This man told me that they aren't prisoner camps or even labour camps. They're... they're extermination camps.'

'What? You can't mean—?'

'I can. I do. He's got proof, Jen. He was in one himself and he escaped when he was working the fields nearby.'

'So they *are* labour camps?'

'Yes. That is, they're labour camps as well. But if anyone is incapable of working, if they're too sick or too weak or too, too young... The Nazis exterminate them.'

'Let them die?'

He grabbed her shoulders, his eyes wild. 'No! They kill them – drive them into big chambers and release poisonous gas into them.'

'They can't!'

'They do. I've seen pictures of the gas. I've seen its technical spec. It's called Zyklon B and it was originally used against vermin. Still is, if you ask the Nazis. They're poisoning people en masse, Jenny. Then they're burning them in giant crematoria and burying the ash.'

'That's impossible.'

'Is it?'

Jenny swallowed. 'OK, it's not impossible but it's... monstrous.'

'Yes. But it's true.'

'Are you sure, Ned? Because it's important. If you tell this to the world, you have to be right.'

'You think I don't know that? He had a label from the gas canister, Jen. He had witness reports. He knows resistance groups who've followed the trains full of Jews from the ghettos to Treblinka and Auschwitz and Buchenwald. People go in and they don't come out. At Treblinka, the trains head into the forest full of people and come back empty. No food goes in, no clothes, almost no staff. It's a human dead end.'

Jenny could see now why he was shaking.

'Is this your story to tell, Ned?'

'It is now. Vladej has handed it to me, trusted me with it, asked me to tell it.'

'It's explosive, though. If you're going to name the Nazis as mass murderers you have to be sure of your facts.'

'I know! But if I don't name them as mass murderers, I'm in

dereliction of my duty, not just as a broadcaster but as a human being. People look to me for the truth, Jen. I've set myself up to bring them the war as it is, right into their front rooms in all its horror and suffering. I did that and, yes, I've enjoyed it. You know I have. You've seen the vain peacock I've become.' He raked his hands through his hair and looked at her like a drowning man. 'I've done this to myself, Jen. I can't pick and choose which struggles I show and if this is true – and it is – then it's the most important story I'll ever tell. The problem is, I don't know how to.'

'I'll help you,' she said.

'Will you? Really? It's ghastly, Jen. They're not the sort of details I'd like my wife to hear.'

'I'm tougher than you think.'

'You're amazing. I don't tell you that enough. I'm sorry. It's the war.'

Jenny wasn't sure it was. The war didn't help, but you couldn't blame it for everything. This, though, this seemed like the worst thing it had thrown at them yet.

'Gas chambers?' she said, feeling her way around the latent horror of even the words. 'Crematoria?'

'Extermination camps,' Ned said. 'That's what we must call them now.'

'Then we will, Ned. Together we will.'

It was not the way she'd seen their marriage going on that happy day when they'd promised themselves to each other and laughed over strawberries. It was not something she'd imagined them sharing, but this was the hand the world had dealt them and they had little choice but to play it. As Ned had said to her in the Houses of Parliament back in 1938, there were more ways of changing the world than becoming an MP.

She picked up a pen. 'Tell me everything, Ned. I'll write it all down and then we'll pick out the right words.'

He nodded and his spine straightened. 'The right words,' he

agreed, his voice calmer now. 'That's what we need, Jen – the right words to tell the world of an evil she doesn't want to conceive of. How do we find those?'

'Together,' she said stoutly and he took her hand and began to talk.

Two days later, Ned delivered the broadcast in an uncharacteristically subdued voice. Jenny sat at his side as he spoke the words they'd chosen into the microphone, and again for several more reports over the next few weeks. They were met with interest and shock, but an element of disbelief and little action. They railed against it to all who would listen and eventually Ned challenged Winston Churchill when he came to collect Jenny from a Bundles meeting with Clementine.

'No one believes me, Mr Churchill,' he complained.

'It's not that, Mr Miller,' Winston told him earnestly. 'It's hard for any normal human to conceptualise the horrors you so vividly present, but you are not alone. Several BBC reporters have brought us similar accounts and the queen herself has had telegrams from Jewish women begging for assistance. It's heart-breaking.'

'So why are we not doing anything?' Ned demanded.

'We are. Did you not hear the statement of condemnation made jointly with the USA and Russia?'

'A statement?!' Ned wailed. 'What use is a "statement" to the poor people shoved into the camps?'

Winston patted his arm. 'Shockingly little on an individual basis, I admit, but it's not entirely useless, especially when it comes to enacting justice after the war.'

'And in the meantime?'

'In the meantime, it is a matter of strategy.'

Ned went a furious red. 'How can the life of who knows

how many people being taken in the most barbaric of ways not be a key part of "strategy"?'

'I mean the strategy for how we stop that, Mr Miller. The quickest and most comprehensive way, as I have personally told the queen, is to win the war and liberate the land on which these monstrosities are built. Trying to go in while they're in enemy territory is a high-risk operation, costing thousands of lives, while also detracting from the main attacking forces driving the Nazis into ultimate defeat. Do you see?'

Ned agreed that he did see, and Jenny had to admit the logic was sound, but it was still hard to think of thousands – maybe even millions – of terrified people stuck behind barbed wire, waiting for the agonising creep of the front line to stand a chance of surviving this ever-more-hideous war. Somehow, as he said to Jenny over and over again in bed at night, the Allies had to go on the offensive. They had to defeat Hitler. And they had to do it before he sucked all that was strong and good out of the world for ever.

TWENTY-SIX

THE WHITE HOUSE, SEPTEMBER 1943

CLEMENTINE

'See, there!' Winston pointed eagerly out of the limousine window as it turned into the White House grounds. 'In there are the people who will help us win this war!'

Clementine prayed her husband was right. Things were certainly going well, with the Allies successfully invading Italy last month. The Nazis had pulled troops out of Russia to defend their European lines and the Red Army were driving them out of their territories with fury. They'd even opened up a narrow supply line to poor Leningrad, still under siege after two impossibly long years, and Clementine spent what time she could directing fund supplies to the starving city. Now, they must ensure the push was on to full victory.

She just hoped she was up to it.

She was meant to be in America to keep Winston well enough for the vital discussions ahead, but her health was struggling. She'd started feeling ill on the boat over. Actually, no, she'd started feeling ill months ago when she'd had an embarrassingly large boil that had had to be painfully lanced, and then caught a fever. Dr Moran had sent her to the seaside for a rest but she'd spent most of it worrying about Winston – and who could blame her? He seemed to be flying all the time now.

He'd gone to Casablanca in January but then insisted, against all advice, on extending his journey home via Turkey to try and persuade President İnönü to join the Allies. The only result of this bold mission, however, had been to bring himself home with pneumonia. He'd had to stay in bed for days, though the damned man had insisted on working through his illness, even holding cabinet meetings propped up on his pillows.

'I can't just stop, Clemmie,' he'd said when she'd objected. 'There's a war to win.'

That was true, she knew, but if Winston couldn't stop, Clementine couldn't either and she wasn't sure she was up to holding them both together any longer. In June, while he'd been preparing to head home from yet another meeting in the States, the popular actor Leslie Howard's plane had been shot down, his tragic and dramatic death splashed all over the papers. It had been hard to see why the Nazis had shot down a small private plane, other than out of sheer spite, but then someone had pointed out that the actor's tax adviser, Mr Alfred Chenhalls, a tubby, cigar-smoking bon viveur who'd been travelling with him, had borne a remarkable similarity to the British prime minister.

'There's no truth in it,' Jock Colville had assured Clementine. 'Bletchley Park have picked up nothing.'

Bletchley Park were brilliant, Clementine knew, but they weren't infallible and the Nazis were surely capable of taking out a prime target in secret. She could only hope that, if Hitler had thought they'd killed Winston, he'd been spitting feathers at the pictures of him celebrating victory in North Africa with Roosevelt. Either that, or working harder to get him next time. If, that is, the ongoing risk of thrombosis didn't do for him first. Her husband had a big, bold heart but surely there was only so much it could take? Was it any wonder she worried?

'The best thing you can do for your husband,' Charles Moran had told her, 'is get yourself well. No one looks after him like you do.'

That was why she'd crossed the Atlantic at his side, but she'd done a hopeless job. She'd been so weak by the time they'd reached Quebec City that she'd had to decline the Roosevelts' invitation to a weekend at their country residence, and rest in the stunning citadel above the St Lawrence River. Thank heavens Mary was also out here, released from her battery to work as Winston's aide-de-camp and doing a marvellous job, efficiently marshalling him to places as on time as was possible and charming everyone with her happy outlook.

The car drew up outside the grand main entrance and Clementine pulled her compact from her bag to check her reflection, then recalled Eleanor Roosevelt's comments about people mattering more than appearances, and put it hastily away.

'Clemmie! Welcome, welcome.' Eleanor was there the moment she stepped out of the car, proffering a kiss on both cheeks and tucking an arm into Clementine's. 'Let me show you inside? Are you better now? I was so worried about you. Illness is such a bind, isn't it?'

Clementine agreed that it was (which was true) and that she was much better (which was not) and tried not to bristle at this woman she barely knew calling her by the name reserved for family and close friends. They stepped into the White House and Franklin Roosevelt wheeled himself forward.

'Mrs Churchill, charming to meet you. Forgive me for not getting up.'

'Not at all.' She rushed to shake his hand. The chair, a necessity after contracting polio in his thirties, must be a huge inconvenience but it did not diminish him. He had powerful shoulders and dark, searching eyes and commanded the room, even from lower down than everyone else.

'Let's get you shown to your rooms and then I'll mix us some cocktails. Do you like cocktails, Mrs Churchill?'

'I'm not a big drinker,' she admitted. 'My mother did rather more of it than necessary which put me off.'

'My brother too,' Eleanor said. 'And my uncles.'

'And most of your family.' Franklin laughed.

Clementine saw Eleanor flinch but she stood her ground. 'Franklin does a tasty Virgin Mary for those of us less keen on the intoxicating side of pre-dinner drinks. I'm sure you'll love it.'

'I'm sure I will,' she agreed. 'And Mary likes cocktails, don't you, my dear?'

'Love them,' Mary agreed. 'I do hope you'll make me that delicious Manhattan again, Mr Roosevelt. It was the best!'

Franklin beamed, the room settled, and Clementine blessed her daughter for her natural way of putting everyone at ease. Lord knows where she got it from. Winston, she supposed, though Mary managed to do it without dominating. Maybe this visit would be 'OK', to use that most peculiar of Americanisms.

Her room was very grand, with a charming view over vast lawns, though too fussily decorated for her taste and astonishingly dirty. Mrs Roosevelt, for all her other achievements, was clearly not on top of her staff.

'When I ran my finger along the mantelpiece, it came away filthy with dust,' she hissed to Mary while the infamous cocktails were being mixed.

'Then don't run your finger along it,' Mary hissed back, which Clementine felt was very much missing the point. Perhaps she should have had the Manhattan after all.

No one, however, could miss the poor housekeeping when it came to dinner.

'I hope you will forgive simple fare,' Eleanor Roosevelt said with her toothy smile. 'It seems wrong to be eating grandly in wartime, does it not?'

'It does,' Mary agreed, adding wickedly, 'do you not think, Papa?'

That made Clementine smile, for Winston believed that eating grandly was his basic right. Sure enough, he spluttered on his soup, the sort of thick, creamy broth that he despised, and buried any answer in his handkerchief.

'I was most impressed by how frugally your king and queen were living when I stayed with them,' Eleanor sailed on. 'If even those in a palace can cut back, then we certainly can.'

'The king has a very moral soul,' Winston said, recovering himself.

Clementine picked up a spoon to eat her soup but, to be fair to Winston, it was a battle. There was simple and then there was, well, disgusting. Thankfully, however, the company was excellent. Franklin was an amusing raconteur and he and his wife sparred enjoyably on various issues, though it was clear that both their hearts lay in the same direction. They were deeply engaged with social reform and a worldwide approach to peace that spoke to all Clementine's basic beliefs. They chatted about Eleanor's social housing programmes, her work with students, and the details of the 'New Deal' that was bringing Depression-wracked America back to prosperity. Clementine was fascinated to hear Eleanor talking about her projects and Franklin deferring to her on them, even when it came to the war.

'Ask Eleanor,' he said when Winston quizzed him about defences on the west coast as coffee was served (all together with not a hint of the women withdrawing). 'She's the one who sorts all that.'

Winston looked astonished and Mary actually clapped.

'Just like Mummy sorts Russia for us,' she said gaily.

'I don't *sort* Russia, Mary,' Clementine protested, embarrassed.

'You don't raise money for their people?'

'I do that, yes.'

'And answer endless letters from them?'

'Well yes, but they're just letters—'

'And gather all sorts of experts to find the best ways to build them hospitals and provide them with food and clothing?'

'I suppose so, yes, but I don't make any war decisions.'

'Listen to her!' Mary said to Eleanor and they laughed together.

'What?' Clementine demanded indignantly.

Eleanor put a hand over hers. 'I'm sorry, my dear. We're merely laughing at your touching modesty. Do you think all war decisions involve guns?'

'No.'

'So, give yourself some credit.' She clicked her fingers in the air. 'You know what, you should do a press conference.'

'Me?' Clementine looked at her, confused. 'With Winston?'

'No! Why on earth would you do it with Winston? Just yourself.'

'Just myself?'

'Oh yes, Mummy!' Mary said. 'You'd be marvellous. Wouldn't she be marvellous, Papa?'

'Your mother's always marvellous,' Winston agreed, though he was studying the bottle of Franklin's brandy and Clementine wasn't sure he'd actually heard the proposal.

'What would I say?'

Eleanor laughed. 'You'd tell them what you're doing for the war – your YWCA work, the improvements to shelters, Bundles for Britain, your Aid to Russia fund.'

'I *could* talk about the fund,' Clementine agreed reluctantly. 'More donations are always helpful. I could tell them about the siege of Leningrad, and the youngsters carrying food packages between enemy lines at night to try to keep the population alive.'

'That would be great,' Eleanor said. 'And you could tell them about you, too.'

'Me?' Clementine repeated.

'You, as the first lady of Great Britain.'

Clementine laughed. 'Oh we don't have that term, Eleanor.'

Eleanor did not laugh. 'Well, you should,' she said, 'because you sure as hell have the job of it.'

Clementine thought she'd never been as nervous as she was standing in a side room of the east wing of the White House, watching what felt like hundreds of journalists flocking into Eleanor's parlour. One journalist was tricky enough; why on earth would you have a 'conference' of them? It was bound to go wrong.

She rubbed her hands down her favourite Kitty Foyle dress, then worried she'd stained it. She should have worn her white gloves, but no one seemed to do that over here. Nervously fingering her stalwart pearl studs, she cast around for escape, but Eleanor was calling her name and saying over-exaggerated things about her work in London, so she had little choice but to step out and take her seat.

'Mrs Winnie, Mrs Winnie!'

An arm waved from the front row and Clementine realised the woman was addressing her.

She smiled. 'Mrs Winnie? I like that.'

'They don't call you that back home?'

'Not to my face.' This got a laugh. 'What would you like to know?' she asked.

'What's it like, Mrs Winnie, living with Mr Winnie?'

Clementine looked around the room. 'I'm sure many of you have husbands and know how demanding and awkward they can be at times.' Appreciative murmurs of agreement ran around the group. 'Well, imagine that when they've got the perfect excuse of having a war to run!'

The women burst out laughing and then they were off, firing all sorts of questions at her, some earnest, about the plight of the Russians, or the sufferings of the Blitz, some domestic about rationing and turbans, and others more random about soldiers' underwear and Winston's V-sign. The hour flew past and before she knew it, Eleanor was saying 'Last question, please, ladies,' and everyone was groaning, even Clementine.

'You're a natural,' Eleanor said, doing that chummy arm-holding thing she insisted on, though today it did feel quite nice.

'They weren't as... intimidating as I thought they would be. Did I say the right things?'

'You said the true things, which is what counts. I find that if you share what you can, the press respect you. It's when you're too aloof that there's trouble.'

Clementine laughed. 'Perhaps that's my problem. I was brought up with aloofness being the gold standard of behaviour.'

'Then let's celebrate bringing you out of yourself. How about some shopping?'

'Perfect!'

They collected Mary and headed 'downtown' to what felt like a wonderland after the deprivations of London. They found nylons aplenty, new dresses with indulgently flared skirts, and an enticing shop brimming with different chocolates in which they spent far too much money. The shopkeeper was thrilled by the presence of 'Mrs Winnie' at his counter and plied them with samples so that Clementine came out feeling drunk on the unaccustomed sugar.

'Books?' Mary suggested, pointing to a palace of a bookstore across the road.

'Books!' Clementine agreed happily.

Books weren't rationed back home but with paper shortages

and distribution problems, they were restricted all the same. Libraries, book clubs and swapping stations kept a blacked-out nation amused but a shop brimming with new tomes was a prize indeed. It was her thirty-fifth wedding anniversary next week, she remembered, and this was the perfect place to find a present for Winston.

Mary bounced off to the romance section, Eleanor went to talk to the bookseller, and Clementine wandered happily into 'History'. The irony of her husband losing himself from the busy task of making history by reading about it wasn't lost on her, but that was Winston – world events, be they past, present or future, had always and would always absorb him.

'Aren't you going to get yourself a book, Mummy?' Mary asked as they met up to head to the counter.

'I suppose I could,' Clementine agreed, 'but what would I choose?' Ever since she'd married Winston, she'd read books recommended by him that they could discuss over dinner. These days, though, they rarely had dinner alone and had far more pressing matters than the prose of H.G. Wells to discuss.

'Virginia Woolf?' Mary suggested.

'A little oblique?'

'Evelyn Waugh then?'

'Isn't he rather racy?'

'So? Live a little, Mummy!'

Clementine felt that was unjust; she was living a lot right now. She turned to look at the shelf of 'bestsellers' to the right of the steps down to the main floor. A novel called *Mrs Parkington* caught her eye, but somehow, as she was grasping it, her ankle caught on the edge of the step and crumpled beneath her. She fell, clutching desperately for the shelf, but missing it and tumbling into the centre of the shop, *Mrs Parkington* flying at a startled young man in the philosophy section.

Everyone in the bookshop, or so it felt, crowded around. Medics were called for, bandages fetched, lemonade, cookies and shots of rum were produced and administered and Clementine just sat there, legs splayed out like a child, in the centre of downtown Washington. Her right elbow throbbed painfully, her favourite dress was ruined, her shopping trip was spoiled and she wanted nothing more than to crawl into her bed. She'd come out here to look after Winston and, instead, she was ruining herself.

It was a relief, in the end, to get to Hyde Park a few days later, though the Roosevelts' country residence was nothing like Clementine had imagined. Set in a sprawling estate alongside the Hudson River, north of New York, the main house was a solid mansion, decked out like a hunting lodge with dark walls and heavy furniture, though with floral brocades everywhere in a strange overlay of old-fashioned femininity.

'Ghastly, isn't it?' Eleanor said happily to Clementine. 'Come and see my place.'

'Her place' turned out to be a whole other house – a sprawling cottage she called Val-Kill (meaning waterfall stream), nestled in the woods at the far side of the estate, complete with tennis court and swimming pool.

'This is heaven!' Clementine said as they sat to tea on the small lawn.

'That's the idea. I built it with some friends as a furniture factory back in the early twenties when things with Franklin were, well, not the best. He was...'

'Demanding and awkward?' Clementine suggested.

'More like inattentive and unfaithful.'

'Oh. I'm so sorry.'

Eleanor shrugged. 'I was devastated at the time but it's worked out for the best. Or, at least, it's worked out. I never would have been able to do half my projects if I'd been more intimately entwined with Franklin. We women tend to put others first, don't we? It's very kind of us but makes it almost impossible to get our own things done.'

'How do men manage it then? I believe most men care for their wives.'

'Of course. I'm not denying it. But they still put themselves first. And really, it's much the most sensible way. If we all put ourselves first and those we loved a close second, I suspect it would work out fine. That's what Franklin and I have found, anyway. We have our own friends, our own... intimates, but we're still very much a team.'

Clementine was sure that was true, but caught a wistful note in her American counterpart's voice, though perhaps she was just projecting her own feelings. She couldn't imagine sharing Winston with anyone, or being able to bear him being 'intimate' with another person. If a little of her independence was the price, then so be it.

'Any which way,' Eleanor said, leaping up, 'I find that one of the keys to my sanity and my energy is having time to myself.'

'That I could not agree with more.' Clementine looked longingly at the water, craving the fresh feel of it on her warm skin and still-aching ankle. 'Can we swim?'

'We surely can.'

They returned to the 'Big House' two hours later, refreshed and invigorated. Clementine even felt lively enough to accept one of Franklin's Manhattans and it was, as Mary had promised, delicious. She looked around the opulent surroundings of the president's country home and smiled. On this day thirty-five years ago, aged twenty-three, she had married Winston and embarked on a life of politics at his side. 'It might be a bit rocky at times,' he'd warned her and he'd been right about that. Scarcely a year had gone past without some sort of crisis to overcome and they were far from the balmy plains of dry land yet.

'To the most wonderful woman in the world!' Winston proposed, putting his arm around her waist and raising his glass to hers. He was in evening dress, his comfy romper exchanged for his finest togs in her honour. Standing with him in her favourite blue gown and the sapphire pendant and earrings he'd presented to her earlier, she felt good – glamorous even. 'I knew from the moment I first saw the beautiful Clementine Hozier that she was the one for me,' he went on. 'And I was bloody well right. I couldn't have done half what I have without her.'

Clementine felt rather tearful and, reaching up to give him a kiss, almost missed Eleanor saying, 'The question is, Winston, how much might Clementine have done without you?'

She blocked her ears to it. That wasn't the point. She'd known what she'd signed up to with Winston Churchill and she'd signed up to it willingly. Their 'team' was not as balanced, perhaps, as the Roosevelts', or their tasks as clearly separated, but they were intricately bound. As dear Nellie had told her, the world needed Winston and Winston needed Clementine. She had to step up, get herself well, and keep him going to the victory they all so sorely wanted.

TWENTY-SEVEN

TEN DOWNING STREET, DECEMBER 1943

CLEMENTINE

Clementine stepped into Ten Downing Street and gasped in pleasure at the sight of the grand arrangement of holly and ivy at the centre of the hallway. There were no candles – they were not to be wasted in wartime – but artfully draped foil strips sparkled from between the leaves and an exuberant red bow brought colour to the display. She clasped her hands in delight. It was Christmas and maybe, just maybe, the last one of the war?

Beneath the bow sat three brightly painted Russian dolls. They'd arrived from Kursk yesterday, a gift from Madame Maslennicova, chairwoman of the council of Kursk. Chair*woman*! Clementine had been unable to believe it – a woman running a whole city council! *We hope you might one day visit us,* she'd written in the accompanying card. *My city would welcome you with open arms, and celebrate the relief your fund has brought to so many of my citizens.* It had been most stirring and Clementine smiled to see the bold symbols of the country she had taken to her heart.

The Russians were driving Hitler out of their country with pride and ferocity and Clementine got letters every day from grateful Russian women, thanking her for the food parcels, clothing or medical supplies the fund had sent to the suffering populations of Moscow, Kiev, Lviv, Leningrad, and many smaller towns and villages in between. Sometimes she almost felt as if she knew them and wished she could see the projects they'd funded. Work had begun on two new hospitals in Rostov-on-Don and, although she'd reviewed the plans and sketches, it would be so satisfying to see the buildings herself and, far more importantly, meet the people.

Winston was in Russia, conferring with Stalin over the French second front he'd been demanding since his first visit back in 1941. It was now tentatively planned for next spring, so Winston had had high hopes for this meeting of the 'big three' as the press were calling him, Stalin and Roosevelt. Clementine had fretted about him flying so far again, and mooted the idea of joining the trip.

'To care for Winston?' Jock Colville had asked.

'That's right,' she'd agreed, adding, 'And perhaps to go out and meet some of the Russian Red Cross staff while he's in conference.'

'Go *out?*' Jock had repeated, horrified. 'Go out where?'

'Kursk?'

'Kursk!' He'd actually thrown his hands in the air. 'Kursk would be far too dangerous. There's a war on, you know.'

'Of course I know, Jock,' she'd snapped, infuriated. 'But you're all going.'

'To a conference in Moscow, Clementine, within the security of the Kremlin, not romping around the country.'

'It would not be "romping", Jock, and Kursk has never been occupied.'

'*Yet.* They're still fighting hard.'

'Then they must need support more than ever,' she'd said

stiffly, but it had been more to stop him patronising her than in any real hope.

'Jock's right about the danger,' Winston had said, when she'd mentioned it to him. 'Imagine if anything happened to you, my Kat. I wouldn't be able to bear it.'

And that really, had been that. No one seemed to think about how *she'd* bear it if something happened to him. Still, nothing had yet and at least she could prepare for a delightful Christmas when everyone got back.

Touching her fingers to the dolls, she forced herself out of the pretty hallway and down to the kitchens to check in with Mrs Landermare. Her cook was in a state of great excitement.

'A goose!' she cried, gesturing to a fat bird in the pantry. 'Lovely King Haakon has gifted us a goose. Ooh, I could kiss him!'

Clementine smiled. The King of Norway might be surprised if her cook embraced him, but perhaps not. It was Christmas after all!

'What else is on the menu?' she asked.

The cook happily produced a raft of recipes and notes. It was icily foggy outside the patched-up window but the Downing Street kitchen was cosy and the plans were fun. It looked as if almost all the family might be able to gather. Mary would be on leave and was excited to see everyone. Duncan's poor feet were much recovered so he and Diana would be there with their children, three of them now, with a daughter born last May.

'You're so good at mothering, darling,' Clementine had told her, holding her tiny granddaughter tenderly in her arms and feeling a rush of love almost as powerful as the relief that it would not be down to her to keep this fragile creature alive.

'One of us has to be,' Diana had said, but with a smile.

Clementine had visited as much as possible but, between the press of her other duties, it had not felt nearly often enough and it would be good to have them around for a few days. Pamela would also be there with young Winston, though Randolph would have to remain in Cairo. Averell Harriman, mind you, would not be there either as he'd been posted to Moscow as US ambassador, taking his daughter Kathleen as his secretary. Everyone, it seemed, was heading to Russia – except Clementine.

Even Sarah was there, having been released from her duties at Medenham to travel with Winston as his aide-de-camp, and she'd been very excited about the trip. She and Vic now seemed fully estranged but she was loving WAAF life, just as Mary was thriving in the ATS. It was a different world for these girls. By Sarah's age, Clementine had had three children and been about to head into what they were now calling the First World War. If today's war was the second, she just hoped, for future generations' sake, that there was never a third.

For now, though, the focus had to be on ending this one. The year 1944 would bring the big push over the Channel into Normandy and, although it was vital to defeat Hitler on his soil, there were huge risks. The Italian invasion in the summer had seemed to be going so well but now the poor soldiers were bogged down in a wet, cold winter and stuck at the hilltop fortress of Monte Cassino, some way south of Rome. Attacking, especially on foreign soil, was harder than defending and the Germans would be ready and waiting for the forces to land in France.

Winston was plotting various subterfuges with Bletchley Park and the Special Ops lot but it would be hard to hide a force of a hundred thousand men. Clementine worried how many of them would be lost in the landings, not to mention the onward fight to Berlin. Hitler, she was sure, would not surrender until his last soldier was no longer standing.

'I can almost taste victory,' Winston had cried in 1941 when America had joined the war. Now they were poised to dish it up, but Clementine feared victory would taste of blood and tears.

'Figgy pudding,' Mrs Landermare said happily and Clementine pulled herself back to domestic concerns.

The invasion would not be until the summer. For now, she had to focus on making this the best possible family Christmas for those she loved.

'Figgy pudding,' she agreed. 'Do we have raisins?'

'We do. Pamela got me some from an American.'

'Did she indeed? She's not missing Averell too much then?'

Mrs Landermare laughed. 'She's sad, but certainly not lonely. She's working on a replacement, she says – or two – all in the name of Anglo-American relations!'

Clementine shushed her cook. It might be amusing to her, but this was her son's wife they were talking about. The marriage had perhaps been rushed and ill-advised but it was a marriage all the same, for now at least, and she should not be condoning the breaking of sacred vows. Clementine sighed. There were far too many things to worry about these days. She glanced again to the window as early darkness descended through the horrible fog.

'Shall we make the pudding now?' she suggested to her cook.

'*We?* That would be delightful. And maybe a small sherry to aid us along...?'

'Why not!'

Clementine rolled up the ruched sleeves of her day dress as her cook fetched the bottle from the cupboard. It was naughty but, goodness, if there was one thing this endless, grinding war had taught her, it was to enjoy life when you could. She took a sip of her sherry and a precious raisin from the jar Mrs Landermare produced reverently from the pantry, then picked up her wooden spoon.

'Telephone for Mrs Churchill!'

The cry came down the stairs and, with a groan, Clementine lowered the spoon.

'I'll just be a minute,' she said to Mrs Landermare and headed upwards. 'Is it important?' she grumbled as she turned into the study, but when she saw Jock's face, she knew it was. 'What?'

He held out the receiver. 'You'd better talk to her yourself.'

Clementine felt her world close in. The sherry seemed to burn in her mouth and the raisin stuck in her throat. 'Clementine Churchill speaking,' she said.

'Mummy? Thank God. It's Sarah.'

'Darling? Where are you?'

'Tunis, Mummy. On our way home.'

Her daughter's voice was determinedly calm, but Clementine could hear the shake beneath.

'What is it? What's happened?'

'It's Papa, Mummy. He's ill. Very ill. I... I think you'd better come.'

Clementine huddled into the back of an official car between Jock and Grace, who'd both volunteered to accompany her on this hellish trip. The icy fog that had made the Downing Street kitchen so enticing now had to be negotiated as aides frantically tried to find an airfield open for flying. In the end, the only possibility was Lyneham, over two hours' drive away. Every minute was agony.

It was pneumonia again, but far more serious this time.

'He's hanging in there,' Sarah had assured her. 'And we have all the best doctors flying from Cairo so he's in good hands, but...'

It had been a big but. Sarah hadn't dared say it and Clementine hadn't dared ask, but she knew that his heart was weak – had known it for a year now – and only hoped that, if this was it, she got there in time to see him. She couldn't bear him to go without her holding his hand, without kissing his lips and telling him how much she loved him. He would be scared, she knew, and fretting about letting everyone down before the war was won. She could imagine him in fevered desperation in the darkest part of the night and longed to soothe him.

'I'm so glad you're there,' she'd told Sarah.

'I won't leave his side, Mummy.'

'Give him all my love, won't you?'

'Of course.'

'And tell him I'm coming.'

'I will. He'll wait for you, I know he will. Just... come fast.'

At last they made it to Lyneham and were driven onto the runway alongside a huge Liberator bomber.

'It's very big,' Clementine said, staring into the open door and seeing a cavernously empty space with a few rugs spread on the floor as if for some sick sort of picnic.

'It's all we could get, I'm afraid, ma'am,' the RAF officer said apologetically. 'It will be cold, but we have padded suits for you.'

He showed them into a stark hut where padded white boiler suits were hanging like bloated corpses on hooks.

'Are they necessary?' she asked.

'Yes,' came the blunt reply.

Sarah's voice echoed through her head – 'come fast' – and she nodded. 'Let's get on with it then.'

They waddled into the belly of the great plane.

'There are no belts, I'm afraid,' the officer said. 'You're sitting where the bombs would normally be, you see, but you can hold these straps if things get rocky.'

'Rocky?' Clementine was desperate to get to Winston but she couldn't help fearing for her life. How ironic would it be if she died on her way to him? She almost laughed but recognised hysteria and clamped her lips shut.

'I'm sure it will be fine,' the officer said. 'At least until you reach the Alps. Hopefully you can get some sleep.'

They sat on the rugs and held onto the straps, tiny figures in the middle of the echoing bomb bay. The engines roared, the plane juddered down the runway, and Clementine thought she'd never been less likely to sleep in her life. Thank heavens Grace had thrown a backgammon board into her bag and Mrs Landermare had sent them with flasks of hot coffee. Already the air was so cold she could see her breath frosting, but at least while it was doing that, she was alive and on her way to Winston. Determinedly, she set out the board, poured the coffee, and gritted her teeth for a long, dark night.

They landed, bruised from lack of sleep, shaking from the cold and unnaturally alert from the coffee, into the glow of a Tunisian afternoon. Clementine blinked furiously against the glare and sent up a prayer of thanks that she'd made it. Then she saw Charles Moran coming towards them and feared it had all been for naught. She ran to him, clumsy in her padded suit.

'Is he alive?'

'He's alive.'

'And well?'

'I wouldn't go that far. Prepare yourself, Clementine. His temperature is very high and he's weak. It was touch and go in the night but he's come through, which is a good sign.'

She grabbed his arm. 'Take me to him, Charles – now.'

It was another agonising half hour to the villa, an imposing white building surrounded with beautiful flower gardens she would normally have loved, but she could focus on nothing save getting to her husband. She sprang from the car, scanning every face for bad news, and was shown inside, up a grand staircase, and to a guarded door.

'Are you ready?' Charles asked.

'Of course I'm damn well ready,' she snapped. 'Let me in.'

The room was darkened by heavy curtains, and the figure in the bed was surrounded by beeping machines and very, very still.

'Mummy!' Sarah, eyes red-rimmed and hair and clothes rumpled, jumped up from the bedside and grabbed her hand. 'I'm so glad you're here.'

'Is he...?'

'Clemmie?' the voice from the bed was hoarse and weak but unmistakable. 'Is that my Clemmie? Is she here?'

Clementine sprang forward. 'I'm here, my darling,' she said, bending to kiss his burning-hot face. 'I'm here for you.'

A shadow of a smile crossed his lips. 'Then all will be well.'

She could only pray that was true...

Two nights later he called out. 'Clementine? Clementine Hozier?!'

She leaped to his side. 'Clementine *Churchill*, my darling.'

His hand fumbled for hers in the dim light, his fingers hot with fever. 'You said yes?'

'You don't remember? In the Temple of Diana, with the rain keeping the rest of the world at bay?'

His brow furrowed. 'And three hundred and fifty thousand men to get back from Dunkirk?'

She squeezed his hand. 'That was another time, my darling. In 1940. We were only pretending to be in the temple then.'

'Can we pretend again?'

His voice was weak as his grasp and she feared this was it, a memory through which to exit life. He'd seemed so much better these last days, even up and calling for his PM's box, but the nights were harder. She clung to his burning hand, willing him to hold on.

'Of course,' she choked out. 'You see the columns, Winston?'

'Ionic?' he croaked.

'That's right. You see the frieze above our heads? You see the glorious, green, English gardens leading down to the lake in front?'

'And the beautiful young woman agreeing to be my wife?' He sat up suddenly. 'You did agree to be my wife?'

'I did, Winston. Of course I did.'

He smiled. 'That, Clemmie, was the greatest achievement of my life.'

Now the tears fell. 'So far, Winston,' she said hoarsely. 'The greatest achievement of your life *so far*. You have a war to win.'

'I do.' His grip tightened around her fingers, cooler now, and his voice surged with strength. 'I do have a war to win. But Clemmie...' He pulled her close. 'Even then, that day in the temple will be my greatest.'

'You're a miracle-worker, Mrs Churchill,' Charles Moran said a few days later as Winston sat tentatively up in bed. The colour in his cheeks was, at last, not the unnatural brightness of fever but a faint glow of returning health, and he had already asked for a whisky – and been refused.

'It is you and your team who have worked the miracle,' Clementine said. 'I'm hugely grateful.'

So many experts had been flown in to keep the prime minister alive that the villa was better-equipped than half the hospitals on the front line. Dr Bedford, an expert on circulation, had administered digitalis, and Colonel Buttle, a specialist in sulphadiazine – a clever new drug to combat infections – had flown in from Italy to supervise its use. Dr Pulvertaft, a Cambridge pathologist running a laboratory in Egypt to produce local penicillin had brought some over, along with two highly experienced nurses. Even Air Marshal Tedder had been recruited to find a bedside commode, locating one made from packing-cases in an RAF mobile hospital seventy miles away. All in all, it had been a superhuman medical effort.

'You've given him the best of care,' Clementine told Charles.

'That's true,' he agreed. 'But you have given him hope, which is just as important.'

It was all rather overwhelming and Clementine had to excuse herself to look at the sea and cry salt tears into the warm air.

Christmas Day was like no other in her life before. Winston rose from his bed, unsteady but pleasingly flamboyant in a silk dressing gown emblazoned with splendid gold and blue dragons that dear Grace had found in a local market. He also wore a broad smile for the many troops who lined his wheelchair-bound route to a touching service in a large corrugated shed, specially cleared of ammunition by the Coldstream Guards to operate as an improvised church.

In two days' time, Clementine, Sarah and Randolph – also flown in from Egypt – would fly with Winston to Marrakech for convalescence in Roosevelt's villa in the foothills of the Atlas mountains. Winston had been keen to go tomorrow but Clementine had put her foot down. That would be far too much work for the staff, she'd told him, and after all they'd done they deserved a Christmas break. Winston had looked disappointed but given way with a cowed, 'yes, dear' that had made Jock laugh and say he really must get her into the cabinet.

'You really must,' Sarah had said crisply. 'Mother is far sharper than half those saggy old blokes.'

Clementine had shushed her but been pleased all the same. As they all stood in the ammo-shed, she looked around at the Christmas service she had not been expecting but now felt blessed to see. There was no goose and no figgy pudding but there was a Winston and for both the world, and for Clementine, that would be enough.

The padre raised his arms and sang the 'Gloria in excelsis deo', the bells of Carthage cathedral pealed up on the hill, and a white dove suddenly fluttered down from the roof and swooped over the altar drawing gasps of pleasure at this sign of God's favour. Looking upwards, Clementine thought she saw the shadow of a small Tunisian scrambling back across the roof, and suspected it was more a sign of their host's cleverness, but that counted for much too.

Next year, 1944, would be a big one for the Allies and she prayed that dove, however it had arrived, signalled a much-needed peace. It had been a terrifying two weeks, and it wasn't over yet. Winston might not survive another scare like this, and if Winston didn't survive, the world as they knew it might not either. She had to get him fully better, and fast.

PART THREE

TWENTY-EIGHT

HALLAM STREET, APRIL 1944

JENNY

Jenny peered out the car window as she was driven up Hallam Street, glad to be home after three long weeks away, but uneasy too. Would Ned have missed her? They'd not been getting on well before she'd left. The RAF had agreed to fly him on bomber raids over Germany at last and he'd gone off excitedly and returned buzzing, the dull horror of the camps subsumed in these more dramatic reports. She'd felt dull and parochial keeping house and there had been no sign of a baby – though no wonder, given how rarely they came together. She had, therefore, snatched at this assignment to tour airfields across Britain, doing a series of broadcasts on the evacuation of wounded American soldiers. It had been exhilarating and satisfying but now she was back and unsure what awaited her.

She stepped out of the car and thanked her driver, a young air cadet who'd leaped out to open her door.

'My pleasure,' he said. 'The boys sure did enjoy your visits.' She flushed. He was obviously a polite young man but he didn't have to say that. 'Like seeing Mom,' he added, which was rather less flattering but, she supposed, kindly meant.

Popping the trunk, he lifted out her suitcase but, as she went to take it, she was swept aside by arms around her waist, lifting her high.

'Honey, you're home!'

Ned kissed her neck, then set her down and spun her round for a deeper kiss. It was very nice but Jenny couldn't help but be aware of the poor cadet shuffling nearby. Still, perhaps she didn't seem quite so mumsie now!

'Lovely to see you too, Ned,' she said when he finally released her. Maybe she should go away more often!

'I've missed you. Come inside, come inside.' He took her case from the cadet and shook his hand. 'Thank you for bringing her home safely.'

'It was a privilege, sir. As it is to meet you. My whole family listens to your programmes.'

'Do thank them from me.'

'I will. They'll be made up that I've met you.'

'That's very kind.'

'And your charming wife,' he said hastily, tipping his cap to Jenny, but it was an afterthought. He'd not said a word about his family listening to her programmes on the whole trip home.

'I shall be sure to give you a mention in my broadcast,' she said, perhaps a little pointedly.

If he noticed, he didn't flinch but simply thanked her again and got back into the car.

'Come on,' Ned said. 'I've made you dinner.'

'You have?'

'Well,' he hedged, 'I've bought it in, but I'll do the serving.'

He swept her through the door and she saw their table laid out with a cloth, a bunch of pretty meadow-flowers and wine glasses for two and felt a rush of joy at being home. He *had* missed her.

'Oh Ned, this is so nice.'

'Anything for you, hon.'

'Did you listen to my broadcasts?'

'Of course.' He poured wine. 'They were fantastic. That one with the poor young man whose foot had been trapped in his ejector door was heart-rending.'

She glowed. He *had* listened.

'He was so brave, Ned. His plane was going into a flat spin and his parachute was tangling and he had to stay calm enough to yank his foot out and then try and land with it broken and bleeding. Thank God it was the French resistance who found him and not a German patrol.'

'And then to have to hide out in Brittany to get that fishing boat over the Channel!'

'He said it was petrifying. He had this letter that he'd written to his parents in case he died and it was so touching – all about what an amazing life they'd given him and how he hoped, if he had to lose it, it would gain them the freedom to live without tyranny.'

'How old was he?'

'Nineteen. Crazy young, Ned. At his age, we were drifting around student conferences, trying to change the world with earnest debate.'

'It's a better way,' he said stoutly.

'That's true, but this poor boy didn't have that choice.'

'At least he made it out.'

'He did. And now he's being evacuated home to his family.'

'Minus his foot?'

'Hmm.'

They looked at each other.

'Bloody business, isn't it,' Ned said sadly. 'And all because one man thinks he has the right to rule others.'

'It's criminal. I really, really hope that when the Allies finally get to Berlin they trap Hitler and put him on trial before all the wounded men and women, and then they make him pay with his miserable life, preferably screaming in terror in one of his damned gas chambers.'

Ned shuddered. 'Let's not talk about such sadness this evening,' he said. 'I've got far better plans for you, Mrs Miller.'

'Do you indeed?'

'I do. In fact, you're looking so delicious that dinner might have to wait while I take you to bed.'

'Hmm,' she teased, looking up at him as too-long-forgotten ripples of pleasure ran through her body. 'I do need a nap, now you mention it.'

He pulled her into his arms and kissed her again. 'There'll be no napping for you, my gorgeous pixie-girl.' Then he was tugging her through to the bedroom, and peeling off her travelling clothes and there was no time for anything but pleasure.

Afterwards, she stretched out happily, watching the last of the spring sunshine shining across their bodies. 'I should go away more often.'

'Please don't.'

His voice sounded curiously desperate and she rolled over to kiss him. 'I might have to, Ned, if CBS send me on another assignment.'

'I'll tell them not to.'

'Don't you dare!'

'I think I have a right to my wife in my bed.'

'As I have a right to my husband in mine. Shall I tell CBS to keep you here too?'

'No! That is...' He sat up. 'Shall we eat now? I'm starving.'

'In a minute.' She reached out to pull him back down but something dug into her side and she squealed. 'What on earth is that?' She rolled over and found, stuck to her side, a dangly gold earring. She pulled it off her skin and held it up, her stomach sinking. 'What's this?'

Ned was already half up but he turned back. 'I don't know. An earring?'

'Yes, but whose earring?'

'Is it not yours?'

'When have you ever seen me wear anything as flashy as this?' Jenny felt fear surge into her heart. 'Ned?'

He shook his head. 'I honestly don't know, Jen.'

She wanted to let it go at that, wanted not to have to ask more, but that would be cowardly. 'Well, unless you've got some very flamboyant male friends, I'd say it means there's been a woman in the apartment – in the bed.'

He frowned again. 'I don't think there has... Oh wait! Brad did bring his new broad over the other night. She was dripping in gold. It must be hers.'

It was almost convincing. Except that...

'Why was she in our bed?'

He smiled. 'She had a headache. There was a bit of an argument about it, actually. She wanted to go home but Brad had just opened a beer and wasn't keen. I said she could have a rest if she wanted, so she came in here and lay down. It must have fallen out then.'

It certainly sounded convincing.

'We'll take it back to Brad then, shall we?'

'I'm not sure he's still seeing her. He said something snide about a lieutenant colonel taking her to dinner yesterday. Why don't you keep it, honey?'

'A single earring? Really, Ned, even you must know that wouldn't work.'

'Fine.' He reached out and plucked it from her hand. 'I'll give it to Brad and he can decide. Maybe he'll enjoy flinging it back at her.'

'How very gentlemanly.'

'Brad's not so good at that. There are too few men in

London these days. It's far too easy for any half-decent single guy with a bit of cash.'

'And any half-decent married one too,' Jenny muttered but Ned was gone.

She heard him toss the earring onto the plate in the hall and head to the kitchen to make the promised welcome-home dinner that Jenny was no longer sure she could face. She could only pray that somewhere in London Brad had an ex-girlfriend who was hunting desperately for her missing earring. With the war grinding painfully slowly towards its close, everyone was looking for fun and sometimes that could be every bit as dangerous as fighting.

TWENTY-NINE

WINDSOR CASTLE, MAY 1944

CLEMENTINE

'Mary, that's hardly dignified!'

Clementine pulled her excitable younger daughter in from the open window of the car, though she had to admit to feeling thrilled herself. They were being driven at a suitably sedate pace up the gracious driveway to Windsor Castle and, after five years of wartime austerity, it was such a treat to be going out that she felt as giddy as a youngster heading to her very first ball.

This event, held by the king and queen to mark Princess Elizabeth's recent eighteenth birthday, had been described on the invitation as a 'quiet dance' but looking at Mary bouncing on the seat next to her, Clementine had a feeling it was going to be anything but quiet, at least once the doors of the castle were firmly shut. Well, they all needed the release. Preparations for 'D-Day' – the landing of seven thousand ships carrying a hundred and thirty thousand men, tanks, guns and even bicycles onto the Normandy beaches – were in full swing and the tension was mounting daily. This evening would be a brief but very welcome escape.

'Have you heard,' Mary said now, her eyes shining, 'the king has persuaded the Ambrose Dance Band to play? Ambrose himself has come out of retirement specially.'

'And why would he not?' Winston said from the front seat. 'It's an honour to play for the king and queen of England.'

'I'm sure it is,' Mary agreed easily. 'But more importantly, it means we get to dance and dance!' She leaned out of the window once more.

'Decorum, Mary,' Clementine muttered.

'Surely there's been enough decorum to last a lifetime,' Pamela said on her other side.

Clementine raised an eyebrow at her daughter-in-law. 'Are you sure about that, Pamela?'

Pam flushed. 'Not from me maybe,' she conceded.

Clementine looked at her in concern. She'd become very beautiful. The plump cheeks of her wedding day, four years ago, had hollowed out into fine lines, her hair was swept elegantly back with a tiara Clementine had never seen before, and her dark green dress made her skin look ivory pale. For once, though, she seemed subdued.

'Is all well?'

Pamela shifted on the seat and looked out at Windsor Castle, looming impressively large as they drew close. 'I'm not sure,' she admitted. 'I need to talk to you.'

'Now?'

She shook herself. 'No. Sorry. It's hardly appropriate, is it?'

'I won't know until you tell me. Come – it will take ages for all the cars to release their passengers.' Mary let out an impatient moan but Clementine was fixed on Pam. 'Is it something we can help with?'

She leaned forward to nudge at Winston, who was going

through a pile of papers on his knees. He glanced back and Pamela twisted her hands in her lap.

'In a way. That is, I feel I need to tell you that I... I think my marriage with Randolph is over.'

'Ah.'

Clementine looked at Winston, who looked impassively back. This was hardly news, but it was sad all the same.

'You do not feel you could be reconciled once the war is over and life can resume more normal patterns?' Winston asked.

Pam shook her head. 'We've tried. When he was back on leave last year, we really tried but, well, we just don't like each other, I'm afraid.'

'I see.' Winston smiled at her. 'Well, we can't have that, can we? It wouldn't be good for either of you. I hope we will not lose you, though, Pam?'

'Lose Baby Winston?' she shot back.

'Lose *either* of you,' Winston said smoothly. 'For you are both very dear to us.'

Pamela looked to Clementine and she nodded urgently. This was important.

'You've become like a daughter to us, Pam.'

'Not a very well-behaved one,' she said ruefully.

Clementine gave a dry laugh. 'Not many of our children are very well behaved when it comes to romance. Even Mary got herself engaged on the way back from America.'

'He was a very gallant officer, Mummy,' Mary protested. 'And he saved my life when that wave came over the deck.'

'He did indeed, but I do not think he required your hand in repayment. Thank heavens we got that one untangled once we were back on dry land.' Mary rolled her eyes at Pam. 'I saw that,' Clementine said.

'You were engaged twice before you married Papa,' Mary pointed out.

'Third time lucky,' Winston said gallantly.

'And we are not talking about me, right now.' Clementine put a hand on Pamela's knee. 'If you truly feel the marriage is irrecoverable, Pamela, then of course we will support you and hope you will stay in our lives always.'

Tears welled up in Pam's big eyes and she put her fingers up to try and catch them. Clementine drew a handkerchief from her bag and passed it over.

'Thank you,' Pamela said, dabbing carefully. 'That means a lot to me. I love you all so much.'

Clementine swallowed. A little tenderness was lovely, but this was getting far too American. 'Oh look,' she said gratefully. 'We're next.' The car was pulling round to the grand entrance of the castle and she busied herself checking her gloves and bag.

Mary, however, seemed quite happy with the conversation. 'Do you have someone new, Pam?' she asked.

'Oh no,' Pamela said quickly.

Far too quickly.

Clementine looked at her sharply. 'I hope he's not married this time.'

'There's no one. Come on, time to get out. Don't want to keep other people waiting!' She leaped from the car as if it had grown too hot for her.

On the other side, Mary was also out and heading eagerly for the steps with her sister-in-law. Clementine edged out, feeling her hips creak, and was grateful when Winston offered his arm.

'May I escort you, my beauty?'

'Winston!' she tutted, but she took his arm and, adjusting the train of her dress, headed gratefully inside.

St George's Hall, when they made it up the sweeping stair-case and into the grand room, was looking magnificent. With night falling, the long, arched windows down one side were already blacked out, but lamps sparkled from every sconce on the high walls, lighting up the gracious ceiling, studded with brightly coloured shields. As they queued with the rest of society for the royal receiving line, Clementine could see musicians warming up on the oak balcony at the far end and assumed this was the Ambrose band that had so excited Mary.

'Will you dance with me, husband?' she asked Winston.

'If I must.'

She laughed. 'Just once?'

'Anything for you.'

They'd reached the line and the king stepped forward, shaking Winston's hand warmly. Clementine was pleased to see it. Every Tuesday Winston went off to the palace for lunch with the king, and more often than not the queen, and having this kind, earnest monarch to share some of the load of running the country had been a great relief for him. And for Clementine.

'I've not much time right now,' she heard King George say to Winston, 'but how about a glass or two together shortly?'

'Marvellous,' Winston agreed, with far more enthusiasm than he had greeted her suggestion of a dance.

Clementine curtsied to the king and then to Queen Elizabeth, who took her hand.

'You look well, Mrs Churchill.'

'We all look better than usual tonight, I think. Thank you so much, ma'am, for giving us a little joy.'

'We need it, do we not? And we had to mark Lilibet's coming of age.'

Clementine looked at her surprised. 'She is eighteen, surely, not twenty-one?'

'She is,' the queen agreed. 'But these days, with all that they're going through, the youngsters seem so much more grown up, do they not? The king is having the Regency Act changed to ensure that Lilibet could take the throne without a regent should...' She faltered. 'Should she need to.'

'Which we all pray she will not.'

'We do indeed, but war spares no one. I was terrified when the king flew to Italy last year.'

Clementine nodded. 'I'm terrified every time Winston takes to the air. All this technology makes the world a smaller place, which may be a good thing, but increases the need to speed around it. It would be exciting, I suppose, if I was as young as they.' She indicated Mary chattering away to Princess Elizabeth, next in line. 'But at our age...'

'It is rather taxing. I couldn't agree more. When the war is over I would like to retreat to Sandringham, or Balmoral, for an entire year and go nowhere I cannot reach on my own tiny legs.' She swept a hand down her elegant dress.

Clementine smiled. 'That sounds heaven.' She could have talked on this subject for hours but the line was clogging up behind them and politeness dictated she moved on. With a smile to the queen, she turned to her daughter. 'Happy belated birthday, Princess Elizabeth.'

The young woman – not so young now – smiled. 'Thank you so much, Mrs Churchill. I am now of an age to serve, am I not?'

'Serve?' Clementine looked at her, confused. 'You serve already, Princess. I've heard tell of several successful engagements.'

The princess shook her head. 'Not serve as a royal, serve in the forces.'

'Oh.' Clementine glanced back and saw the king and the queen looking their way, even while they greeted the next guests.

'You wish to join up, Princess?' Winston asked.

She turned eagerly to him. 'Yes, Prime Minister, I do. Everyone else has to, after all.'

'You are not like everyone else, Princess.'

'I don't see why not. *Your* daughter is in the ATS, is she not?'

'Jolly well am,' Mary agreed, rejoining them. 'It's splendid.'

'See!'

The princess's eyes went to the king and queen, who shifted. This was clearly a matter of some contention in the royal household.

'There are many ways to serve, Princess,' Clementine said hastily.

The queen shot her a grateful glance, but Winston was sadly oblivious.

'Few as glorious as in his majesty's forces,' he said pompously.

Clementine grabbed his arm. 'The princess is already a colonel of the Grenadiers, is she not?'

'Purely ceremonial,' Princess Elizabeth said.

'As is only correct for such a jewel,' Clementine shot back. She sounded ridiculously obsequious and knew the princess was not impressed but this was a royal quagmire and she did not intend to get caught in it. 'Happy birthday again,' she said and steered Winston hastily away.

'She's a good gal, that Princess Elizabeth,' Winston commented. 'Knows her duty.'

'Which is surely at the king's side,' Clementine said pointedly.

He glanced back. 'Ah. Ah, I see. The king does not want his daughter in the line of fire?'

'His daughter and *heir*.'

'Quite. Absolutely right. Thank you, Clemmie. I shall tread carefully.'

Clementine wasn't sure her bluff, determined husband knew how to tread as carefully as might be required, but right now the band was striking up a merry tune and the youngsters were rushing to the carpetless area in front of them and the only path that, praise God, needed to be trodden for the next few hours was around the dance floor.

'That dance, Winston?'

'Shortly,' he said and, with a winning smile, extricated himself from her grip and made for the drinks table.

The evening unwound in a happy run of tunes. Clementine watched Mary and Pamela dancing enthusiastically with the princesses and the ecstatic company of grenadier guards, usually on duty protecting the castle, but today released to provide the sparkling young ladies of London with partners. She was escorted onto the floor herself several times and the whole company looked on with joy as the king and queen performed a dazzling double-time waltz.

Clementine watched them spin and hoped Hitler got wind of this. From the lowliest dockworkers in their makeshift dance halls, to the highest pair in the land, the Nazis had not stopped the British dancing. Their bombs and tanks and poisonous ideas had not trampled British spirits and soon they would be coming for him, making sure he never stopped anyone living a decent, normal life again. She even got Winston onto the floor when Princess Elizabeth called for the Palais Glide. This simple parade dance involved lines of eight processing in easy steps around the ballroom, and Clementine found herself lined up with Winston, the king and queen, the princesses, and Mary and Pamela.

'We seem a little outnumbered, Winston,' the king called down the line.

'We have been for five years, your royal highness.'

'A good job, then, that we have such fine women around us.'

Winston tipped an imaginary hat in agreement and, as the band struck up a jaunty tune, they slotted their arms around each other's waists and danced. Clementine felt the war fade into the background as if, beyond the giant blacked-out windows of St George's Hall, men were not killing each other for the privilege of redrawing boundaries in their favour. As if her husband was not reading casualty lists over breakfast and flying through enemy airspace to talk with Soviet dictators and American presidents. As if there was little more to life than meeting friends and sipping champagne and falling in love.

She looked along the line and saw them all laughing and tripping over the steps, little caring for the exactitudes of the dance and simply being swept up in its spirit, and she felt an unutterable sadness when the final bars sounded and they palais-glided to a stop.

'A drink?' Winston suggested, as ever, and she allowed herself to be steered to the side with the king and queen as the youngsters rushed into the next dance.

'It's almost as if there's no war,' she said, watching them wistfully.

'Soon there will not be,' Winston said. 'We are poised.'

The king leaned in. 'Are you sure, Winston? I hear tell the landing exercises at Slapton did not go entirely to plan.'

Winston flushed and Clementine felt the war knocking at the long windows once more. Two weeks ago, a mass landing exercise had taken place in Devon with thirty thousand men. It had not, as the king had quietly said, gone well. Confusion over communications had ended up with ships arriving at odd times, drawing friendly fire that had, tragically, taken a number of innocent lives. The next day, a German U-boat, presumably unable to believe its luck, had happened on one of the craft, carrying American soldiers, and sunk it. More had died, many from the unforgivably simple issue of not knowing how to inflate their lifebelts correctly. The incident had been hushed up, the press forbidden to report on it, but the pain of it had kept Winston awake for several nights.

'We have learned many lessons, sir,' he said now. 'Radio

frequencies must be perfectly synched and we must up lifebelt training and provide small craft to reach any stranded men quickly.'

'You will not, then, be cancelling the invasion?'

King George's voice was low, his words covered by the trill of the dance music and the happy rapping of a hundred young feet, but Clementine felt as if they were booming around the vast hall taking all her happiness with them. The invasion of Normandy, D-Day as they were calling it, was scheduled in less than a month and although she longed for this final push to victory, she dreaded its dangers. So much could go wrong, as Slapton had so painfully proved.

'We will not,' Winston said. 'We cannot. Remember Dunkirk, sir?'

'How could we forget it?'

Clementine saw the queen draw closer to her husband and he placed a comforting arm around her waist.

'We have been on the defensive ever since,' Winston said, 'bar in Africa and Italy. Now, we must attack. We must finish the bugger off, whatever it takes.'

The king nodded grimly and then, as if Mr Ambrose, up on the balcony, had heard them, his band struck up a tune that had the young people cheering and clapping.

'When that man is dead and gone,' the singer crooned into the microphone and soon everyone was taking up the familiar lyrics – a song written by Irving Berlin, hailing the glorious day when Hitler would be dead.

It would, indeed, be a glorious day, Clementine thought as the crowd sang along, and the sooner it came the better – before Princess Elizabeth had to put herself into uniform, before more young soldiers were mown down on the battlefields, or more helpless civilians bombed out of their homes. They would dance, the entire nation, when that man was dead and gone, but how long would that take? In a month's time, some of the young men whirling Mary and Pamela and the princesses around this fairy-tale dance floor would be leaping into the froth of the Channel and racing up Normandy's beaches into Nazi fire, and who knows what else...

'We must finish the bugger off, whatever it takes,' Winston's voice said in her head and she clutched her arms around herself and prayed the price of victory would not be too high.

THIRTY

JENNY

Jenny chewed on the end of her pen, seeking the right words for her next broadcast. With invasion surely imminent, CBS had upped their scheduling of both news and features and today she'd visited a munitions' factory run by a company called Plessey who were working all the hours to provide the weapons needed for the final attack. The place, built into 300,000 square feet of unfinished Tube tunnels between Leytonstone and Gants Hill, had been extraordinary, and the women so brave and dedicated to their tough and very dangerous job.

Frowning in concentration, Jenny sought the right words to do them proud, trying to block out the banter from next door. Reporters had been flooding into London with the troops, and Ned and a couple of his established friends were entertaining them between broadcasts. Brad was not among them, making it impossible to ask after his dangly-earringed sweetheart, and as it had all got a little heavy on the adulation of her superstar husband, she'd left them to it. Unlike the men in the next room, she had a day-job and was due into the Special Relations Committee offices at 10 a.m.

'She was desperate for you, Chuck,' someone roared and, with a sigh, Jenny put her notepad down. She'd never be able to concentrate and might as well try and get some sleep. She reached into the bedside drawer for her earplugs, hearing Chuck boasting that, 'It's my killer dance moves.'

'More like they've never been with a black man,' Ned countered. 'And good on them for choosing you.'

Jenny smiled, glad that her husband was promoting integration, albeit in a rather racy way. There had been a lot of trouble in Britain about the ongoing segregation of black and white troops in the American army. Some public houses, disgusted by the attitude of white GIs to their black compatriots, had, to her and Ned's great amusement, put up signs saying 'Only Brits and black Americans welcome'. It had provoked fury among thirsty white soldiers but Jenny had heard one burly publican telling his rejected customers that 'segregation is what Nazis do' and been proud of her adopted country. She was glad the women were being similarly welcoming.

'That girl was hot for it,' Chuck said. 'But, gee, she's not a patch on your broad, Ned.'

Jenny felt a shiver of pride and held back from inserting the ear plugs.

'Yeah, she's a fancy piece all right!' someone else said.

Fancy piece, she thought, puzzled. She'd been called a few nice things, though usually more 'cutie' or 'pixie-girl'.

'Ssh,' Ned laughed, then added on a hiss, 'the missus is through there!'

Jenny's blood ran cold. She sat, rigid, every fibre of her being focused on the conversation next door. The men's voices had dropped, but not enough.

'How did you catch her attention, though, man?'

'I'll have you know I'm famous around here,' was Ned's low-voiced retort.

Jenny clutched her arms around herself. She'd been so stupid, fallen for the oldest excuse in the book. There was no Brad's ex and the exotic earing had belonged to Ned's equally exotic 'fancy piece' who, it seemed, he'd brought into their marital bed. She wanted to cry but had to hear more. Who was she?

'Even so,' Chuck said, 'Pamela Churchill, man – that's classy!'

Jenny's whole body turned to ice. Pamela Churchill? Her husband was cheating on her with Pamela Churchill, daughter-in-law of her supposed friend? She'd heard Clementine debate whether it was right to let her son's wife 'consort' with Americans many times, but it seemed she had no qualms about it at all. And with Jenny's husband! A double betrayal. How long had it been going on? Had Clementine been quietly encouraging it, buttering up Ned to keep his all-important broadcasts hooking Americans into the war? The questions raced around Jenny's brain. She knew her friend was fierce in her promotion of British interests, but how could she have done that to her? And how had she kept on being friendly, if she'd known what was going on?

It made Jenny's skin crawl to think of Westminster gossiping about her husband and glamorous Pamela Churchill and she sat up again, listening intently for the departure of Ned's crass guests. At last, the music clicked off and she heard the men heading out the door. Her eyes were gritty with tiredness and unshed tears, but she jumped out of bed and headed into the living room. Ned was sitting amongst the detritus of the evening, smoking a final cigarette, and startled as she walked in.

'Jenny! What are you doing up?'

'Waiting for you.'

'That's nice,' he managed, but his voice quivered with uncertainty.

She looked at him, not wanting to have this conversation but knowing she could never respect herself again if she did not. She sucked in a deep breath. 'I know you're having an affair, Ned.'

He looked indignant. 'An affair? Don't be ridiculous, Jen. Why would I—'

'And I know it's with Pamela Churchill. I heard you talking about it just now.'

That stumped him. He stared at her, mouth opening and closing, and as she watched him flounder she was coldly, miserably certain. This wasn't just a flirtation, or a one-nighter, this truly was an affair.

'Why?' she asked.

'I'm sorry,' he groaned. He pushed himself up to come towards her but she held up her hands to ward him off.

'Why?' she asked again.

'Because I'm an arrogant, conceited fool?'

That much she knew already but hearing him offering it as if it were sufficient excuse for profaning their marriage only made this more painful. 'I'm your wife, Ned. You swore vows to me.'

'I know. And I meant them – *mean* them. You're everything to me, Jen.'

It was so patently untrue that she felt welcome anger bubble up. 'Not when you're in her bed. Does she make you feel young, Ned? Sexy? Exciting?'

His eyes narrowed and he planted his feet more firmly, on the defensive now. 'Yes,' he flung back. 'She does actually. You just make me feel irresponsible and self-serving.'

'Because you *are*.'

'Maybe, but so what? We're still young, Jen, still free, but you never come out. You never want to dance, or have fun.'

'There's a war on, Ned.'

'I know! Life is on the line, so all the more reason to live it to the full.'

'All the more reason to live it to keep safe, to fight for justice, to defeat the enemy.'

He pouted. 'I'm bored of safe.'

'And bored of me?'

'No!' he said, but it was a token protest.

Sorrow washed over Jenny. She'd known for a while that her husband loved the glamour of becoming a feted reporter, but it seemed he also now loved the cocktail-life that came with it. And how attractive it had made him to the hot girl about town. How very, very shallow of him.

'Does she help you with your broadcasts, Ned?' she demanded.

'Of course not.'

'Does she talk to you about the state of the world?'

'Jen, you're being silly.'

'Silly? I don't think I'm the one being silly here. I don't think I'm the one running into someone else's bed because they make me feel like an inflated version of myself. I know who I am, Ned – I'm your wife, your friend, your life partner. Or I thought I was.'

'You are!'

'You just want her too?'

He hesitated too long. The pain was deep but she would not let it wash away her pride.

Putting her hands on her hips, she shook her head at him. 'You can't have that, Ned. I'm not going to share you. You have to choose. And soon, or I might not be here at all.'

'Jen... Please. I'm sorry.'

'Good. You should be. I'm sorry too, devastated, in fact; hurting, pained, miserable. Take any of the words you wish. The question now, is what are you going to do about it?'

He bit at his lip. Then the phone rang. He looked at it, buzzing on the side table between them, then moved to it like a man saved.

'Might be a story,' he mumbled as he scrabbled for the receiver. 'Might be D-Day.'

Jenny watched him, feeling contempt for his weakness and hating that. This was not her Ned, not the man she'd fallen in love with, not the man she'd married.

'This is our D-Day, Ned,' she flung at him, biting back tears. 'The story is *us*. The question is whether you want to keep writing it.'

THIRTY-ONE

THE ANNEXE, JUNE 1944

CLEMENTINE

'Please, Mrs Churchill. He might listen to you.'

Clementine groaned and heaved herself off the daybed where she'd been trying to rest. D-Day was tomorrow and since the blissful night of Princess Elizabeth's ball, their lives had been endlessly bound up in preparation. The exiled leaders were gathering, keen to aid the restitution of their countries, and General de Gaulle, imperious leader of the Free French forces, was annoying everyone with his high-handed ways. Clementine rather liked him. He was a man of principles and the only one who'd been brave enough to stand up to the country's cowardly collaborationist leader, Premier Pétain. Besides, he loved speaking French with her and it took her back to her youth. For so long, Dieppe had felt like a place tarnished by memories of Kitty's death, but sharing that with the people of Southwark shelter, and then talking it over with Jenny, had taken away some of the sorrow and allowed her room to remember the joy once again. Now, if all went well, it might be free to visit in weeks.

If all went well...

Clementine's stomach churned with nerves for the men, and the pressure of keeping it all secret. She'd barely seen her family, and friends had been impossible for fear of leaking the all-important date. Grace was a godsend as always but Clementine felt as if she hadn't spoken to anyone bar officers and ministers in weeks. Even those they considered padlocked could not know the date of D-Day; the risk was far too high for everyone. She'd invited Jenny Miller for tea the other day, thinking they could talk about the excellent broadcasts the young woman had done on American evacuation of the wounded, but she hadn't even replied to the note. It had been odd, but probably for the best. Plus, as always, looking after Winston took up most of her time.

Her husband was frenetic with activity, desperate for this to work, and she understood that. Having one life as your responsibility was hard enough; having a hundred and thirty thousand was almost impossible to bear. Even so, his current plan was ridiculous and she couldn't believe he hadn't given it up already. Since they'd nearly lost him last Christmas she'd rededicated herself to keeping him safe but, really, if he wouldn't work with her, it was impossible.

'He's still saying he's going to go then?' she asked Jock.

He was standing before her, turning his handkerchief in his hands like a fretting schoolboy. 'He is.'

'Such nonsense! Come on, let's get this sorted once and for all.'

It was about two days ago that Winston had conceived the notion of going to Normandy with the troops. He and King George had decided, almost certainly over a brandy or two, that they would best serve their nation by leading them into battle in person. The king, at least, had realised it was a poor idea sometime the next morning, but perhaps Queen Elizabeth was a stronger influence on her husband than Clementine.

'How did you stop him?' she'd asked Queen Elizabeth when they'd met at an Aid to Russia fundraiser the day before.

'I pointed out to him that for a man who did not want his daughter putting herself in the way of harm by joining the navy, this would be making him a remarkably foolish role model.'

'And he agreed?'

'Immediately.'

There was an ongoing battle between Princess Elizabeth and her parents over her joining the armed forces, so the queen had strong leverage; Clementine was not so lucky. Besides, Winston had always been like a moth to the flame of danger. She could still remember the long months when he'd had himself posted to the front in the First World War, the proximity of his death seeming to bring him more fully to life. He'd been a battalion commander back then, but now he was in charge of the entire Allied war effort. All the chiefs of staff were against him sailing, the cabinet had argued against it until they were blue in the face, and the king had obediently told him to abandon their ill-conceived plan, but still he could not let it go.

Clementine followed Jock through their private entrance into the buzz of the War Rooms. The narrow corridors were filled with people hurrying between the cabinet office, map room and chiefs of staff's chamber. In between were the various studies-cum-bedrooms of Winston and his key aides. Even his group of dedicated female secretaries and telephonists were working away like moles beneath London to keep the orders filtering out to the army, navy and air force on the brink of the biggest attack of the war. And, pray God, the final one.

Clementine had a bedroom down here, alongside the chiefs of staff's chamber, though she'd rarely slept in it since the Blitz had ended. She thought back to that now – the nightmare of the planes coming every night, the injuries, the loss of lives and homes, the battle to get shelters habitable and hospitals equipped, all in the shadow of imminent invasion. It had been frantic and immediate and Britain had stood so very alone for so long. Alone and strong.

Back then, however, they had simply been defending their territory; now they were taking the huge risk of moving onto Hitler's. Last time they'd done that, they'd had to flee Dunkirk in a thousand tiny fishing boats and if they got it wrong again, the war, which had been quietly turning their way, might turn right back. Their country might fall. Millions might die.

For now, though, Clementine had to concentrate on just one.

She found Winston in the map room, wearing a khaki romper and jabbing his cigar at the wallcharts marked with pins to show the ever-changing Allied and Axis locations. Bletchley Park and SOE had been waging a war of information – or, rather disinformation – to convince Hitler that the Allies were going to attack across the Pas de Calais. It had been constructed via a network of fake spies and messages, a network so deep it had included such elaborate subterfuges as the body of a supposed order-carrying officer dropped into the waters off Spain, and a camp of cardboard tanks outside Dover.

So far it seemed to be working as all reconnaissance and reading of Enigma suggested the majority of the German troops were down near Calais while the Allies were poised to hit the Normandy beaches three hundred miles west. But maybe Hitler was playing a double game himself? There was only one way to find out and Clementine felt sick every time she thought about it.

She poked her head around the door. 'Winston? May I have a word, please?'

'Is everything all right, my dear?' He sidled out, attempting a placating smile.

She wasn't falling for it. 'Of course everything is not all right. Jock tells me you're still at this fool notion of going with the men.'

He bristled. 'It is not a fool notion, Clemmie. It is the only decent thing to do. Leaders lead.'

She tutted crossly. 'This isn't the Middle Ages, Winston. Who do you think you are, William the Conqueror?'

'Not at all, I—'

'You think the men will only follow you?'

'No.'

'You think they need a portly chap in a homburg waving a cigar in the direction of the Nazi gun emplacements to give them the courage to charge?'

'Clemmie, you're making me sound pathetic.'

'Because in this, my darling husband, you are. The men need you here, coordinating operations from your brilliant map room. They do not need you getting in their way on the beaches.'

'They need to see that I am with them.'

'They do not. They need to be able to focus on their commanders, on their orders, on staying alive. They do not need some self-seeking prime minister riding up and down in front of them on his metaphorical horse.'

'Clemmie, that's mean!' Winston looked hurt.

She reached out and stroked his face. 'It's true, my darling. If you went, you would not be going for the men, but for yourself, to feel like a leader in the cut and thrust of battle. But the truth is, Winston, you *are* a leader, you *are* an inspiration, and you *are* vital to the forward conduct of the final stages of this horrible, horrible war. You are too precious to go.'

'I am no more precious than the next man.'

'You are to the nation.' She stepped closer. 'And you are to me.'

He looked into her eyes and she saw sadness in his, and the weight of the many impossible decisions he was making every day.

'I don't want to let them down, Clemmie,' he whispered.

She put her arms around him. 'Then stay here and make sure this operation is conducted in the best possible way.'

He nodded slowly, wearily. 'Very well.'

'Thank you.'

'I'll be up later, for supper.'

She kissed him. 'It will work, Winston.'

'Let us pray so.'

He shuffled back to the map room, leaving Clementine to Jock's effusive thanks. She waved it away and headed back towards the Annexe, but she was reluctant to leave this hive of activity, so diverted to her bedroom. It amused her to see the pink blanket on her bed, in place of the khaki ones for the men, and she sank into the small floral armchair she'd brought in when they'd first moved down back in 1940. She spotted a jewellery tray half-hidden below the mirror and, with a gasp of delight, recognised the pearl drop earrings she'd thought lost.

Jumping up, she removed her amethyst studs to put the pearls on, feeling almost as if she were trying on her old self, the one from the start of the war, full of energy and excitement at being in Number Ten. She picked up the first earring, remembering it surviving her fall to the floor when Downing Street had been bombed. That had been five years ago but she felt at least ten years older. Still, they were surely close to the end now? D-Day *had* to work.

She'd left her door ajar and it was noisy down there but the hum was comforting. As with Dunkirk, this wasn't only Winston's operation to run. Many highly competent men were involved, from across a number of nations, and a few smart women too. With them all working together, this would surely succeed.

Clementine pushed an earring into her right ear, listening to two junior aides chatting outside her door.

'I can't wait for this to be over and for us all to go back to drinking and dancing!' one joked gruffly.

'From what I can see, you've never stopped,' his friend retorted.

'True, true. It feels a bit desperate though, when every dance might be your last.'

'Which is why you always have it with the prettiest girls, hey?'

'Too right! Thought I was going to get a chance with Pamela the other day.'

Clementine froze, second earring halfway to her left ear.

'You dreamer!' the second man laughed. 'Pamela Churchill's far too good for the likes of you.'

'I know, I know. Besides, that smarmy broadcaster's got her in his bed now.'

Clementine jumped and the earring stabbed into her neck. She bit back her cry, listening intently.

'Bloody Ned Miller with his slicked-back American style and his velvety voice!'

The men laughed heartily, then someone called order on a meeting down the corridor and they were gone, leaving Clementine staring at herself in horror. Ned Miller, Jenny's husband, was having an affair with her daughter-in-law? How awful!

This is all your fault, she told her reflection. She'd turned a blind eye to Pamela consorting with Americans, encouraged it even. She'd known it was wrong, but told herself it was for the good of the war. Did that not, though, on a very small scale, make her as bad as Hitler? Principles had to be held to, whatever the challenges, or else what was the point of them? She had to see Pamela and warn her off. There were a thousand men in London who'd kill to go out with her, so she could leave Ned alone.

Clementine put a hand to the small prick of blood on her neck. She had to see Jenny too. No wonder the poor woman had been avoiding her. She felt her insides curl at the thought that she might believe her in some way complicit. She had to tell her friend that she hadn't known, that she didn't approve.

But not today. Today they were on the brink of the largest cross-Channel attack since the Conqueror she had so recently accused her husband of wanting to be. Another woman's distress, however great, would have to wait.

THIRTY-TWO

HALLAM STREET, JUNE 1944

JENNY

'The sand clings to my trousers, as it must have clung to those of the brave soldiers in the first wave of the Normandy attacks, but today no Nazis fire at me. They are fled, gone from the concrete pillboxes and the abandoned houses that were their nests until the Allied forces drove them out last week.'

Ned's voice both soothed and pained Jenny, but, either way, she found herself unable to resist listening to his compelling reports. Even now. The wireless whined as the apartment shook under the impact of a nearby bomb and she reached out to retune it, unsure which was more scary – listening to Ned in Omaha or cowering under his desk as bombs fell around her here in London.

She put her hands over her eyes like a little girl and listened in cold fear as the skies above filled with terror. It sounded, as one young lad had so accurately said when she'd interviewed his mother yesterday, like a motorbike in the sky. That was terrifying enough but the worst bit was when the noise stopped and a loaded silence hung over you, meaning the bomb was about to drop.

Hitler had launched his first V1 rocket at London three days ago and had already sent hundreds more after it to wreak destruction on the capital. The press were calling them 'revenge weapons', launched in response to D-Day, which had catapulted thousands of Allied troops into Normandy while Hitler and his forces had been napping near Calais. The people were calling them buzz bombs, for their scary noise, or doodlebugs for their insect-like appearance. Neither name took away the fear and the novelist Evelyn Waugh had called the attacks an 'impersonal plague' on long-suffering London.

'Along the topline of the sand,' Ned's voice went on, 'a row of rough wooden crosses mark the bodies of fallen men. As the sun goes down behind them, a single bugle calls out a mournful tribute to their sacrifice.'

Jenny shuddered at the thought. Ned had betrayed her but she hated to think of him in danger, though it was probably safer over there in France right now than it was here. Winston Churchill had even been to the beaches, so she'd heard, though she tried not to think of the Churchills these days.

The deadly sky-motorbike sound stopped, horribly close by, and Jenny pressed herself into the side of the desk, knowing it would be useless to protect her if the bomb landed on Hallam Street. These things were brutal. They could take out entire streets, destroying homes, shops, pubs and, above all else, lives. It was like the Blitz all over again, only worse.

Yesterday, back down in the Southwark shelter, Jenny had done a heartbreaking interview with two mothers who'd lost children to the blast the night before. Their daughters had been playing together at the entrance to the small shelter the families had taken refuge in, and been left utterly helpless when someone had opened the door just as a rocket exploded mere feet away. The shrapnel and flying rubble of the blast had burst into the shelter, killing everyone at the near end and leaving the others, the poor mothers included, trapped behind a wall of rubble and bodies. Jenny could not imagine anything more traumatic for the two women, but there they'd been the next night, cowering in the depths of Southwark Tube station, clutching their remaining children to them and calling down curses on Hitler.

'Why can't someone shoot him?' one had wailed. 'There must be some good people in Germany still? Why can't one of them pick up a gun and shoot the bastard dead before he murders us all?'

It certainly felt as if he might right now. The troops had landed in France, but here in London, ordinary men, women and children were paying the price and it was a heavy one. Jenny had heard tell that Churchill was sending all the anti-aircraft batteries he could spare to the south coast to try to shoot down the doodlebugs before they reached the city. Even his daughter had been posted there and Jenny admired her courage – but did not want to think about that treacherous family.

The walls of their apartment rocked and she heard a huge bang surely only a few streets away. Wails filled the air and she quivered to the cacophony of loss. What, in all this, was one husband's pathetic infidelity?

Nothing.

And yet, for her, so much.

Jenny gritted her teeth. On the radio, Ned was interviewing a wounded young American sending a brave message to his mother. It was nicely done, she thought from her hidey-hole. It would move the American people with the bravery of their boys – and the brilliance of their reporter. Ned Miller, golden boy; so golden Pamela Churchill was prepared to take him into her busy bed.

Jenny tutted at her spite, but it was the only thing that kept her sane. Clementine had sent several messages asking to see her and called several times. Every time Jenny heard her voice, she hung up. She knew it was irrational as it was hardly down to Clementine what her wayward daughter-in-law did or with whom, but the hurt of Ned's betrayal was too much to bear, without adding the hurt of Clementine's possible collusion. She'd thought they were friends. Clementine had even called her one of the family, but believing that had just been vanity. The truth was, she was alone in London and a bloody V1 might as well fall on her.

'Jenny Miller!' she scolded herself out loud. That was an unforgivable way to think. She was her own person – a daughter and a sister and a woman with a life to lead, not just an appendage of her husband. If he was done with her, so be it. It wasn't even like she had any children to tie her to him...

At that, the tears came. She meant none of it. She was just a scared woman hiding under the desk of a man who might not even want to be her husband any more. She hated him for doing this to her, and she would not stand for being second place, but she'd told him he had to choose and she was terrified he would opt for glamorous, light-hearted, fun Pamela. She didn't want her marriage to end. She didn't want to lose all they'd had together. She didn't want to be without him.

She cowered, waiting for the next motorbike of death in the sky, but the noise that came instead was the curiously merry tinkle of the doorbell. Unpeeling her hands from her eyes, she leaned out of her near-useless shelter as it rang again.

'Who's there?' she called, which was stupid because she'd never be heard over the next roar filling the skies. Whoever it was, she couldn't leave them on the street. Crawling out, she ran to the door as the bell went again, more frantic this time. 'You?!'

Clementine Churchill stood on the doorstep wearing a smart summer coat, a pretty turban and a mulish look on her still-beautiful face. 'I didn't know,' she said.

Jenny stared at her. 'You didn't know your daughter-in-law was bedding my husband?'

Clementine flinched but nodded. 'Correct. I didn't know and I'm so sorry. I've been to see her, told her to leave him alone.'

'And she'll do what you tell her, will she? Is that how it works in your world?'

Clementine sighed. 'I have no idea what Pamela will do. She's a little...'

'Wild? Irresponsible? Sluttish?'

Clementine grimaced. 'All of those, yes. I'm sorry. I hate that she's hurt you, Jenny. Can I come in? Please?'

There was a sudden silence. Clementine glanced nervously up and Jenny tugged her into the apartment and through to her under-desk shelter. They both scrambled in, pressed together as a bomb exploded far too close for comfort. The building shook and plaster fell onto the oak above their heads.

'You shouldn't be out in this,' Jenny said over the noise.

'I had to see you.'

'You'd be a terrible loss to the nation.'

'And you'd be a terrible loss to me.'

'Hardly, Mrs Churchill.'

'Clementine, please, and you would. You've been such a good friend – so calm, so efficient, so trustworthy.'

Another damned bomb filled the skies over London with its thunderous doom and Jenny took a detached moment to consider what this poor woman valued in a friend – not fun, not laughter, not shared experiences or jokes, just calmness and trust. She did feel for her, adrift at the heart of this war. But that didn't mean she wanted to be around her.

'It hurts,' she said.

'I know.'

Jenny looked at her curiously. 'You do? Has Winston been unfaithful?'

'Not in that way. His mistress is his work, though she's a demanding one. But I've known loss.'

'Kitty?'

Silence above them. The two women instinctively clutched at each other in the agonising space before the explosion. It was the closest yet, shaking the entire apartment and sending ornaments crashing to the floor.

'Not just Kitty,' Clementine said.

They sat there, willing the building to settle, willing the bricks not to fall on them. Wails mere doors down told them how close they'd been to death and they clung on to each other as another ominous roar filled the skies.

'Marigold,' Clementine said, more a moan than a word.

'Your daughter?' Jenny hazarded, remembering the brief mention of the child the first time they'd visited Fircroft together.

Clementine pulled back and looked at her, eyes wild. 'I don't tell many people about her,' she said. 'I don't even talk to the other children about her. It's too painful.'

'So why are you telling me?' Jenny asked, intrigued her self-controlled friend was suddenly opening up.

'I don't know. Maybe I feel I owe you? Maybe I want you to know what you mean to me? Maybe I'm just terrified we're going to die here and she won't be remembered. That she'll slide into the rubble of this blasted war with everything else.'

Another bomb exploded and again the building shook. Jenny wanted to be angry. She wanted to rage and shout and blame someone for what she was feeling, but Clementine was not the right person. If she was going to rage, it had to be at Ned. Right now, there were more immediate concerns and she'd take any distraction she could.

'I'd love to hear, if you can bear to tell me.'

Clementine nodded and looked at the side of the desk as if

she could find in the whorls of the polished oak the lines back into a past she rarely visited.

'It was the summer of 1921 and Marigold was two and a half. She was a lovely child, so sunny and happy. She'd sing all the time. Her favourite was "I'm Forever Blowing Bubbles". She loved bubbles. She'd sit in a bath for hours playing with them and singing. We called her Duckadilly. Our dear little Duckadilly.' Clementine clutched her arms around herself and rocked.

Jenny sat, her body pressed against the older woman in the small space but unable to reach her in her pain, and willed her to continue.

'She was in Broadstairs, with Diana, Randolph and Sarah, looked after by Rose, their nurserymaid. It was a place we went every summer, a cosy boarding house with a kind landlady. Winston hated it. He was never as keen on a British seaside holiday as I was. But I wasn't there then. Like a selfish, miserable fool, I wasn't there.'

Silence fell. They both froze, but they were spared again – for now.

'Where were you?' Jenny asked urgently.

'Cheshire. Eaton Hall. There was a tennis tournament. I was quite good back then and I loved to play.' She grabbed at Jenny. 'Can you believe that? My child was dying and I was off playing tennis. I'm a bad mother.'

'You weren't to know.'

'But I was. She'd been coughing for weeks. It was one of the reasons we sent them to the seaside – the air, you know.'

'It's meant to help.'

'That's what we thought and it had with various of the children before, but it didn't this time. Rose was too young and inexperienced to realise how ill Duckadilly was. It was only when the landlady sent me a telegram that I knew something was seriously wrong.'

'So you went?'

'Oh yes. I shot down there, so did Winston. We were in time, but only...' Tears ran down her soft cheeks. 'Only in time to see her die. Two days and two nights we sat with her. We tried everything – cold baths, compresses, syrups, herbs. Nothing brought down her fever. Her throat was infected, you see. Septicaemia, the doctor said. Nowadays we might have cured it with sulphonamides, like they gave Winston in Tunis, but we didn't have them then. She only had her own defences to fall back on and she was small. So very small.'

Clementine ran a finger around a whorl in the wood of the desk as tenderly as if it were her baby girl's cheek and Jenny felt her heart breaking for her.

'On the last night she asked me to sing. "Sing "Bubbles", Mummy," she said. I thought it was a good sign. I thought it meant she was perking up. So I sang. Winston held my hand and I held Marigold's hand and I sang.' She paused, drew in a deep breath. 'I only got through the first line. "I'm tired, Mummy," she said. "Sing rest in morning." Then she closed her eyes and... and never saw any morning ever again. I never finished the song. I never even got to finish the song.'

Clementine was weeping now and Jenny put her arms around her and held her close.

'We buried her two days later. I took the other children to visit the grave before they went back to school. They put flowers down – marigolds for Marigold – and a white butterfly came and perched on them, fragile but beautiful, just like my baby girl had been. The children were very silent on the way home. We were all, I think, very silent for a very long time.'

Jenny was crying too now and Clementine pulled out a handkerchief and passed it to her, as if Jenny's grief was more important than hers.

'I'm so sorry,' Jenny said. She wiped her eyes and handed it back.

Clementine wiped her own. 'It was terrible,' she said simply. 'I think of it all the time. Whenever I see a mother weeping for a baby lost to a bomb, or a son lost to an enemy gun, I think of Marigold. Whenever I visit a hospital, I see her, whenever I look at my surviving children, I trace the imprint of her upon them. Except, perhaps Mary. Mary came after, Mary was part of the healing.'

Jenny thought perhaps the healing was still going on.

'Your troubles are greater than mine,' Jenny said, ashamed.

But at that Clementine spun round and took her face in her long, slim hands. 'No. That's not the point at all. I didn't tell you this for your sympathy. I told you to show how useless I was, how I failed my child. If I'd been there earlier, I could have saved Marigold, could have got her treated and she'd be alive now.'

'Or killed by the war.'

'Or that,' Clementine agreed, as the dark buzz of yet another V1 filled the skies above them. 'It's a constant worry with the girls all over the place and Randolph off in Africa. He's injured again, a plane crash in Yugoslavia. He's on the mend – the boy has nine lives – but it's upset Winston terribly, which isn't good for him, not with his heart. I worry all the time about losing him, not just for myself, you understand, but for everyone.' She grabbed at Jenny again. 'I have to keep him safe, Jenny. I *have* to.'

Jenny patted her hand. 'You will,' she offered weakly. 'And there are others to help.'

Clementine waved this away. 'They don't understand him like I do. They—' She caught herself. 'But here now, I did not come to your apartment to burden you with my problems. I came to see you. I came to see if I could help you deal with *your* hurt.'

'That's very kind of you but I don't think there's much you can do. Ned's caught up in being the star of CBS and the darling of London society and there's little I can do to compete.'

'You shouldn't have to compete,' Clementine said indignantly. 'You're his wife. He swore himself to you, for better and for worse.'

'Well, it's got better for him,' Jenny said bitterly. 'Just worse for me.'

'He'd be sorry if he lost you.'

There was another dark roar and then a deeply loaded silence that seemed to go on forever. The explosion was so loud Jenny felt it physically reverberate in her eardrums. Screams sounded from the room next door and Clementine threw herself over Jenny as their flimsy desk-shelter leaped in the air. Jenny waited for her chest to be ripped open, waited for the air to be sucked out of her lungs and the blood burst from her body, but all she could feel was her friend's body heavy upon her.

'Clementine?' She shook her. 'Clemmie, are you all right? Are you alive?'

'Just about,' came a muffled voice, 'though I think the buggering desk has scuffed my best shoes.'

Jenny had no idea whether to laugh or cry. She squirmed out from under Clementine and saw that, on landing back down, the desk had indeed scraped the shine off the prime minister's wife's smart leather shoes.

'I'm sorry.'

Clementine let out a shaky laugh. 'Shoes can be replaced, my dear. People cannot.'

Jenny's laugh was just as shaky. 'I bet Ned would be sorry if I died,' she said darkly.

Clementine grabbed at her. 'Come to America, Jenny.'

'What?' Jenny wondered if her eardrums were still ringing, because she couldn't have heard correctly.

'Come to America,' Clementine said again. 'I'm going with

Winston at the end of the summer, for a conference in Quebec to monitor the final stages of the war. You should come on the ship.'

Jenny remembered Clementine offering her the same escape back when they'd sat on the roofs of the Treasury watching for incendiaries and waiting for the Nazis to invade. That was when she'd told her she was family. It seemed she still felt the same way but this was different, this was Jenny's real family falling apart. Another motorbike sounded in the sky and she cringed, wondering how much more of this she could bear.

'I thought you shouldn't flee your enemies?' she challenged.

Clementine sighed. 'This isn't fleeing, this is a tactical withdrawal. Do you want him still?'

Jenny jumped at the starkness of the question, but did not hesitate. 'I do, if he gives her up. He's my soulmate, Clementine. Or he was...'

'And will be again. You need to leave him, Jen.'

'What?'

'Let him see what he's missing.'

'If he misses me at all.'

'He will. Pamela is a lovely girl but vacuous. He'll tire of her in no time.'

The roar of the bomb grew louder.

'And if he doesn't?' Jenny shouted over it.

Clementine shrugged. 'Then I suppose at least you'll know. Life goes on, my dear. Sometimes we cannot see how it will, sometimes we don't even want it to. But while we have breath in our bodies, it goes on and perhaps what this war has taught us is to honour that – to seize it and make the very most of it, however hard that might be.'

Jenny sighed. Deadly silence filled the air once more and she huddled against her unusual friend, steeped with loss, and waited. The bomb landed several streets away. It felt like a sign.

'You're right,' she said. 'Thank you. If I need to, I'll come.'

It was so kind of Clementine; she just prayed it wasn't a kindness she would need.

THIRTY-THREE

THE QUEEN MARY, SEPTEMBER 1944

CLEMENTINE

Clementine leaned over the railings of the *Queen Mary* and felt the sea air tug at her hair. She put up her hands to tie her turban tighter but, really, what was the point? A glance in the cabin mirror earlier had showed her an old woman. The war, like a sadistic artist, had carved worry lines deep into her once-lauded face and she must accept her injuries like everyone else.

Her worries over Winston, sadly, persisted. He had recently travelled to Italy, now secured, with Rome falling just before D-Day in a triumph of accidental orchestration. He'd enjoyed himself enormously in victorious camps with the men, but had returned home with a raging temperature, and only swift administration of sulphonamides had kept pneumonia at bay once more. Infection, Clementine was certain, had its claws into her husband's veins, waiting for any show of weakness to attack, and she had confined him to bed for the five days of the sea journey in the hope of him regaining some strength.

'Blast it, woman,' he'd objected. 'The *Queen Mary* is the height of luxury. I'll be very rested in the saloon bar.'

'Very rested until 3 a.m. and halfway down a bottle of cognac,' she'd told him, 'which will do you no good at all, will it, Dr Moran?'

Charles Moran had gladly backed her up, so Winston was in his cabin, sulking – and hopefully sleeping – and Clementine was free to walk the decks with Mary, back in place as aide-de-camp, and Jenny. The poor woman had contacted her two weeks ago, asking to come along, and she looked thin and far too grey for someone so young. She had not spoken about her marriage much but Clementine had noted that several telegrams had arrived at the ship's wiring room from Ned, full of concern for Jenny's welfare. She could only pray her advice to leave him for a time would pay off. It helped, perhaps, that Pamela had contracted scarlet fever and was confined to her bed with a swollen neck, high fever and constant headache – no fit companion for any man.

'Maybe God has a sense of humour,' was all Jenny had said on hearing this. Clementine admired her restraint.

She looked west. It was evening and the sun was dropping ahead of the ship, lighting her route in gold. They would arrive in Quebec in two days' time and Mrs Roosevelt – Eleanor – had sent messages saying how much she was looking forward to seeing Clementine again. Remembering their happy afternoon in her cottage, Val-Kill, in Hyde Park, Clementine thought perhaps she was looking forward to it too. Eleanor was exhausting, yes, but she felt she understood why, now, and was keen to talk further.

There was much to talk about, and a great deal of it good. The troops had advanced through Normandy and west towards Holland, thankfully driving the V1 launching sites beyond reach of Great Britain. Then, two weeks ago, Paris had been liberated. It had felt like a huge moment – the restoration of freedom to the French capital, city of poets, thinkers and lovers.

There had been talk, amongst the British and Americans, of

trying to impose an Allied government on the collaborationist country, but De Gaulle had been having none of that. His Free French had moved swiftly through liberated towns and cities, setting up bureaucrats in the *mairies*, and hailing the restoration of true French government. It was, as Winston had said the other night, 'a bit of a cheek' but Clementine admired him for it. Why look back?

'Mummy, there you are! You must come! Colonel Williams is making the most divine champagne cocktails in the bar and there's to be dancing.'

'Dancing?' Clementine stared at Mary, coming up the deck towards her in a stunning off-the-shoulder evening gown that had once been hers. 'I'm too old for dancing.'

'Nonsense. No one is too old for dancing. Come on!'

Clementine laughed and let herself be pulled away from the railings. The sun was almost gone and maybe a dance would be nice.

'Even Papa says he might take a turn,' Mary said gaily.

'Papa? He's in the bar?'

'He is.' Mary saw her face and grimaced comically. 'Is he not meant to be? Oh dear, have I got him into frightful trouble?'

'No, Mary,' Clementine told her. 'He has done that entirely by himself.'

In the end, she didn't have the heart to send Winston, resplendent in the amber romper she'd given him last birthday, back to bed, especially when he rose and waltzed her sedately around the room to the applause of all.

'You don't even like dancing,' she said, laughing.

'I do with you.'

It was all charm, of course, but far too delightfully done to resist. Here, in the middle of the Atlantic, with the Nazi U-boats chased back to their own waters and the war that had been weighing on them all so heavily for so long finally, pray God, turning their way, they dropped their cares for a night.

Mary was the belle of the impromptu ball, dancing with every officer in turn, and Jenny was even persuaded onto the floor, blushing like a girl. Clementine, hovering at Winston's side, watched her friend smiling up at Jock Colville as he demonstrated impressive prowess at the quickstep and cursed Pamela.

'Do you know,' she whispered to Winston, 'that our daughter-in-law is having an affair with Jenny's husband?'

'Is she, indeed? Poor form!'

'Did we think that when it was with Averell Harriman?'

'We *did* think that, my dear, but we overlooked it. For the greater good. There seems no benefit to the war effort in Pamela having a relationship with Mr Miller.'

'I'm not sure we get to pick and choose like that, Winston.'

He looked at her. 'This troubles you, my dear?'

'Very much. Jenny is a good friend of mine and she's upset. I hate that I've had any part in that.'

He took her hand. 'Love is perhaps like war, my dear – it only truly affects us when it touches our own.'

'Oh Winston,' she said, 'you are far, far too wise.'

He grinned. 'I'm glad that, after almost thirty-six years of marriage, you have finally realised that. Does this revelation, perhaps, merit a small cognac...?'

'No,' she said, kissing him. 'In that, husband, you are never wise enough.'

'And you, wife,' he groaned, 'are always far too much so.'

The conference, held in Quebec's impressive citadel, went well, at least as far as Clementine could tell. She and Eleanor were not invited, a decision that was a relief to Clementine but a huge frustration to her new friend.

'What's the point of having us here if we cannot be involved?' Eleanor raged as they took a walk around the edges of the stunning hexagonal citadel in which the men were busily hammering out the first ideas for a post-war world.

'So we can support our husbands?' Clementine suggested.

'Pah! I could support Franklin far better if I was in the room with him.'

'A fair point.' Clementine thought about it. 'The issue, I suppose, is that we are not elected by the people so cannot speak on their behalf.'

Eleanor nodded reluctantly. 'Also a fair point. But your daughter is in there, as is my son.'

'As officially appointed aides.'

'So officially appoint me!'

Clementine laughed. 'I really hope the American people have the wisdom to do that. You'd be an excellent leader.'

'No, I—'

'And in the meantime, you will have to content yourself with talking to Franklin about it afterwards.'

Eleanor ground her teeth. 'But that's the problem – he doesn't talk to me about it. Not in detail.'

'Ah.' Clementine thought of all the times she'd had to sit up with Winston telling her his dilemmas and concerns. Often she'd cursed the knowledge his role had brought her. She could still remember the heavy feeling of knowing from the Bletchley Park code-breaking that the Germans were massing just over the Channel. But maybe not knowing was worse.

'Perhaps we can all discuss it over dinner.'

'That would be good.' Eleanor took her arm. 'You're a wonderful woman, Clemmie.'

Clementine smiled as naturally as she could because it was kind of her to say so, but, really, she wished this dynamic American woman wouldn't be quite so familiar.

Dinner was, for once, a small one – just the four of them plus Mary and Elliott, the Roosevelts' second son – and Clementine was glad of it. Winston was up and charging bullishly around but Clementine could see the shadows around his eyes and the stoop in his shoulders and knew the conference was wearing him out. Franklin Roosevelt looked even worse. His skin had an ashen tone and if he tried to get out of his chair, leaning heavily on his son's broad arm, a sheen of sweat broke out on his greying temples. The war was taking a heavy toll on the Allied leaders and Clementine could only hope it was doing the same to Herr Hitler.

Bearing Eleanor's earlier comments in mind as they all sat down, Clementine asked, 'How was business today?'

'Endless,' Franklin said with a laugh.

'In what way?'

He looked surprised but Winston stepped readily in. 'We're trying to decide on the extent and division of occupation zones in defeated Germany.'

'Occupation zones?' Eleanor asked.

'Germany will have to be ruled by us until such time as we believe she can be trusted again.'

'There must be some good Germans around,' Eleanor suggested. 'We have a number in exile in the States. You must be the same?'

'Yes, but we can't just catapult them back into leading a country riddled with Nazism, can we?'

'Why not? Is France not ruling itself, despite many of their leaders collaborating with the Nazi regime?'

'Well yes, but De Gaulle is in charge.'

'And is a jumped-up, pompous ass,' Franklin fumed. 'Do you know—'

But Eleanor was not to be deflected. 'Will the Norwegian government not simply return and take up the reins again in their country, despite it collaborating?'

'The exiled government has not been collaborating,' Winston said. 'Quite clearly.'

'But many of the country has. Can we trust *them*?'

'We cannot occupy the whole of Europe, dear lady. That would make us as bad as Hitler.'

'Quite!'

Clementine felt her husband's disapproval coming off him in waves. She could see, now, why Franklin didn't talk things over with Eleanor; she was so combative.

Winston squared his shoulders. 'So you would have us leave Germany to govern herself, Eleanor? Put in a few academics and artists we've been harbouring overseas and hope they're strong enough to do the job?'

'We could support them from the edges.'

The irony of this was not lost on Clementine.

'Is it possible,' she couldn't resist saying, 'to support from the edges? It's so much easier if one is actually in the room.'

Eleanor looked at her. Her eyes narrowed and Clementine experienced the sinking feeling that she'd gone too far but then, to her surprise and relief, the American burst out laughing.

'Touché, Clemmie! I asked for that.'

Franklin looked as relieved as Clementine. 'So what are you ladies up to tomorrow?' he asked.

Eleanor groaned. 'Lady Fiset is hosting a luncheon.'

'That sounds excellent,' Winston said. 'I love a good luncheon.'

'It will be rather formal, I fear,' Eleanor said. 'Lady Fiset is very... colonial.'

'Even better. Gin and tonics and kedgeree. I miss those days.'

Eleanor looked at him sideways. 'When you British were occupying half the known world? Oh, but you still are, aren't you?'

Winston squared his shoulders; Clementine braced herself. Here they went again!

'Do you know,' Mary piped up, 'they put taps in trees here in Canada to get the maple syrup out?'

Winston's head turned to his daughter. 'Actual taps?'

'Yep. I was talking to a darling colonel who's a maple syrup farmer when there isn't a war on and he told me all about it. Isn't that the best?'

Clementine could have leaped up and kissed her daughter. The conversation swung to farming and tempers remained even, at least until the clock struck eleven.

'I suppose we should retire,' Eleanor said. 'You must have a big day tomorrow, gentlemen.'

Winston shifted in his armchair. He'd had his usual nap at 6 p.m. and was just getting into his stride.

'Maybe a final nightcap...?'

'Just one,' Franklin agreed. 'To see us to sleep. You ladies go up.'

The president looked pathetically eager. Clementine glanced to Eleanor. Both men were frail and Franklin, in particular, looked weary.

'I think you said, dear,' Eleanor tried, 'that you wanted an early night?'

'It's not late.'

'It is for you.'

Franklin visibly bristled. 'I am president of the United States, *dear*, I think I can decide my own bedtime.'

Eleanor looked stung. 'As the wife of the president of the United States, I am simply reminding him what he said earlier.'

'And I am simply telling you that he has changed his mind.'

'I see.'

Clementine winced. Telltale beads of sweat had appeared at the president's temple and she felt for Eleanor.

'Well,' she said, 'Winston is under strict doctor's orders not to stay up, aren't you, my dear?'

'I am,' he agreed reluctantly. 'But—'

'And I am here to support him and ensure he stays in the very best of health, so come along, let's retire.'

'Just one more...?'

'I'm afraid not.'

Winston looked up at her and she gave him a tiny nod in the president's direction. He huffed but pushed himself reluctantly to his feet.

'Best do as the ladies say, hey, Franklin? They've only got our best interests at heart.'

Franklin did not look convinced but had little choice. Clementine bade the first couple goodnight and kissed Mary, who had the wisdom not to say anything of her plans, though judging by her racy dress it did not involve retiring.

Clementine led Winston up the corridor to their adjoining rooms. 'Thank you,' she said to him at his door.

'I do, occasionally, have some tact, Kat. I will be having a nightcap in my room, though, and you can't stop me!'

She laughed, feeling ridiculously fond of her bluff, loving, entertaining husband. 'On the contrary, Winston, I shall join you.'

Lady Fiset's luncheon was like nothing Clementine could have imagined. It was a gloriously hot day and she chose a soft, floral dress and light hat, but arrived at the spreading villa to find tables set for seventy in the 'grand hall', with the curtains firmly closed. Candles flickered up the centre of the table and the menu promised seven courses.

'Good Lord,' she murmured to Eleanor, 'my stomach will explode.'

'She's showing off,' Eleanor said.

'Well, I'd be much more impressed by a salad on the terrace.'

Eleanor laughed. 'And much less sleepy for our broadcast later.'

'Broadcast?'

'Did I not say? CBC, the Canadian sister station of our own CBS, are keen for us to talk to the Americas.'

'You and I?'

'Yes.'

'Today?'

'Yes. They've found a slot for us this evening. Is that a problem?'

Clementine looked at her. 'You want me to address "the Americas" this evening? What on earth will I say?'

'We can sort that later. They'd like it in French and English, if possible. I said that would be fine. You're fluent, are you not?'

'I am, but—'

'Me too. I went to a school in England run by a marvellous Frenchwoman, did you know that?'

'I think you've mentioned it—'

'Madame Souvestre. A wonderful headteacher and an inspiration for me. She unlocked the woman I've become. Now, let's get this over with and we can go and do some proper work.'

Clementine followed her reluctantly into the buzzing, darkened crowd, thinking that if she could ever have met this Madame Souvestre she might have had a few words with her. A joint radio broadcast? Tonight?! Her heart quailed.

By the time she reached the studio, Clementine was so befuddled from the rich food and the endless wine her hostess had insisted she try with every course, that she could easily have spoken gibberish, not French. She wished Jenny were with her to help but she'd gone over the border to her home in Connecticut, so she was alone with her nerves. She thought of all the times she'd listened from the sidelines as Winston had spoken his speeches carefully and deliberately into the microphone, and tried to do the same.

Eleanor was a natural but, then, she did her show every Sunday evening. Clementine felt stiff alongside her but she read the words they'd suggested and, a sentence or two in, found it strangely compelling. The microphone proved a seductive confidante and the nodding technicians a pleasing affirmation. For the French section, she imagined herself sitting with her sister Kitty outside the Place des Tribunaux in Dieppe and the language flowed off her tongue as if conjured up direct from her past. Kitty was long gone but maybe a spark of her had remained inside Clementine waiting to pop up and help when most needed. Or maybe that was just the wine!

'You were marvellous, Clemmie!' Eleanor gushed afterwards and for once she didn't object to the familiar name.

'It was quite fun,' she admitted.

'Have you not done it before?' Eleanor looked horrified.

Clementine laughed. 'The odd formal appeal for the Red Cross, that's all. Nothing so... chatty.'

'I'm so sorry I flung you into it then, but you were excellent. You should do it more often.'

'Oh no.'

'Why not? Talk to people about the work the Red Cross are doing in Russia.'

'I could,' Clementine agreed cautiously, buoyed up by her success. 'We've helped rebuild all sorts of homes, schools and hospitals, you know. The Russians write to me all the time and have invited me to go out and see our work in action.'

'How exciting. You should.'

'Go? To Russia?'

'Why not? Russia is liberated now and they're our allies, aren't they?'

Clementine stared at her. 'Well yes, but Winston is very suspicious of Stalin's motives.'

'All the more reason to keep him close. I'm sure he'd be delighted to host the woman who's raised...?'

'Nearly six million pounds so far.'

'Six million! That's astonishing. So, yes, I'm sure he'd be delighted to host you. He certainly should be.'

Clementine shook her head. 'I don't think it would be politic for me to travel there.'

'Why not? Winston did.'

'Well, yes, but Winston is the prime minister.'

'And you are the prime minister's wife. More importantly you are you – wonderful, marvellous you!'

Clementine looked at her generous, endlessly enthusiastic host and smiled. It was very kind of her but really… Maybe Eleanor had been at Lady Fiset's wine too!

As they stepped into a car to return to the citadel, however, she couldn't help her thoughts drifting to the far-off women of Russia who wrote to her every day. Could she visit? Of course not. This time last year she'd taken her eye off the ball, had spent more time on her new projects and not enough on her true one – her husband – and had been rewarded by that dreadful call from Tunis summoning her to what she had been certain would be his death bed. A Soviet trip would be as much for her vanity as Winston sailing on D-Day and it was an indulgence neither she nor the nation could afford. Her job was, as it had always been, at Winston's side.

THIRTY-FOUR

BROOKLYN DOCKS, DECEMBER 1944

JENNY

Jenny fidgeted on Pier Twelve of the Red Hook Terminal in Brooklyn. The *Queen Mary* was docking and people were thronging along the pier, eager to see their loved ones. Many were soldiers who'd been injured in the African campaign and were now returning home and it was clear from the noise that they'd been much missed. Only Jenny, amongst the crowd, seemed to be nervous about her upcoming reunion. She pushed her fingers into the pocket of her slacks, feeling Ned's latest letter.

I long to see you, honey, he'd written, but did he mean it, or was it just the rhetoric of a man used to using words to paint believable pictures? Did he long to see her to take her in his arms and beg forgiveness, or to tell her he wanted a divorce?

She shuddered. Divorce! It was such an ugly word. Her parents would be mortified. *She'd* be mortified. And upset. She'd lain in her old bed back home, staring at the dreamy picture of James Cagney she'd pinned to her wall as a teenager, and tried to imagine life without Ned. It had been impossible.

They'd only been married nine years – nothing compared to, say, Clementine and Winston – but they'd been the years in which she'd grown into herself, in which she'd travelled and seen the world and learned about the shape she wanted it to take. She'd met Ned when they'd both been passionate student activists and she still felt like that youthful person deep inside, very deep some days, but there all the same. It had been an amazing journey for her and she thought it had for him too. She just prayed he agreed.

She stared up at the vast steel hulk as men secured the ship with giant ropes and the gangplank was manhandled into place. People squealed and wept and called out to the men lining the railings, and Jenny wanted to do the same but had no idea how Ned would respond. He was here, at least, and he'd booked them a 'fine holiday' down in Florida for Christmas, which must mean he was keen to be with her. But even if that was true, could they sustain happiness when they were together?

Men began tumbling down the gangplank into the waiting arms of their loved ones but Jenny just stood, numb, remembering Ned's face when she'd told him she was leaving. She'd waited for him to return from Normandy, given him time to rest, and then quietly asked if he was giving up Pamela. He'd hedged painfully and the arguments had swiftly spiralled, Ned offering only reasons for his discontent in the marriage, as if his affair was in some way her fault. After weeks of increasingly bitter wrangling, she'd had enough.

'I'm leaving you, Ned,' she'd finally told him.

That had caught him up short. 'What do you mean?'

'What I said, Ned. I'm going.'

'Where?'

'Back to the States.'

'How? We can't afford a ticket, we—'

'Firstly, we *can* afford a ticket. I expect it costs less than the cocktails in the damned Ritz. And secondly, I don't need us to. I have an invitation to join a friend.'

'A friend?' His eyes had narrowed. 'Are you—?'

'Cheating? No, Ned, that's just you, I'm afraid. But you're not the only one who knows a Churchill. Clementine has offered me a place on the *Queen Mary*.'

'She...?'

'And I'm going.' She'd fetched her ready-packed suitcase and made for the door but spun back, her heart aching. Ned had been standing in the middle of their carefully put-together apartment, his feet on their special Navajo rug, his back to the oak desk under which they'd hidden together from bombs so many times. But she'd hidden there with Clementine too, when she'd offered her the escape that it now seemed she needed. She'd had to stay firm. 'It won't be for long, Ned. Just long enough for you to think about this – about us, about what you want.'

He'd leaped forward, finally jolted into action. 'I want you, Jen. You're my wife, my love.'

'But not, sadly, your lover. *Think*, Ned, please, for both of us.'

It had taken all her strength to walk out of the door, and every mile across the Atlantic had felt like a mile away from her marriage. Now Ned had closed those miles, and she could only pray it was not for more arguments.

'Jenny?'

He was standing before her, hat in one hand, suitcase in the other.

'Ned!' He looked wonderful and suddenly she felt as shy as a kid at a high school dance. 'It's good to see you.'

'You too. You look beautiful.'

It was kind of him to say but she wasn't a patch on Pamela. *Stop that*, she told herself. She couldn't spend her life in comparisons; that way madness lay.

'I've been resting.' That sounded so gauche. So pathetic. 'Playing a lot of golf,' she added hastily.

'You've always been good at golf.'

'I'm better now,' she said, daring herself to look teasingly up at him.

His eyes darkened and her pulse quickened in instant response. This was like a mid-afternoon radio drama. Next thing she knew, her heart would be fluttering and probably her eyelashes besides.

'I'll have to take you on once we're in Florida,' he said.

'See if you dare.'

Aaah! She sounded so stupid! Ned didn't seem to notice, though, and stepped closer, dropping his hat and case to the floor.

'I've been an idiot, Jen, a total idiot. Can you forgive me? *Please.*'

Could she?

'Why?'

He drew in a deep breath. 'I've thought about that a lot, like you asked me to. I've thought about what life might be like without you and I can't bear it, Jen. I know things have been... difficult. *I've* been difficult. I've thrown myself into work too much and let it all go to my head. I've changed, and not necessarily for the better, at least when it comes to us.'

He swallowed. The other passengers were swarming around them, but they were locked in their own space, as if no one else existed.

'The thing is, Jen, I like myself better with you, because of you. You're so interesting and challenging – in a good way. You understand my ideas. You talk to me about them, you help me expand them, you have ideas of your own. You care about the world and you want to make it a better place. I want that too, Jen, really I do. I love a party, I admit it, and they're so very tempting when everything else is so tough. But more than that I love exploring the world, interrogating it, interacting with it. And I can do that with you better than with anyone else because you're so clever and honest and caring.'

Jenny swallowed. This wasn't blame. This wasn't complaint. He'd done what she asked and thought about their marriage, and maybe honest and caring didn't feel quite as good as sexy and exciting but it did feel more solid, more real.

'I got dull, Ned,' she admitted. 'London felt so hard and... and not having a baby made me sad.'

'I know.' He reached out his arms and she stepped closer. 'I should have been there for you. But it's not too late, you know.'

She looked up at him. 'To make a baby?'

He smiled softly. 'To make a marriage, honey. It's you I want, and if a baby comes, it will be a bonus.'

'Oh, Ned.'

Now she did fall into his arms, and then his lips were on hers and if they looked like a mid-afternoon radio drama, so what? All she knew was that Ned was back.

'Do you forgive me?' he whispered against her lips.

Did she? He'd said he liked her for her honesty...

'I'm working on it.'

'That's the most I could possibly ask.'

Then he was kissing her again and leading her out of the shadow of the giant ship and she knew that love, like integrity and humanity and everything else they'd come up against in the last five years, was truly worth fighting for.

THIRTY-FIVE

THE ANNEXE, FEBRUARY 1945

CLEMENTINE

A shrill ring pulled Clementine from sleep and she started up, scrabbling for the telephone that Winston had insisted on having installed by her bed in the Annexe 'in case'. Neither of them had gone into details about what 'in case' might be, but it would never be good. Right now, with him a thousand miles away in the Russian city of Yalta, meeting Roosevelt and Stalin, it might be terrible.

'Clementine Churchill,' she said, her voice coming out hoarse and afraid.

'So sorry to disturb you, Mrs Churchill.' She couldn't place the voice. It was a woman, though. Was that good or bad? 'This is Nurse Morrison.'

Nurse!

'Is it Winston?' Clementine gasped. 'Is he ill?' Visions of her husband in a Russian hospital, gasping out his last breaths under communist care, raced across her mind. She thought of the hospitals in Rostov-on-Don, as yet only half built, and wondered if this was some cruel twist of fate.

'Winston? Oh no, ma'am, I'm so sorry.'

'Sorry?' Her world went black at the edges.

'That is, I'm sure Mr Churchill is fine. It's Fircroft.'

'Fircroft?' The words weren't matching up in Clementine's head and she wondered if she was still asleep, but the February cold creeping into her toes told her she was very much awake.

'It's taken a hit, Mrs Churchill. A V2.'

Clementine came to her senses. Hitler had launched his V2 rockets last September while she and Winston had been dancing on the *Queen Mary*, and they were even deadlier than the V1. They could fly unpiloted for two hundred miles, so be launched from German territory in the Netherlands, and the British people were reeling from yet more attacks. If you listened to the strategists, pushing their pins around the map room beneath Whitehall, the war was almost over. But it didn't feel like that on the streets of London. Now, it seemed, they were attacking the countryside too.

'Is anyone hurt?' she asked, stretching the telephone cable so she could pull back the curtains. Traces of dawn crept in through an icy mist. She shivered.

'Thankfully no, Mrs Churchill. The bomb hit the empty dining area, though young Millie Ecclestone had been there barely minutes before fetching a bottle for her Thomas. She's very shaken.'

'I can imagine.' Clementine's mind was racing. 'Where's everyone now?'

'We've had to evacuate. There was all sorts falling down in the bedrooms and one section of the roof looks unstable. The warden said it wasn't safe, so the poor mothers and babies are on the lawn.'

'In this weather?'

'We're not sure where else to go.'

'Ask for shelter,' Clementine instructed. 'There must be

people out from the houses nearby? If there aren't, knock them up. We can't have those little ones in the cold.'

'Will do.'

'Good. I'll be there as soon as I can.' Clementine rang the bell for her maid, already pulling off her nightwear. 'I need warm clothes, Molly,' she instructed the girl. 'And my coats. Plenty of them. Wake Grace, she'll know which ones are best. Blankets too. And fuel in the car.'

'Yes, ma'am.'

The phone rang again as Clementine was pulling on her gardening slacks, the closest thing to hand.

'Answer that please, Molly.'

The girl nervously picked up the telephone. 'Hello? Yes? Oh no! Of course. Yes. She's right here.'

Clementine stared at her – what now?

'There's a lady on the line saying something about exploding cows.'

'What?! Who is she?'

'Says she's called Cousin Maryott?'

'Maryott!' Clementine grabbed the receiver back. 'Are you all right?'

'Totally fine, Clemmie. I just thought you should know we've taken a bit of a hit down here.'

'Chartwell?' Clementine pictured the mish-mash old house, Winston's pride and joy. If it was gone, his heart might truly break.

'Not the house, thank God. Blasted rocket landed on the far side of the grounds. Tree house has taken a bit of a knock.'

'Tree houses can be rebuilt. Is anyone hurt?'

'No one human.'

'The cows? Molly says they've exploded.'

'Then Molly wasn't listening properly,' came the thankfully crisp reply. 'The bomb exploded *near* the cows. Sent shrapnel all over their field. It's cut their feet up terribly, but Joseph is tending them, or he will be when we can get the silly things to stand still.'

'Can you cope?'

'Of course we can cope, dear! I just wanted you to hear it from me before some reporter poked his nose in.'

'Thank you, Maryott.'

'I'd best get on. Bastard Nazis aren't going quietly, are they?'

Clementine would have laughed if it hadn't been so very tragic. The Russians were halfway through Poland, making a beeline for Berlin from the east, and the Anglo-American forces were approaching the Rhine from the west. Thousands of Wehrmacht soldiers were being captured or killed every day but Hitler was refusing to surrender. The delusional megalomaniac was going to go down fighting, and he was going to take as many people with him as possible – both his and, it seemed, theirs.

Clementine and Grace sped to Fircroft through the first grey threads of day, only a nasty encounter with a patch of black ice slowing them down. Even so, it took over an hour and Clementine was horrified to see several women still huddled on the lawn, wrapped in big coats and talking stridently to a broad-beamed nurse.

'Why are these women outside?' Clementine demanded.

'Beg pardon, Mrs Churchill,' said the nurse, 'but they want to help.'

Clementine looked to the women, who nodded.

'Our babies are safe over there,' one said, pointing to a nearby house. 'And we want to do something useful.'

'Like what?'

'Put the house back together, of course.'

The nurse threw her hands in the air. 'I told them—' she started.

'That would be marvellous,' Clementine finished brightly. 'We're going to need all the help we can get.'

'But—' started the nurse.

'Nurse Morrison, I assume?'

'Yes, Mrs Churchill. It's an honour to meet you. I—'

'Very kind, but there's no time for that. As these good women have just said, we need to put the house back together.'

'We can't just, just—'

'I think we can. Now, let's see who and what is about to help.'

One of the mothers, Peggy, had worked for the last three years in a carpentry shop and took charge of the splintered rafters. Her friend, Marg, 'knew a bit about electrics', which turned out to be quite the understatement as she soon had the fuse box located and the broken wires reconnected. Two other mothers emerged, saying they'd been land girls up until their pregnancies and could 'hulk stuff like no other'. Grace soon had the mish-mash group organised into an efficient work team and even Nurse Morrison, shocked into action, rolled up her sleeves and got stuck in.

As the sun burned off the mist, their activities attracted others. Clementine drove to nearby Fulmer Chase and brought back the resident handyman and three local lads. He'd pulled them from their beds, by the blurry-eyed look of them, but they got stuck in, encouraged by the tea and buns the locals brought out. By midday, the house looked almost habitable and Clementine felt quite misty-eyed with pride in her impromptu team.

She gathered everyone in the patched-up dining area as the mothers flocked back inside with their babies, most of them wearing Clementine's coats like a bizarre personal fashion parade. They were chattering and smiling, helping the kitchen staff assemble a hearty soup to feed the hungry helpers, and she paused to look around the house, remembering the first time she'd seen it back in 1941 with Jenny Miller.

Clementine had had a Christmas card from her friend, saying that she was with Ned and suggesting that all was, thankfully, well. Pamela had been rather quiet since her scarlet fever and had told Clementine she was missing Averell.

'Perhaps,' Clementine had suggested gently, 'you should try to heal the hole he's left in your heart, rather than rushing to fill it with someone who fits it less well?'

'Perhaps,' Pamela had agreed, though not very convincingly, and Clementine could only hope she would find a nice single man to keep her company.

Jenny was on the boat back to London with Ned, both of them, she'd written, keen to 'see victory in Europe' and Clementine admired their bravery. London and her surrounds, as tonight had so bitterly proved, was no place for the faint-hearted, even at what must, surely, be the end of the war. She looked at the motley collection of people gathered around the soup pot and felt blessed. There was work still to be done but the house was sound and life could go on safely while they brought in professional workmen to complete the repairs.

'Thank you all so much,' she said. 'This has been a tremendous effort and I'm so, so happy we've restored Fircroft for these brave mothers and their infants.'

'No,' Peggy said, standing up, her baby in her arms. 'We should thank you, Mrs Churchill. This house, along with Fulmer Chase, has been a lifeline to me. My mam was killed in the Blitz, my pa in the Great War, and my Reg is fighting his way to Berlin. I'd have been all alone without these hospitals, so a bit of work is the least I could do.'

'Tell your Reg to find the sites they're launching these evil weapons from, and stop them,' Marg suggested and everyone cheered.

'Send Mrs Churchill over,' someone else cried. 'She'd get this blasted war sorted way quicker than her husband and all those stodgy men.'

The cheers for this were even louder. Clementine looked around the women, astonished. She opened her mouth to protest but her words were drowned out in a chorus of 'For She's a Jolly Good Fellow'. She felt something sting at her eye and fumbled for her handkerchief, but then realised it was not the irritation of dust, or even the prickle of embarrassment. It was pride.

These women had been a marvel today but she had brought them together. She had responded to the crisis, mustered a team, and got the job done. She might be knocking on the door of her sixtieth birthday but those long and full years of life had given her experience and maybe even confidence. She wouldn't get the war sorted – that was just nonsense – but maybe, like all the others around her today, she was learning to become someone who could act not just as a wife, but as a person in her own right. It was a heady feeling, but not, she had to admit, entirely unpleasant. Maybe, with women like these – herself included – they could win not just the war, but the future too.

THIRTY-SIX

YWCA HOSTEL, LONDON, MARCH 1945

JENNY

Jenny looked around the dining hall as it seemed to almost physically swell with applause. Today was a celebration of the YWCA's hostel work and the dining room was packed to bursting. There were the residents, plus a bunch of workmen and women, and an elegantly dressed clutch of dignitaries, trying to look relaxed in such an eclectic crowd. One factory girl put two fingers to her scarlet lips and let out a loud wolf whistle and Jenny nearly broke down laughing as a bejewelled older lady in front of her jumped out of her fox-fur stole. Clementine Churchill, recipient of this raucous adulation, simply smiled and waved a grateful hand.

'Please, ladies and gentlemen, it's very kind but none of the successes of the YWCA hostel group would have been possible without your hard work. The safe, comfortable living that so many of our young people have enjoyed' – she had to pause for another wolf whistle – 'has been down to those who built the hostels, kitted them out, and maintained them. It's been down to those who repaired the roofs and made the beds, and it's been down to those who've done the books, cooked the meals, and cleaned the latrines!'

The crowd laughed.

Fox-fur lady fanned herself. 'Clementine really has become quite coarse,' Jenny heard her say to her husband.

'She has,' he agreed, adding, 'it suits her.'

His wife looked horrified and Jenny smiled again. Clementine's attitude wasn't what she would call coarse, but it *did* suit her. Her friend looked newly confident, her eyes sparkling, her skin rosy and her shoulders relaxed. Jenny remembered how hunched they'd been the night she'd joined her on the roof of the Treasury in 1941, as if she were the very guardian of the government, and was pleased to see her looking so much less tense. She stood taller than ever in a dark green suit and today's turban which, if Jenny was not mistaken, was patterned with words from Winston's speeches. How very Clementine – even her signature garment was imprinted with her husband's ambition!

'Above all,' Clementine went on, 'the success of the hostels has been down to you girls, who've been brave enough to leave your homes to come and give yourselves to the war effort. A house is nothing without a family in it and you girls, you are the YWCA hostel family.'

More applause, laced with whistles and cheers.

'And you're our mam!' someone shouted.

Clementine blushed furiously. 'Then I hope...'

She caught herself, but looked momentarily lost and Jenny knew she was thinking that she was no use as a mother. She remembered her crouched beneath Ned's desk amidst the bombs, telling her about losing Marigold. It had been one of the saddest things she'd ever heard – a reminder, if they needed it, that life was fragile even outside the brutal boundaries of war.

Jenny leaned against a pillar and put a hand to her belly, feeling giddy with hope and worry. It was early days yet but all the signs were there that her and Ned's Florida reconciliation had borne fruit. Perhaps, all along, their baby had simply been waiting to be born in peacetime? If so, he or she would be as smart as their parents had once thought themselves.

It had been a happy holiday. After the initial few days of awkwardness, they'd slipped into the pattern of their first days of marriage – going out together to see places, play golf, and watch plays and films. They'd talked and talked, of all they'd seen and all they wanted to see. They'd made a list of countries to visit once borders opened again, and discussed where they might live once the war was over.

Once the war was over...

Those were words Jenny heard more and more these days, spoken not just with the wistful longing of the early years but with real hope, even impatience. The hideous V2s were still hitting targets in London and other cities, but with less frequency, and reports from the front suggested the launch sites would shortly be overwhelmed. It was nearly April, nine months since the Normandy offensive, and both sides of the Allied pincer were close to Berlin. The Russians were closer, though, and Jenny knew from Ned that Winston was furious at Allied strategy to let them take the German capital.

'He says Stalin's playing the long game,' Ned had told her the other night, after he'd come back from 'a wee whisky' with the prime minister. 'He says Stalin doesn't care about throwing the Germans off foreign territory as much as he does about taking it for himself. He says Stalin's forging an eastern empire and the Americans have been fooled by the "Uncle Joe" image into thinking he's far more benign and cooperative than he really is.'

'Is he right?' Jenny had asked.

'Probably,' Ned had said gloomily. 'We might have to cross the Balkans off our to-do list for a few years, honey.'

Then he'd taken her in his arms and pulled her to bed and

she'd gladly acquiesced, far happier to talk present love than future war.

She'd been nervous about coming back to London, afraid that once Ned was sucked into the CBS social scene he'd be seduced by Pamela Churchill again, but he'd been far too busy flying bombing raids over Germany. In a few days he would join General Patton's 89th Infantry to chart the Allied march over the Rhine. Jenny was scared for him, for the fighting was intense and she couldn't bear to lose him in this final run.

Her hand went to her stomach again. She would tell Ned before he went to Germany; it would give him an extra reason to stay safe.

'As you know,' Clementine was continuing, 'we are honoured to have extended our work onto the continent. I'm newly back from touring several hostels housing our brave ATS women in Belgium and they tell me that it's lovely having a "home from home" on foreign soil.'

'Hope you took them some decent teabags,' someone shouted. 'My son's over there and says they've got no idea how to make a good brew.'

'As it happens, we did,' Clementine agreed. 'At the request of my daughter.'

More cheers greeted this and Jenny let out a whoop. Clementine had written to tell her that Mary was being posted to Brussels, as commander of her anti-aircraft unit. She'd sounded proud but nervous, and little wonder. These young women were defiant in the face of danger. Even the king and queen had, after long resistance, let Princess Elizabeth join the ATS and the papers had been full of pictures of her doing mechanical work on army trucks. It was amazing to see the girls standing up to do their bit, but terrifying too, and it had clearly done Clementine good to see her daughter.

'No Brit likes to work without a decent cup of tea,' Clementine went on with a broad smile. 'And on that note, it's time to serve up our own. Do sample the cakes made by the residents, which look delicious. Thank you again, everyone, and enjoy your refreshments.'

The applause was long, stopped only by the whistle of the kettle.

'Thank heavens,' Fox-fur lady muttered.

Jenny thought perhaps she'd have some fun.

'Good afternoon,' she said, stepping in front of her. 'Jenny Miller, CBS reporter. I'd love to know your thoughts on this afternoon's celebration.'

'Mine?' The lady's hand fluttered to her chest. 'Oh, my dear, I'm just a humble observer.'

'That cannot be true,' Jenny said. 'Everyone here has been part of the YWCA effort.'

'Well, yes. But all I did was turn over one of my houses for use as a hostel.'

One of her houses, Jenny noted.

'And...' her husband said, 'personally made twenty beds for the young ladies to sleep in.'

'Made the beds?' Jenny asked, trying not to sound scathing though, really, how hard was it to throw on a few sheets?

'Hammered them together from planks of wood, yes.' Jenny gaped and the man winked at her. 'And stuffed the mattresses to boot. My Hermione is a dab hand.'

He was glowing with pride, though his Hermione gave him an embarrassed nudge.

'It was nothing,' she said to Jenny. 'I did hundreds of them in the first war. This was pathetic in comparison, but the arthritis in my silly hands makes me so slow these days.'

Jenny made a note and felt mean for thinking she could tease this amazing woman when she was prepared to get stuck in and graft with everyone else. 'I think it's wonderful,' she said sincerely. 'Women do so much these days and it's your generation who have shown the way.'

Hermione frowned. 'It's been easy so far, my dear. War can be surprisingly liberating. It's the young girls like yourself, trying to hold on to your new-found powers once the men are back to resent them, who have the tricky road to forge.'

Jenny supposed she was right. Part of her troubles had come from Ned being torn between being proud of her achievements and wanting her in the home supporting his. They would have to find compromises, but together they would manage it.

'Jenny, my dear, how lovely to have you back!'

Clementine descended and, to Jenny's huge surprise, engulfed her in a warm hug.

She hugged her gladly back. 'It's good to be here.'

'You look well.'

'As do you. How was Belgium?'

'Superb! It was so good to see Mary, of course, and to view the hostels, but I'd forgotten how much I love to travel. I used to do it a lot, you know.'

'Hunting dragons,' Jenny said.

Clementine gave her braying laugh. 'You remember!'

'Of course. It was quite a story.'

'It was quite a journey, my dear. I was less cautious back then. Brussels reminded me how staid I've become.'

'There's been a war on,' Jenny reminded her.

Again the laugh. 'Still is, sadly. Surely Hitler will surrender soon?'

'You told me once that you don't believe in last stands.'

'Did I? Heavens, Jenny, you pay far too much attention to what I say. That's certainly true but I fear Hitler does not share my opinion and is going to go on killing all the way to his death – unless we can get to him first.'

'And put him on trial?'

'Exactly. D'you know, until a few weeks ago I just wanted him gone and myself free to live a peaceful life, but I've been watching what our youngsters can achieve and now I believe we can do better than that to set up a bright future. I hope we capture Hitler and we make him squeal. I hope all his evil ministers are forced to answer for their crimes before the whole world so that they never, ever happen again.'

'Quite right. What changed?'

'Spending time with strong, courageous women who deserve the best.'

Jenny smiled. 'Delighted to hear it. How's Winston?'

'Miraculously well. Damn man is talking about running for PM again.'

'You're not keen?'

'I'd rather travel.'

'You could go back to Brussels?'

'I could, though I don't want Mary thinking I'm hovering over her.'

'France perhaps?'

'Perhaps. Madame De Gaulle says I'm welcome whenever I wish and Eleanor's extended an open invitation to the States, but the place I'd really like to go...' She stopped herself.

'The place you'd really like to go...?' Jenny prompted.

Clementine looked around surreptitiously, but everyone was chattering away. 'I've been invited to Russia,' she confided.

'Really?' Jenny clapped her hands. 'How thrilling!'

'Do you think so? Winston thinks it could be dangerous to pander to Stalin, though also that it might be valuable to keep him close.'

'And you? What do you think?'

Clementine considered. 'I couldn't give a monkey's about Stalin, or believe I could do anything to influence him either way. But I would love to meet some of the women who write to me. I'd love to meet the chairwoman of Kursk, and I'd love to see the hospitals in Rostov.'

'Then go!' Jenny urged. 'You deserve it.'

Clementine nodded earnestly. 'I realise that. When we had

the bomb at Fircroft I saw very clearly that I can do things on my own these days.'

'That's great! Then—'

'But I'll turn sixty in April.'

'What a trip to mark that milestone!'

Clementine laughed. 'I like your optimism, Jenny.' But then her face dropped. 'It's not just about me though. Last Christmas, when I got the terrible call from Tunis, I saw very clearly what can go wrong if I'm not there. Winston nearly died, Jenny.'

'But he didn't.'

'Thank God. He's been so committed to winning this war, so courageous in his convictions. He stood alone back in 1940, when all of Europe was falling and America was refusing to join the fight. He stood all alone.'

'He stood with you,' Jenny corrected gently. 'For you stood with him, as you always do.'

'I do!' Clementine nodded her head. 'As I should. You're right, Jenny – I won't go.'

Jenny was horrified. 'That's not what I said. You should definitely go. You should go for international relations, you should go for yourself, and you should go for the generation of women fighting to continue to do things of their own.'

'Heavens, really?'

'Definitely. Go for your daughters, Clementine,' she urged. 'Go for everyone's daughters.' She put a hand to her stomach and swallowed. She hadn't even told Ned yet but this was important. 'Go for *my* daughter.'

'Your daughter...?'

'Or son.'

Clementine stared at her. 'You're...?'

'I believe so, yes.'

'Bravo!' Clementine swept her up in another hug. 'That's

delightful, Jenny, the best news I've heard in weeks. I'm so pleased for you.'

Jenny felt emotion flood through her and clung to this most unlikely of friends. 'Then,' she urged through tears, 'go to Russia!'

But at that Clementine clammed up again.

'I can't. It may seem stupid to a liberated young thing like you, but I can't. When I married Winston, I promised I would stand at his side. It's not been easy, but I've done it and I'm proud of it and I can't let him down. It just wouldn't be right.' She set her chin. 'Now, let's be sure that everyone has a cup of tea, shall we?'

And, with the consummate change of subject Jenny had grown to expect from her reserved host, she was off into the crowd, talking to people and checking on them and making them comfortable. Jenny watched, her heart aching for this woman who gave so much to others and took so little for herself.

Then an idea came to her – a surely mad, certainly insolent idea. Dare she...?

She set her chin. Of course she dared. Clementine Churchill had done so much for her; it was time she did something in return.

THIRTY-SEVEN

THE WAR ROOMS, MARCH 1945

WINSTON

Winston sat, whisky glass raised, spy-like, to hide his face as he scrutinised his wife's. She was at her desk, reading a letter from the top of an enormous pile, and for the first time it struck him how much time must go into correspondence. People said it all the time, 'she's just doing her correspondence', making it sound so light and genteel – a few lines asking after someone's health or inviting them to tea. Watching Clemmie now, as he'd so rarely had time to do in these last years, he could see that it was a full-time job.

'Who writes to you?'

She looked up, surprised. 'Many people. Women mainly, but men too, if they need something badly enough.'

'Something like...?'

She turned towards him. 'The condition of the shelters. I got that a lot during the Blitz.'

'When you made Jock go down with you?'

'Jock and many others besides. They had to see, Winston.

Sometimes it's not enough to simply know; you have to *see*. And to taste and to smell.'

'I'm not sure he ever got over those latrines.'

'Good. That's the point. The war may be a big game of tin soldiers to you lot in the War Rooms, but to the people in the streets it's hardship and sorrow, hunger and fear and loss.'

Winston took a puff on his cigar, offended. 'That's why I went to visit them in the Blitz, Clemmie – or tried. You usually stopped me.'

She rose and came to sit next to him.

'That's true and I'm sorry but the thing is, Winston, you're precious. You're what we need to win the war, so we can't afford to lose you. I had to keep you safe. *Have* to keep you safe.'

There was an urgency in her tone, and a strange light in her eyes. Winston set down his whisky and looked at his wife, properly looked at her. Maybe the young woman was right...

THREE DAYS AGO

Winston looked at Jock, surprised to be told Jenny Miller was asking for an audience, but nodded his assent. She was a bright girl and a hard worker, or so Clemmie had told him. She did all sorts of charity work and broadcast on CBS and the BBC too. He'd listened to a couple of her programmes on American history and they'd been good. Simplified for the audience, of course, but intelligently so. What on earth she wanted with him, however, he was unable to think.

Then he remembered Clemmie telling him something about Pamela having an affair with her husband and his throat tightened. Was this some domestic issue? Did she want him to intervene? Lord help him, surely not! He waved her inside cautiously.

'I'll come straight to the point,' she said.

He braced himself, but her next words bowled him over like a skittle.

'You're holding your wife back.'

'I'm what?!'

She flinched, perhaps surprised at her own audacity. 'Sorry, but it's important. Clementine is so amazing—'

'As I know far better than you, young lady.'

'Of course.' She swallowed, then pushed her pixie chin high and said it again, 'But you're still holding her back.'

He was tempted to throw her straight out, because it was patently untrue. He loved Clemmie. He'd do anything for her. He'd made her prime minister's wife, hadn't he? Though that, he had to admit, had been very much his own ambition. Still, he'd given her adorable children, albeit rather troublesome ones on occasion. On quite a few occasions actually. And he'd bought her a beautiful house – that she hadn't actually wanted. He'd been a bit ashamed of that trick. Buying Chartwell while she was giving birth to Mary hadn't been up to his usual gentlemanly standards, but he'd known she'd love it once she came round to the idea. And she did, sort of. If not as much as him.

'In what way?' he asked Mrs Miller reluctantly.

'She thinks it's her job to keep you going, to keep you safe, to keep you happy and well and up to fighting for the nation.'

'Isn't it?'

'In part, yes. But she also runs the YWCA Wartime Appeal and the Aid to Russia fund. She also keeps the shelters up to par, and hosts hundreds of charity teas and luncheons to keep everything together. She also answers thousands of letters, and makes sure the important issues get acted on. She does more, sir, than ten of your cabinet ministers put together.'

That reminded Winston of something Clemmie had done out in Tunis (possibly getting him to bed 'on time', whatever 'on time' was) that had led to Jock saying he should get her in the cabinet. 'You really must,' Sarah had told him straight away. 'Mother is far sharper than half those saggy old blokes.'

Was she? He knew she was. He knew she was special. He remembered that time she'd leaped across the platform in Bristol to save him from the shrill suffragette who'd been trying to horsewhip him under a train. 'If all women were like you, I'd definitely give them the vote,' he'd told her and he'd meant it. So what was Jenny Miller going on about?

'In what way am I holding her back?' he demanded.

The answer was even more surprising than the initial statement.

'You won't let her go to Russia.'

'Russia? Good God, does she want to go to Russia?'

'Yes! Very much.'

'Then she only has to say.'

'No, sir, begging your pardon – *you* only have to say.'

He squinted at her. 'You're talking in riddles, young lady.'

She folded her arms. 'Then let me be plain. Your wife has been working on the Aid to Russia fund since Sir Philip Chetwode asked her to do so in October 1941. In that time she has raised almost seven million pounds, raised it by hard graft, by going to fundraising events, and doing radio appeals, by visiting schools and associations, and walking into the centre of the stock market to demand cash.'

'I remember. Good show that.'

'Brave show, sir. She was the only woman in the place. But she did it, not for herself, but for the people of Russia who write to her every day, who talk directly to her about their hospitals being bombed and their sons being burned alive and their daughters being raped.'

'Young lady!'

'It's true, sir! It's what she has to read, day in day out. She's carrying the weight of all those people's sorrows.'

'I'm sorry for it.'

'You should be, because she's carrying them on top of the weight of carrying you.'

He felt rather indignant at that. They were so strident, these Americans, so damned pointed. But then he remembered how blunt his mother had often been and how much he'd loved her for it, and tried not to overreact.

'She's my wife, Mrs Miller,' he reminded her. 'I think I have the right to support from my wife.'

'You do. As she does from you.'

'I... Well, yes, of course. It's just that I'm rather busy, you know.'

'I know.' She tipped her head on one side, looking at him most disconcertingly. 'But so is she. The world needs Winston to win the war, and Winston needs Clementine. The buck, sir, stops with her.'

The metaphor was poorly chosen – his Clemmie had never liked poker – but perhaps that had been the point. She *did* keep him going, however hard it got. He could still remember the raging nights of illness out in Tunis, the dark, dragging sense that he was going to die, like some Greek hero but without achieving anything heroic. Without winning the war.

He'd hated that. He'd fought against it with everything he'd had, but it had felt so hard. And then, through the fug and the pain of drawing even one more breath, he'd heard her voice and he'd been back in the Temple of Diana, asking her to be his wife, and he'd known that if she just said yes, he could do it. With her at his side, he'd always known he could do anything.

'I don't want to hold her back,' he told Jenny Miller.

'Then tell her to go to Russia, sir. Let her have this chance to see the fruit of all her hard work. Let her meet the people who've been writing to her for help for so long, and let her be thanked, as she so deserves to be thanked.'

'It's that simple?'

She smiled then, the bright young American. 'Probably not, but it will do for starters.'

Remembering the startling conversation as he looked at his wife three days later, Winston reached out and took her hands. 'This Russia trip, Clemmie...'

'I won't go, Winston.'

'Why not?'

'It's poor timing. The war is coming to a head. I can't just leave.'

'Can't just leave *me*, you mean?'

Her eyes slid sideways. 'It's nearly done, Pug. You've nearly done it. I can't waltz off when you're so close.'

'When *we're* so close. And it would hardly be waltzing, Kat. It would be a long, hard, very valuable trip.'

'Valuable?' She looked up at that.

'You've worked so hard on the fund, Clemmie, done so much good. Don't you want to see it on the ground?'

'I do, Winston. I really do. But—'

'No!' He stood up, pulling her with him. 'No buts. You should do this.'

'For the Red Cross?'

'No.'

'For Britain?'

'No.'

'For you?'

'No! No, woman, no, no, no – for you, for yourself.'

She looked stunned. 'That's what Eleanor Roosevelt said.'

'Is it?' She'd talked about it with the president's wife? Goodness!

'And Jenny Miller.'

He smiled at that. 'I know. She told me.'

'Jenny did? How dare she!'

He kissed the indignation off her lips. 'She dares because she cares. She thinks I'm a grumpy, demanding, boorish old husband.'

'That's not true!'

He chuckled. 'Come now, it's a bit true.' A smile crept onto her lovely lips and his heart gladdened to see it. 'I've been a pain to you in so many ways, my Kat, and you've stuck with me.'

'Because I love you.'

'And I you, but I am not as good at showing it as you are – not in real, practical support.'

'You've been busy.'

He chuckled again. 'That's what I told Mrs Miller.'

'And what did she say?'

'She said you'd been busy too.'

'We're all busy, Winston, there's a...'

'War to win.' They said it together.

He kissed her again. 'And it is nearly won,' he assured her. 'You don't have to protect me any longer, my Kat. You can go out there and start the long, long process of peace.'

'I can?'

He gripped her hands tight. 'You can, my dear wife, you truly can. Do you remember when the Millers came to dinner? It must have been back in '42, after America had joined the war. We had a jolly time, I think, but something that young woman said then came to me when she tackled me again.'

Clementine looked at him quizzically and he shifted. He wasn't good at humility, he knew that. No one got anywhere bleating about how hopeless they were, but sometimes it was important.

'I was doing my gallant act. I said, as I have often done, that you are the light that lets my star shine.'

'It's a charming metaphor.'

'I thought so,' Winston agreed. 'Now I'm not so sure. Do you remember what she said?'

Clementine shook her head.

'She said, "But who, sir, lets Clementine's star shine?" She had a point. She still does. So I want you to go to Russia, Clemmie. I want you to permit me to let *your* star shine.'

A tear sparkled in her eye. 'It's not about that,' she said. 'I don't need to shine.'

He kissed the tear away, his heart full of love for this bold, brave, unassumingly wonderful woman he'd been blessed to have at his side for so much of his life. 'And that, my dear, is precisely why you do.'

THIRTY-EIGHT

MOSCOW, APRIL 1945

CLEMENTINE

Clementine steeled herself and tried not to look at the stern-faced guards standing in tight formation either way up the long corridor at the heart of the Kremlin. It was hard, for the Russian soldiers all held huge, imposing guns that drew the eye and shook the heart. Clementine glanced at Grace and was glad to see her unflappable secretary was similarly rigid.

'Do you think,' Grace whispered, 'that the size of their guns is converse to the size of their—'

'Grace!'

Clementine was horrified at her irreverence but buoyed by it too. There was surely no need for Stalin to impose this bristling show of masculine strength on them and she wasn't going to let it get to her. She'd been in Moscow for two days, arriving to quite astonishing crowds at an airport draped in alternate Union jacks and hammer-and-sickles. There had been much cheering and she'd managed to choke out the Russian thank you she'd been practising all the way there without, apparently, saying anything rude or inappropriate.

Since then, she'd been gracefully entertained by Ambassador Sir Archibald Clark Kerr and his immaculate staff at the British embassy, as well as Averell Harriman and his daughter for the Americans. Averell had asked assiduously after her family, working his way through them all with careful charm before finally getting to Pamela.

'I miss her,' he'd said with American candour.

'She misses you too,' Clementine had conceded, and his eyes had lit up.

Clementine's official hosts were Monsieur Molotov, the Soviet minister of foreign affairs, and his remarkable wife, Polina, head of textiles production for the Ministry of Light Industry. They'd entertained Clementine with grace, taking her to the Bolshoi ballet and around St Basil's Cathedral in a weekend of luxury before the real work of visiting the fund's projects began. The one person conspicuously absent in his welcome had been Stalin himself, but now she'd been summoned for a personal audience.

She'd dressed carefully, selecting a modest tea-dress and the hammer-and-sickle turban she'd had specially made for the visit, but she was already longing to pull it off for it was clear that this was not going to be a cosy chat. She and Grace had been kept waiting in an opulent but empty antechamber for over half an hour until a guard had finally entered, stood to fierce attention, and told them that, 'Marshal Stalin will see you now.'

It had been hugely tempting to ask to visit the lavatory first but she'd not quite dared. Now they were approaching the grand doors of Stalin's study and Clementine tried to remember all Winston had told her about the Russian leader.

'He's a slippery customer, Clemmie. He can be brilliantly jovial – Franklin's Uncle Joe – but he'll turn in an instant if something displeases him.'

'Like a cat?'

'Exactly like! But he'll meet his match in my Kat, I'm sure.'

She put a habitual hand to her earrings, twisting the stunning diamond roses for reassurance. Winston had sent them with Grace for her sixtieth birthday, which had, in the end, been celebrated en route in Cairo. She'd missed her family on the big day, but had to admit she'd been thrilled to mark it on a diplomatic mission in an exotic destination, rather than at home in her slippers. The mission felt scarier now but touching Winston's gift settled her nerves. She couldn't quite get over him insisting on her taking this trip, or over Jenny Miller having the audacity to tell him to do so. The young women of today were a different breed from her generation but, goodness, they were exciting. Clementine envied them their path in life, but not right now. Right now, her own path was exciting enough.

The head of their escort (two soldiers in front and two behind, in case the twenty lining either wall were insufficient to contain two ageing English females) banged on the large doors at the end of the corridor and, after a pathetically long time, a voice said 'enter'. The doors were flung dramatically back and Clementine stepped through to find herself in a room nearly as long as the corridor, also ranged around with armed guards. Stalin was sitting at a large desk at the far end, forcing them to walk all the way up to him. A classic small-man move, she thought and, drawing herself to her full six foot, plus heels, strode forward.

Either she was too fast for him to rise, or he had never intended to do so, but he waved them into two elaborate chairs in front of him with a big smile and a patter of a greeting that a uniformed woman at his side translated as 'Welcome, kind ladies, to the Kremlin, seat of my government.'

'We're delighted to be here,' Clementine said. 'And looking forward to seeing the projects our fund has assisted with.'

The words went through the translator and Stalin's came back to them: 'The marshal is very grateful for the help of your kind people and, of course, your gracious self.'

'It's our pleasure. You are our allies.'

'Allies,' Stalin agreed in clipped English.

'And our friends,' Clementine suggested.

He did not repeat that one; perhaps he did not know it.

'The marshal understands that you have an excellent journey planned around his country,' the translator said.

'I believe so. I am to travel to Leningrad and then down to the Caucasus and Rostov-on-Don, before coming back through Kursk.'

'He knows. He has put his personal train at your disposal so you can travel in luxury.'

'That is very kind.'

'And stay in privacy. With the KGB experts for your protection. You will not have to associate with the local people.'

There was an emphasis on this that Clementine chose to ignore. 'I am very much looking forward to meeting the local people.'

A jumble of words passed between Stalin and the translator, who flushed.

'And they you,' she said eventually. 'But it is important you stick to your programme and do not... wander.'

'Wander? Very well.'

Clementine could not wait to talk to Winston about this. Speaking of which... She felt in her bag. Several guards leaped forward, and she flinched, but Stalin waved them back as she drew out the rectangular leather box she'd sought.

'I bring a gift for you, Marshal Stalin, from my husband.'

She placed it on the desk and he picked it up and lifted the lid. Inside was a gold pen that Winston had chosen with care. And expertise, Clementine reflected looking around her, for it matched the ostentatiously ornate office perfectly. Stalin lifted it out, looked it up and down, then passed it to the translator with a rush of words. She flushed deeper.

'The marshal says thank you very much. It is a beautiful

gift, though...' Her voice dropped as if ashamed to repeat his words, 'he says he only ever uses pencil.'

Clementine felt a treacherous urge to laugh and had to bite on the inside of her mouth to keep it in. Of course the Russian leader only used pencil – that way no one could hold him to account on anything he'd written.

'Perhaps,' she said smoothly, 'he will use it to sign the terms of Hitler's surrender.'

This, finally, drew a smile from Stalin and he rose and held out his hand. 'Perhaps,' he said in smooth English. 'A pleasure to meet you, Mrs Churchill. Winston is a lucky man.'

'Thank you.' She shook his hand and felt it cold against her own. 'I hope we will meet once more on my return to Moscow.'

'Perhaps,' he said again. 'Though I am a busy man. There is a war to win, you know.'

Then he laughed heartily, waved the escort back into place and, just like that, they were being marched across the room, along the corridor and back into the central courtyard of the vast Kremlin fortress at the heart of Moscow.

'Where now?' Clementine asked Polina Molotov, who was waiting for her.

'We have a hospital to visit if you are not too tired?'

'A hospital!' Clementine said. 'Thank goodness.'

The hospital was a miracle of modern medicine. Stark and bare, it offered little in the way of aesthetic comfort but the beds were clean and comfortable, the equipment up to date, and the place spotless. The staff buzzed around efficiently and the patients sat eagerly up in their beds when Clementine was shown into their ward. She took the time, despite the hovering KGB officials, to talk to each and every man or woman. The language barrier was tricky but smiles and gestures were all that was required as it was apparent from the horrific injuries what these men had been through and how much they valued the care they were receiving.

'You are doing wonderful work here,' she told the doctor showing them around.

'Thanks to your money. People can give care, but only money can provide medicines.'

'A shame then,' she said, 'that people seem to spend so much of it on weapons instead.'

'A shame indeed.' He looked as if he might say more but a glance to the KGB officers silenced him. 'In here, please,' he said instead. 'This is our new ward for reconstructive surgery, built with money from your fund. In here, we hope to graft skin and repair some of the ravages of war. We hope to give our patients back something of themselves.'

'How clever.'

'I am glad you think so, for this will be the Churchill Ward.'

'Really?' Clementine's heart skipped happily. 'You're naming it after my husband?'

He looked at her quizzically. 'We are naming it after you, madam.'

'Oh! Oh, how very kind.'

'You are the kind one, Mrs Churchill, we are simply grateful. Now, let me show you the equipment you have bought.'

'And the people you will use it on?'

'If you can bear it. Some of them are rather disfigured.'

'If they must bear it every day, Doctor, I'm sure I can manage it for a few minutes.'

He bowed and escorted her to several beds at the rear. In one lay a man who was so badly burned his flesh was puckered and raw and his left eye fought to peer out of a closed-up slot.

'Nikolas was an early victim of Nazi terror. He was tied to a tree and set alight.'

Clementine's hands went to her mouth. 'Why?'

'Spite? He was fourteen and trying to run away. They shot him in the ankle and then burned him. He was rescued by Irena, a brave girl who dared to put out the flames when the Nazi backs were turned. He will be eighteen in three weeks' time and we hope to gift him a full skin graft. There is only so much we can do, but if we can heal Nikolas's face it will, perhaps, give him the confidence to ask Irena to dance.'

'That's so very sad.'

'It was a war crime, Mrs Churchill. One of very many. The Nazis must be caught and they must be made to pay.'

Clementine nodded. She was more certain than ever that war crimes must be exposed once victory was secured. The perpetrators had to be publicly punished and the world had to know the extent of the horror so that, somehow, they could make sure it was never allowed to happen again.

'Tell Nikolas I will personally gift him a fine suit for his birthday to complement his new face.'

'Truly?'

'It's the least I can do.'

The doctor conveyed the message to the young man, who grabbed Clementine's hand with his fire-gnarled one and cried tears from the slit of his eye as he said, 'thank you, thank you,' over and over.

Clementine squeezed Nikolas's hand and smiled. She thought of Stalin safe in his Kremlin with his million guards and wondered if he ever came out to see the suffering of his people. Maybe he did, but one thing she knew – *she* was going to spend every possible minute of her time in Russia with those people. Let the men battle for the end of the fighting, she was here to battle for the start of restitution and repair. It might only be a hand held, a smile offered, or a story listened to, but she would do it with all the energy she had, in every town and city she visited.

. . .

Three days later, Clementine felt she had smiled so much it physically hurt. She had travelled from the grand Leningradsky station in Moscow to the identical Moskovsky station in Leningrad, the bookends of Russia's oldest and longest railway. The train had been ordered to travel the four hundred mile stretch at a 'sightseeing' pace of twenty miles per hour to let Clementine appreciate the vast reaches of the 'glorious Russian countryside'. It had been vast indeed but what Clementine had really seen, as they'd crawled through myriad towns and villages, had been people lining the track to wave and call out her name.

There had been soldiers everywhere, keeping control of the crowds, but little had masked the poverty of the peasants' clothing, the hollowness of their cheeks, or the desperation in their eyes. Clementine had no idea if this was from the ravages of war, or the ravages of communism, but there was no doubting their suffering. She had annoyed their guards by insisting on any leftovers from their sumptuous dinners being sent out to the next platform they came to.

'It will be too rich for peasants,' they'd protested.

'Is that not for them to decide?'

They'd scratched their heads and muttered to each other in furious Russian, no doubt cursing the eccentric Englishwoman who did not understand. But Clementine had seen the people falling on the food and understood all she needed to.

Now they were approaching Leningrad and she was excited to see the famous city. Her fund had sent much clothing and food here during their nine-hundred-day siege and she had received many letters that must have been smuggled out along the daring supply runs maintained by brave Russian couriers. The citizens had written to thank her, but also to bear witness to their suffering, and she had been honoured to be their conduit. Now, she was here in person.

She thought of Eleanor Roosevelt urging her to take up this opportunity and Jenny telling her to do so for her daughters, for all their daughters. It was a grand idea, for in truth she was here simply for her curiosity and satisfaction, but if she provided some sort of role model for other women, then she must take that seriously too.

A guard knocked on the door. 'We will be arriving in around ten minutes, Mrs Churchill. There is a large crowd.'

'Oh cripes!' Clementine looked to her secretary. 'Will you run over that Russian thank you with me one more time, Grace? I don't want to fluff it.'

They went over the words with care, but as the train drew in, there was a curious absence of cheers from the crowds on the platform. Clementine looked nervously to her secretary. Were the people of Leningrad not pleased to see them?

The train pulled to a stop and a guard rushed to open the door. Clementine, peering out of the window, saw a small group of dignitaries standing on a dais before her, their faces solemn and their clothing a rigid, funereal black.

'Has someone died?' Grace asked.

'Winston?' Clementine whispered.

Her secretary gave a shocked gasp. 'Surely not. They wouldn't do that to you, Clementine, not in public.'

'This is Russia, Grace. Who knows how they do things here?'

'But there's Polina Molotov. She's a sophisticated woman, she wouldn't...'

Clementine looked to the woman stepping forward to greet her, her eyes low. She must have rushed from Moscow specially, which could only mean bad news. Clementine backed away from the door, panicking. She knew she shouldn't have come.

She knew she shouldn't have left him. Who cared about liberation, or equality, or doing things for yourself? If Winston had died without her there for him, she would never forgive herself.

'Tell them to come on board,' she stuttered to Grace. 'Tell them I will talk to them here.'

She stumbled back into the carriage. Grace ordered the blinds shut and hovered at her side as Polina Molotov entered.

'Is it Winston?' Clementine gasped.

'No!' Madame Molotov rushed forward and took her hands. 'No, Mrs Churchill, it is not Winston. It is Franklin.'

'Franklin Roosevelt?' Clementine gaped at her.

Polina nodded. 'I'm afraid so.'

'He's dead?'

Another nod.

'How?'

'A heart attack at his spa in Warm Springs. It was mercifully quick.'

'Was Eleanor there?'

Polina shook her head. 'She didn't make it in time, but she has escorted his coffin home to the White House in state.'

Clementine thought of her American counterpart, her friend. She remembered exchanging glances with her in the White House as they'd conspired to get their fragile husbands to bed on time. They had worried that the war would be too much for the men in charge and it seemed that, for Franklin, that had come true. This could so, so easily be Clementine facing widowhood now.

'Fetch me a black dress,' she said to Grace, 'and I need to get to a telegram office as soon as possible.'

She wired two telegrams from the stark bureau in Leningrad. The first was to Eleanor sending her condolences. It was stiffly worded but she found it hard to do anything else with the KGB breathing down her neck and a city outside waiting for her. She would write more later, when she'd had time to take this in.

The second telegram was to Winston and said, quite simply: *I love you. Stay safe.*

Then she turned back into Leningrad, feeling suddenly very, very far away from all she knew and loved.

THIRTY-NINE

HALLAM STREET, APRIL 1945

JENNY

Jenny stirred the pot and tried not to throw up from what should be a delicious smell. Ned was due home from Germany and she'd managed to get hold of a rabbit to make him a welcoming dinner. She'd followed a recipe out of *Woman and Home* and it looked right, but it smelled nauseating. Then again, so much did. The doctor said it was a sign that baby had taken a strong hold in her womb which was good, but she'd been desperate for this for so long that she'd expected to feel happy rather than tired, teary and sick.

She reached into the cupboard for the preserved ginger Clementine had brought her before she'd gone to Russia.

'It will help the nausea,' she'd assured her. 'Simply infuse a piece in hot water and sip slowly.'

It had been an interesting visit.

'You went to see Winston?' Clementine had asked.

There'd been no point in denying it. 'I felt I should.'

'You didn't think it impudent?'

'Oh yes!' she'd agreed. 'Terribly. But I thought it important too so I decided it was worth the risk. Did I offend you?'

Clementine had considered that for longer than was comfortable.

'A little,' she'd said in the end. 'But you touched me too. Plus, you made Winston stop and think and that, my dear girl, is quite an achievement!'

It had been a huge relief, and the ginger had been very kind. Boiling the kettle now, she spooned a glistening piece into a mug and poured the water on top. That smelled... rather nice actually. How strange. Already this child, barely bigger than a grape according to the books, was turning her world upside down.

She put the lid on the rabbit and retreated from the kitchen. Sinking into an armchair, she propped her feet on the coffee table and sipped at her tea. The nausea receded and she let out a sigh of relief.

'Cheers, Clementine!' she said, raising her mug in a very British toast to her absent friend.

She hoped she was having a good time in Russia, hoped they were looking after her. Ned had come home last week with worrying reports about the Russian advance into Germany. Many soldiers, furious about the treatment their women and children had received at the hands of the Nazis back in 1941, were meting out the same to German women and children. There were stories of mass shootings, of tortures, of rapes. It was perhaps understandable, but why did man have to repay violence with violence? When would it all stop?

The Roosevelts had been talking about replacing the ineffectual League of Nations set up after the first war with a more robust 'United Nations' group – a worldwide alliance to establish rules for civilised co-existence going forward. That had sounded thrilling to Jenny and she'd been keen to report on it, but now Franklin was dead and Harry Truman, his vice president, had been inaugurated as president and who knew what would happen.

Jenny stared sadly into her tea. The news of the president's sudden death had been a shock. Roosevelt had been in charge since 1933. Jenny had been twenty-three then, newly graduated from Mount Holyoke and deep in a heady courtship with Ned. All her married life had been overseen by the FDR administration and it felt disturbing to have that come to an end. Plus, of course, it was a tragedy for Eleanor and their children.

Jenny had written to the now ex first lady, addressing the letter to the White House, although by the time it made it across the Atlantic, she would be long gone. Presumably some kind clerk passed these things on. It was a curiously mundane thought in the midst of death and war.

Jenny drank some more of her tea and watched the door, willing it to reveal Ned. He'd sent her a curious telegram from Germany on 12 April, the day of Roosevelt's death: 'All very sad here; can't wait to see you.' He'd been a Roosevelt supporter, of course, but she hadn't expected the president's death to touch him so. Perhaps this baby was making itself felt on its father too.

The sound of footsteps outside sent her leaping to her feet. Hot ginger splashed onto her dress but she barely noticed as she ran to open the door.

'Ned! It's so good...' She ground to a halt at the sight of her husband. He was gaunt and haggard and his eyes looked hollow in their sockets. 'What's happened?' She tugged him inside, taking his bag and coat and ushering him to the sofa.

He went like an automaton. 'April twelfth,' he said.

'Roosevelt?'

He stared at her, uncomprehending, then shook himself. 'Of course. Same day. No, not Roosevelt, though that's sad of course. Very sad. Just not *as* sad.'

'As what?' He was scaring her now. 'As sad as what, Ned? Talk to me, please.'

He drew in a shaky breath. 'Remember when I told you I'd found out that the Nazis were murdering people in their concentration camps?'

'Of course.'

Jenny recalled them sitting up together for hours working on his broadcast, fighting to tell the world that these were extermination camps – sites of systematic, cold-blooded murder.

'No one listened, did they?'

'They did but it was hard to know what to do, deep behind enemy lines. Winston felt the best possible solution was to win the war.'

He grabbed at her. 'He was wrong. That is... not wrong, but we could have done more. We *should* have done more. We should have tried to stop that, that... hell on earth.'

Jenny swallowed. 'You've been in one?'

He nodded, hanging his head, and Jenny was horrified to see a tear drop onto his knee.

'Buchenwald it was called. That means beechwood. Sounds pretty, right? Well, it wasn't. It wasn't pretty at all.' He spat the words out with a bitterness she rarely heard from him.

'What did you see?'

He looked up, tears flowing freely. 'There are no words, Jenny, for how gruesome it was. The people – the few that were still alive – were like the walking dead. They were so thin, as if they'd been totally and utterly hollowed out. The Nazis had them crammed into rough wooden bunks, three high, with barely room to sit up, and straw mattresses so sparse they had cuts and bruises on their bony hips. They were crawling with lice and coughing from typhoid and there were rats running around as fat as dogs. It was awful.'

She put her arms around him, squeezing tight, trying to take some of the pain, but he was shaking with it.

'They showed us the chambers where...'

He retched and Jenny felt a fool for fretting over a little baby-induced nausea when there was such horror in the world.

'Where they exterminated them?'

He nodded. 'There were grooves in the concrete walls, scratches where the poor souls had clawed at them as the gas came down. The Nazis were very pleased with their Zyklon B because it was so "efficient" but it still took minutes – minutes trapped with hundreds of others having the life poisoned out of you in an "efficient" way.'

'Those poor, poor people.'

'And then there were the crematoria – not places of respectful burial, but great cavernous ovens into which they forced workers to throw the bodies of their fellows like charnel, all in the interests of "purifying" the Aryan race!'

'That's terrible, Ned.'

He shook her. 'It's more than terrible, it's inhumane, barbaric, despicably horrific. It's... it's beyond words. How anyone is still alive I have no idea. Even if they weren't sent to the gas, they were worked to levels surely beyond any human endurance, on the sort of food that wouldn't keep a baby alive.' His hand went suddenly to her stomach and his eyes found hers. 'Are you well, Jenny? Is Baby well?'

'We're very well. Couldn't be better.'

Who cared about a little tiredness, a little sickness?

'Good. That's good. We have a big job ahead, Jen. I've seen, first hand, what humankind is capable of and it's horrifying. Thank God America came into this war because if the Nazis' hateful doctrine had spread across the world while we sat behind the Atlantic thinking it was nothing to do with us, we would have been damned to hell.'

'We knew that, Ned. We said it from the start. *You* said it from the start.'

'Yes, and then I got so carried away with the celebrity that saying it gave me, I forgot the message. While I was being feted at gala dinners, thousands were being herded to their deaths for no crime other than the circumstances of their birth and the way they chose to honour God.'

'That's not your fault.'

He shook his head. 'It *is*. A bit. I *knew*, Jen. I knew at the start of 1943 and I let it drop because Winston promised me we'd win the war and stop it.'

'Which we have done – nearly.'

'Yes, but in the meantime, for those two whole years, more and more people have gone to their deaths in the most horrific way. That's millions of lives on my conscience.'

'You can't take it on yourself, Ned.'

'Maybe not, but I can't excuse myself of it either.' She held him close and his arms went around her, holding on so, so tight. 'I'm sorry, Jen. I've been a fool. I got my values all twisted up and confused and I hate myself for it. I'm so glad you're still here for me.'

'Of course I am.'

'Not of course at all. I don't deserve you. But I will. I promise. I'll make it better, I'll make it all better.'

He was shaking again and she sat back, taking hold of his arms to steady him, and looking into his eyes.

'We must look to the future, Ned. We must honour those people by making sure their stories are told. That's what you're good at, that's what you do.'

He nodded fiercely. 'You're right. You're so right. I made so many notes, most of them blurred by tears, but I know what they say anyway. I'll never forget it, any of it. But I didn't want to broadcast live. I didn't want to dramatise it or trivialise it in any way. I have to somehow find words where no words are truly available to express the evil. Can I do that?'

'You can,' she told him firmly.

'Will you help me?'

'I will.'

He kissed her, running his hands over her face as if wanting to be sure she was still there, still intact. 'This has been a bloody, bloody war, Jen, but a vital one. Hitler didn't just want land, he wanted souls. He wanted to turn everyone into carbon-copy machines for some misplaced utopian ideal, and he didn't care what he did to achieve it. Our differences are what make the human race so exciting, so special. We should celebrate that, not seek to destroy it.'

'We will,' she promised him. 'We'll unite nations and we'll prosecute crimes and we'll lay down rules for a better future.'

'God, Jen, I hope so.' He put one hand around her waist and pressed the other gently to her belly. 'We must make a better world for you and I and this little one we've been blessed with. He or she is *our* future, yes?'

'Yes.'

'And we'll bring them up safe and secure and knowing right from wrong.'

'We'll do our best.'

'We will,' he agreed and, at last, the shaking receded. 'Together, Jenny, we will do our very best.'

It was all she needed to hear. The ginger tea had cooled on the table but it didn't matter. She'd take all the sickness this child threw at her because she was here, alive and well and safe, and as this terrible war drew to its close, that was a gift. Now, they had to turn that gift into a future worthy of all the suffering – a world fit for their children to live in.

FORTY

CLEMENTINE

Clementine sat on the podium alongside two female metro engineers and listened to Madame Maslennicova, chairwoman of Kursk city council, addressing a vast meeting with poise, control and elegance. Her audience were attentive and respectful. When she talked about her plans for expanding the city metro system into something to match Moscow's (translated for Clementine and Grace in a low whisper), the assembled people cheered. No one heckled the idea of a woman designing or running the project. No one suggested they should be at home bringing up babies and cooking their husband's dinner. No one asked why they weren't wearing a pretty skirt instead of their smart engineer's suits. It was fascinating.

'Do you think we'll ever see this at home?' Clementine quietly asked Grace.

'It feels a long way off. Parliament are already calling for women to give up their factory jobs in case there won't be enough work for the returning men.'

'Or that the women will be better than them!'

'That too. Maybe communism has some things right.'

Clementine sighed. 'They definitely do, but they come with a heavy price tag.'

Her travels, taking her six thousand miles around this vast country, had been enthralling but bruising. The Russian people were wonderful – warm and passionate, quick to cry, even quicker to dance – but they had a hard lot under communism. Her time in Rostov, seeing the hospitals, had been amazing, and she had pledged them twice the money originally promised. It would mean the fund continuing to run after the war, but it was badly needed.

Now she was in Kursk, a bold city that had somehow resisted German occupation all through the war.

'God must have been on your side,' Clementine had suggested to Madame Maslennicova.

'God?! Pah! You still believe in God after all of this? Man must rely on themselves – or, better yet, on woman!'

She'd laughed gaily and moved the subject on but Clementine had been struck by her vehemence. Women were achieving much in this striking country and it was good to see but as the time to return to Moscow drew close, she felt the oppression of Stalin's supposedly benign rule weighing heavily on her.

She'd spoken several times with Archie Clark Kerr about reports of Russian atrocities on the front line, but any mention of the Red Army advance that did not include the words 'glorious' or 'heroic' brought their omnipresent KGB escort threateningly forward. She'd dared write nothing home that did not praise her hosts, and her conversations with Winston, on the rare occasion they'd found a line, had been necessarily guarded. They had stuck to expressions of love; it had been enough.

Clementine missed him. Theirs had never been a cloying marriage. Even at the start they'd often holidayed apart, recognising the difference in their interests and agreeing to pursue them separately before enjoying coming together again. This, though, was different. Out here she felt cut off from her husband in a way she rarely had before, and at the most important time in the last five years. She was ready to go home.

Grace nudged her and for a horrible moment she thought she'd missed Madame Maslennicova introducing her, but no, a messenger had arrived on the stage and the chairwoman had paused to read his note. Clementine watched as the expression on her stern face changed from incredulity to delight.

'Mrs Churchill,' she said in English. 'I think you should join me for the announcement of some most important news.'

Clementine rose and went over. Her hostess passed her the note but it was written in Cyrillic script – attractive but meaningless to her.

'What does it say?'

Madame Maslennicova stepped away from the microphone. 'It says that Hitler is dead.'

Clementine gasped. This was it then – this was the end.

'How?'

The Russian woman gave a bitter laugh. 'He committed suicide in the safety of his bunker, the coward. Married that idiot woman, Eva Braun, presumably drank a glass of champagne, and then went peacefully to his rest, having wrecked it for most of the known world.'

Clementine swallowed. 'He's really gone?'

'He is. And Goebbels the same way, with his cosy, well-fed, treacherous family around him. The hellfires will be burning high tonight!'

'I thought you didn't believe in God?'

'I don't, but I sure as hell believe in the Devil. And now he's dead.' She gave Clementine a broad smile and turned back to the microphone to make the announcement in sharp, passionate Russian.

The auditorium erupted. Men and women cheered and danced. Even the KGB officers nearly smiled. People produced vodka bottles and began passing them round, and the planning meeting transformed into a party.

Clementine sidled over to Grace, who looked utterly bemused.

'Is the war over?' she asked.

'Not officially,' Clementine said, 'but Hitler is dead, so surely it will come.'

Her secretary and friend hugged her. 'Thank God,' she said over and over. 'Thank God! And thank Winston.'

Clementine wasn't sure her husband deserved the same credit as the Almighty but she could picture him receiving the news of the death of the man he'd decried to the world way before anyone else was brave enough to do so and longed, again, to be with him. The end must be close and suddenly she was desperate to get to Moscow and from there, home, to celebrate with her people – with Britain and with Winston.

THE BRITISH EMBASSY, MOSCOW, 8 MAY 1945

The joy was palpable. The embassy was crowded with an eclectic mix of people, dancing and laughing and shouting with the giddy joy of children finally released from the darkest of schools. Clementine stood in the middle and felt elation surge through her, so powerful it was hard to even stand up and enjoy it. Especially alone.

You're not alone,' she chided herself. She was with Grace and Archie Clark Kerr, she was with the Harrimans and the Molotovs and all sorts of kind, happy people.

But she wasn't with her family.

She wasn't with Winston.

She'd asked to leave Moscow for London as soon as she'd got back to the Russian capital, but the chargé d'affaires had urged her to stay.

'Your presence in Russia as peace is declared will symbolise the ongoing friendship of our two countries,' he'd assured her, and Winston's advisers back home had agreed.

It was all very flattering, she supposed, but today, of all days, she would rather be a wife than a symbol.

'Victory tastes so sweet,' Madame Molotov said, bringing Clementine a glass of champagne.

Clementine smiled and clinked glasses and sipped, but she could not truly taste victory without her husband. She'd longed to at least speak with him but the telephone lines had been jammed and the Russian operators uncooperative, so she'd had to settle for a telegram.

Congratulations, darling, she'd sent. *I cannot wait to celebrate with you.*

It was true. And, best of all, she didn't want to be with her husband to be sure he was safe, that he was sleeping enough, eating well, not drinking too much, that his heart was still beating and his temperature was still normal and he was intact and thriving. No, she just wanted to be with him. She just wanted to be together.

The climate for the last few days had been extremely awkward. Stalin was playing games. He'd announced that he wished to give Clementine the Order of the Red Banner, but at the last minute had sent his deputy to do the honours. He'd also been curiously obstructive about the peace declaration. As a result, today, 8 May, Victory in Europe was being celebrated all over Britain, America and western Europe, while Russia and the Baltic states had to wait until tomorrow. No wonder the embassy was so crowded – it was a tiny bit of British soil released to happiness a day ahead of those around them.

But it was not the same as being in London.

Clementine had been there when war had been declared. She had moved into Admiralty House and then into Downing Street. She had cowered in shelters below Whitehall and sat on the city's roofs keeping watch against incendiaries. She had worked with victims of the Blitz, travelled around factories and hostels, seen babies born and babies, sadly, killed. Now, as the people of England's brave capital danced in the fountains of Trafalgar Square and sang up the Mall, she was trapped in a colonial villa on the banks of the Volga. Doing your own thing, it seemed, came with drawbacks and none more painful than today.

'Ssh, everyone,' Archie declared suddenly. 'It's nearly time.' He turned on a wireless set at the head of the room. 'Clementine, my dear, please, come and join me. Your husband is about to address the British nation.'

All eyes turned her way and a corridor opened up to let her through, as if she were Winston himself. Grace nudged her forward and she went, trying to keep her head high and her smile broad. She was a symbol after all and she had to do him proud, but as his voice came over the airwaves, crackled and broken but still unmistakably him, she felt tears well and longed to be able to listen in private.

She could not really hear what he said, but she felt his passion and his pride. The commentator talked of him standing on the balcony of Buckingham Palace with the royal family and she remembered him railing against the king and queen inviting Chamberlain up there when he returned from Munich. 'As if he was a bloody hero, Clemmie,' he'd wailed, hurt. But now *he* was up there and he *was* a hero, loudly acclaimed by the crowds. She knew that tomorrow, as VE day rippled out to Russia, she would see pictures of him with his hat and cigar, signing V for victory to the world, and ached to be there sharing his great moment.

She thought of him in bed in Tunis at the end of 1943, almost as close to death as poor Franklin a year later. She thought of him boarding a plane to Russia in the darkness of a night in 1942, his heart already loaded with more than it ought to be able to take without a frozen flight across war-torn Europe.

She thought of him heading into the Blitz in 1941, the only way to keep him from the dangers to suggest she went with him.

She thought of him becoming prime minister in 1940 just in time to evacuate thousands of stranded men from Dunkirk, and of him turning flight into a form of victory with the power of his speeches so that Britain had been brave enough to fight on. Ned Miller had told Winston that voice was power and he had proved that, finding his way into every battered and broken front room in Britain. She thought of listening to Chamberlain declaring war from their apartment in Westminster Gardens, Winston still on the fringes of power. And she thought of him railing against Hitler at Chartwell for year after infuriating year in the 1930s when something could still have been done about the power-mad Führer if only anyone had been listening.

They were listening to him now. And they were celebrating him, as well they should. And she had done it with him. She had played her part, both as his sworn helpmeet and as a campaigner and activist in her own right. It was hard not to be in Britain on this glorious day, but she was in Russia because of *her* works, *her* achievements. Elated, Clementine leaped onto the nearest chair and thrust her champagne glass in her hand.

'To victory!' she cried, as Winston had done on the day he'd been made PM, sitting in Sarah's apartment with their family around them.

'To victory!' the cry came back from the whole British embassy, loud and clear and joyous.

Finally, victory was not a hope, or a plan, or a gritty determination, but a fact. A magnificent, glorious fact and they would have, God willing, years and years of peace in which to enjoy it.

EPILOGUE

'Look down there, Mrs Churchill, ma'am. That's Blighty, that is. Good old Blighty.'

Clementine peered out the window of the plane and saw a mass of green fields, misted with rain. She laughed. 'She looks amazing.'

'Ten minutes to landing, ma'am.'

Her heart swelled. Winston had said he would be here, Sarah, Mary and Diana too, and suddenly the next ten minutes felt longer than the hours and hours she'd been travelling home. She soaked up the views of England unrolling beneath her. Somewhere below was Chartwell, cows' feet mended and their family house forever safe from the grounded Luftwaffe. Then the fields were giving way to houses and Clementine pressed her face against the glass to look at London, battered and broken, but free.

The plane flew on, heading for RAF Northolt, close to Chequers and to Fulmer Chase and Fircroft where, even now, mothers would be nursing their babies and telling them Daddy would soon be home. Those hospitals would be disbanded, but Clementine was determined to keep a facility for giving new mothers much-needed time with their babies. Family, that was what counted now – family and friends, and alliances, big and small. The world must stop hating each other and where better to start than with children?

She thought of Jenny and prayed she was well and her baby was sticking in her womb. It would be wise to do so for she was a wonderful woman – kind, intelligent and caring. Thank God Ned had come to his senses and realised that too. The war had been as tough on marriages as it had on so much else and there would be bridges to build in as many homes as there were over Europe's ravaged rivers. But there was time to do it now, time and freedom.

The plane turned on itself and Clementine tutted with frustration. 'Where are we going?' she called to the pilot.

He glanced back, his cheeks flushed. 'Just, er, waiting clearance to land, ma'am.'

'Clearance?' She peered at the empty grey sky. 'Are there many planes waiting?'

'Not as such. But things need to be, er, ready.'

He looked flustered and Clementine felt a flutter of panic, then she saw, speeding up the road towards the airbase, a bright red Napier, skewing wildly as it screeched into the car park.

'Winston!'

He was late, as usual, doubtless caught up in the endless business of state. For a moment she felt the familiar rush of impatience at her self-centred husband, but then the plane turned and she saw him dashing onto the runway and all other feelings were overwhelmed by a desperate, burning desire to be in his arms.

As they came in to land, she could see her daughters in a row at the edge of the runway. Diana held her young daughter and Clementine was touched she was prepared to bring the baby into the night to be here. Sarah was proud in her WAAF blue and Mary in ATS khaki, and all three were smiling and waving and looking for all the world like daughters keen to see their mother home. Perhaps she hadn't done such a dreadful job with them after all...

She grabbed her compact to check her reflection, thinking, as so often, of Eleanor Roosevelt and hoping she was well. Her marriage could, perhaps, have gone the way of her American friend's, but somehow she and Winston had steered a path through the mire of political life. She had stood by his side throughout his travails. She had listened to him and helped him and waited for him and now here he was, waiting for her.

She unclipped the safety belt and got to her feet. Her limbs ached and her back was stiff but she shifted impatiently from foot to foot as steps were wheeled up outside. Finally, the door was opening and she was in the gusty drizzle of an English spring and there was Winston, standing below her with a bedraggled bunch of flowers – prime minister of England, victor of the Second World War, and her own, dear husband.

Taking the steps at a trot she fell into his arms.

'We made it,' was all she could say as he kissed her. 'We made it.'

Only they, perhaps, would know how close they had come to not doing so, how so nearly this most terrible of wars had claimed him. She pictured him lying in a darkened room in Tunis, his hand reaching for hers, burning hot and shaking. He had needed her that day. But she had needed him too. She had not just kept Winston alive for the world, but for herself and now, at last, she could have him. She pulled back to look into his eyes and as she did so the sun broke through the drizzle, sending a misty shaft of light down upon them.

'Look, my darling,' he said instantly, 'how your star shines.'

It was so very quick, so very apt, so very Winston.

'I'm no star...' she started to say, then stopped herself. She looked to her daughters and held out her arms. 'Come, girls, step into the light, for it is you who will take it forward. It is you who will shine now.'

They came, hugging her and clamouring for tales of her visit and Clementine drew in their beautiful enthusiasm like the finest wine. If these women, ironically released into their full potential by Hitler, were the future of Britain, then it was in safe hands.

'Let's get home,' Diana said. 'So many people are desperate to see you, Mummy.'

Clementine nodded and watched her daughters clatter ahead to the car. She turned to Winston. 'It's so good to be back.'

He smiled. 'Sometimes it is leaving home that makes us aware of how very precious it truly is.'

She kissed him. 'Have I told you how wise you can be, husband?'

'More times than I deserve. I love you, Clementine Hozier.'

Instantly she was back in the Temple of Diana, him standing before her, plucking up the courage to ask for her hand.

'And I you, Winston Churchill.'

She stepped up, taking his hands, as she had taken them for the first time that day, thirty-seven years ago. The plane that had returned her from Russia receded from her view. The creases in both their faces, worn to grooves by the last six years of war, were smoothed away. Even their chattering daughters faded as if a soft rain had fallen, shutting out the rest of the world. They were the two of them, again, in a temple at the start of a shared life, a shared purpose that had got them, against all the odds, to victory.

'I like this temple,' she said softly.

'As you should, my darling girl.' Winston took her in his arms, 'For it is made not of columns or carvings, but of every minute of our time together – a temple to our marriage.'

She smiled. 'I'm glad you found the courage to ask.'

'And I'm glad you found the courage to say yes. Getting you to agree to be my wife was, as I have told you before, my greatest achievement.'

She laughed at the man who had done more to secure victory against the Nazis than any other in the known world. 'Even now?'

He did not laugh. 'Even now.'

Then he kissed her and at last Clementine tasted victory and it was not, thank God, the taste of blood and tears – though there had been far, far too many of them – but of love and decency and kindness. Of a world they had fought for and a world they had, at last, together, truly won.

A LETTER FROM ANNA

Dear reader,

I want to say a huge thank you for choosing to read *The English Wife*. We all, I think, know a certain amount about Winston Churchill, but so few of us know anything about his wife and I really hope that this novel does a little to correct that as she was a fascinating person.

If you want to keep up to date with all my latest releases, and receive a free short story, *The Woman Who Hoped*, just sign up at the following link. Your email address will never be shared and you can unsubscribe at any time.

www.bookouture.com/anna-stuart

Until writing this novel I have mainly concentrated on telling the stories of the lesser-known people and events of World War II. I believe Clementine fits that mould, but the people around her are hugely well-documented and explored in many books, films and plays so I felt a huge responsibility in providing my own interpretation of the story of those at the heart of power during the war. My intention was to open the human, and especially the female, side of Number Ten up to readers and I hope you felt welcome.

If you enjoyed this novel, I'd be very grateful if you could write a review. I'd love to hear what you think, and it makes such a difference helping new readers to discover one of my books for the first time. I also love hearing from my readers – you can get in touch via social media or my website.

Thanks for reading,

Anna

www.annastuartbooks.com

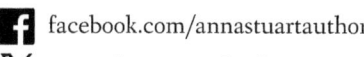 facebook.com/annastuartauthor

𝕏 x.com/annastuartbooks

⊙ instagram.com/annastuartauthor

HISTORICAL NOTES

It was while researching another novel that I came across the astonishing information that Winston Churchill's wife was in Moscow on VE Day. She was not at his side on the balcony of Buckingham Palace with the king and queen, or devotedly waiting at Number Ten, but thousands of miles away in Stalin's Russia. How on earth had this come about, I found myself wondering, and what sort of woman was Clementine Churchill? The answers were to lead me to writing this novel.

What I discovered was a woman of intriguing contradictions: Clementine was a blue-blooded aristocrat, but she had known considerable poverty. She was shy in society, but had been engaged twice before she married Winston. She was considered the plain one of her sisters, but hailed as a society belle when she came out. She was six foot tall and very athletic, winning multiple high-level tennis tournaments, acing it on the croquet lawn and taking up skiing aged fifty (before lifts, so you had to trek up the mountain with your skis on your back for one short run down!), yet she was a known whizz at house decoration and a gentle, caring hostess.

These contradictions carried into her marriage. It was very

much a love match and yet she and Winston would argue fiercely – he usually, from the evidence of their letters, being the first to seek reconciliation. They spent a lot of time apart. She loved hearty British seaside holidays and active, sporty trips abroad; he was devoted to the French Riviera and an easy life of wining, dining and, later on, painting. They also had a topsy-turvy history of buying and renting houses that were hard to maintain – of which Chartwell was the ultimate example. Their marriage, it is safe to say, was more a roller coaster than a merry-go-round, and yet they stuck together, their need and love for each other strong enough to weather the storms of his political career and their chaotic domestic life.

Winston Churchill was an astounding man. Undoubtedly stubborn, bullish, self-absorbed, and astonishingly self-confident, he was also witty, knowledgeable, caring, emotional and very good fun. It is, perhaps, to his credit that, in an age when a man might seek a wife merely to run his house and give him children, he chose an exciting, intelligent woman who would be not just his supporter but his true partner. He told her everything and listened to her opinion. It would be exaggerating to say that she was as critical to winning the war as he was, but it is undoubtedly true, as is, I hope, shown in this novel, that she was critical to keeping him fit, happy and aware enough of others to help him do so. Her position as prime minister's wife gave her a platform to find her own projects and increasingly she did so. The more I looked into this too-little-known woman, the more I admired her.

I wanted this to be a story not just of Clementine, but of the world in which she was operating – the world of British politics and society, but also of transatlantic dealings. Most people are aware that Winston Churchill was desperate to bring the Americans into the war and that his relationship with Franklin Roosevelt – also an enlightened pursuer of world politics – was critical to the eventual defeat of the Nazis. I explored the Churchills' relationships with various Americans in my research and kept coming back to one woman – Janet Murrow. The characters of Jenny and Ned Miller are inspired by the real life couple, Janet and Ed Murrow.

Ed Murrow was relatively famous, especially in America, as a pioneer of live broadcasting, but Janet – as is so often the case with women – was far less known. She was an intelligent woman who gained an economics degree in the early thirties, when this was still unusual for women. She was politically active, which is how she met Ed, then president of the National Student Federation of America. They married in 1934 and came to England in 1937 when Ed was made CBS's European director. Both Ed and Janet were, as shown, welcomed into the 'padlock' of people the beleaguered Churchills knew they could trust.

Clementine and Janet genuinely seem to have become friends. When I then found out that Ed went on to have an affair with the Churchills' daughter-in-law Pamela, it felt as if Janet and Clementine's stories were intimately intertwined and I sought to use that to bring a fresh angle to both. The details of the relations between the fictional Millers and the Churchills are my own invention, but there is no doubting the enduring friendship between Janet Murrow and Clementine Churchill. In the late 1940s Janet sent Clementine food parcels; they were still sending each other books in the sixties, and met several times in 1969 and 1971. The last recorded letter from Clementine to Janet is in 1974 thanking her for the 'glorious lily'. I felt that this was a fascinating cross-Atlantic friendship that merited exploration and I hope readers have enjoyed it.

There are also a number of events, political issues and places covered in the novel that merit more detail for those with an interest:

Winston's health was not good and, having seen so many pictures of the portly man, famous for his cigars and drinking, that was little surprise to me. It wasn't until I was researching this novel, however, that I realised how close he came to dying during the Second World War. The most critical time was in Tunis at Christmas 1943 but he had pneumonia on several other occasions. Mary recorded in her diary that Dr Moran told Clementine he feared his heart would not survive the many high altitude flights he asked of it. Mary and Clementine talked it over and decided not to tell him, realising it would make no difference to how he acted. Winston was going to get the job done, whatever the personal cost, though I think he was also buoyed up by a firm belief in his own invincibility. That luxury was not available to Clementine.

The details of Clementine's terrifying emergency trip to Tunis are true, as are those of the many doctors who were flown into Tunis to keep the prime minister alive. There were certainly points, especially at night, when the doctors feared he wasn't going to make it and all reported that he improved as soon as Clementine reached his side. Maybe she happened to arrive as the drugs kicked in, or maybe she gave him the love and hope needed to battle the disease – maybe a little of both. There is no doubt, however, that she was critical to his happiness and, therefore, his health, and in this novel I explored the weight of that on a woman who was often unwell herself.

Sulphonamides were the first antibiotics – that's to say, the first artificially synthesised drug that could effectively treat bacterial infections in the human body. Ironically, the first sulphonamide drug, trade-named Prontosil, was created in the early thirties by the German company Bayer AG, a branch of the German chemical trust IG Farben that would cruelly use camp labour in the war. They patented it, but it emerged that the key compound, sulphonamide, had actually first been synthesised in 1906. Its patent had expired and the drug was available to anyone, so there was a 'sulfa craze' in the late thirties with hundreds of manufacturers producing and testing various drugs, including those which most likely saved Winston Churchill's life in Tunis.

While researching this novel I became truly aware of how much time people had to spend resting in bed in times past. In my head before, this had been in the rather indulgent way of the weaker Jane Austen characters having 'the vapours' and taking to the couch, but looking into it further I realised that before antibiotics, if you got flu or a chest infection, or even an infected cut, your only chance of healing was to lie still and give your body the best possible chance of fighting the issue itself. Churchill did not have the time for that in 1943 and it seems likely that without sulphonamides he would have died in Tunis and the course of history could have been very different.

The second 'Blitz' in London was something of a surprise to me when researching this novel. I'd long been aware of 'the Blitz' of September 1940 to May 1941, but I was far less aware of the second one, occurring just after D-Day, when the Germans launched first their V1s and then their even more lethal V2s on the capital.

These rockets were Hitler's secret weapon – the first unpiloted bombs that could be launched from far away, removing the need to send pilots into enemy territory, and they were very scary. The first V1 bombs, soon known as doodlebugs (perhaps in an attempt to make them feel less threatening), fell on London on 13 June and very quickly an average of seventy-three would fall every twenty-four hours with up to two hundred if the weather was too bad for the British anti-aircraft batteries. As shown in the novel, they arrived with a loud buzz, then went eerily silent for several seconds before smashing down on those below. They were mainly launched from sites in the Pas de Calais and thankfully the Allies soon got close enough to stop the bombs. On 7 September 1944, Herbert Morrison, the Home Secretary, wrote in *The Times* that the V1 attacks were dropping and the worst was over; on 8 September, the first V2 hit.

The V2s were supersonic missiles, fired from Nazi bases in the Netherlands. They took just four minutes to reach London so were impossible to catch with air defences, and they were lethal, often taking out whole streets in a single strike. Between September 1944 and March 1945, five hundred landed in London, killing 2,500 people and injuring well over 6,000. We tend to think of spring 1945 as a romp to the Berlin finish-line, but there was a bitter battle going on in our capital for much of that period and this second Blitz was, in many ways, more devastating as everyone was weary of war and desperate for an end to it all. There was little 'Blitz spirit' in 1944.

Chartwell was, as many will know, the country house of the Churchill family, although not an ancestral one. Winston was born in Blenheim Palace, owned by his cousin 'Sunny', the ninth Duke of Marlborough, but had no real family house of his own. He was always, therefore, on the lookout for one and fell in love with Chartwell, mainly for its beautiful views across the Kentish Weald. Clementine, too, loved the views on first sight but she was far more practically minded than her extravagant husband and immediately saw the potentially ruinous sums required to make the house liveable in the modern age. They'd already had their fingers burned buying Lullenden Manor near East Grinstead in 1917, which had proved very hard to get under control and which they'd gratefully sold to old friends General Sir Ian and Lady Hamilton after just two years. Clementine had vowed not to make the same mistake again – Winston, however, had not.

Ignoring his wife's protests, he bought Chartwell secretly

(later saying it was the only time he'd not been truly honest with her) just after Mary's birth in September 1922 and took the older children to see it, relying on their enthusiasm to win over their mother. It did not! As it turns out, Clementine was absolutely right about how much it would cost and there were times in the thirties when it nearly ruined them. Only the income from Winston's prodigious writing, and some help from kind friends, kept them afloat and, although they had many, many happy times at Chartwell, Clementine's letters show she never truly loved it as the rest of the family did which makes me rather sad for her. I would strongly recommend a visit as it's a stunning and fascinating place. Plus, you can stand in Clementine's bedroom at the top, preserved just as it was, and get a real sense of her and her life.

The pre-war policy of appeasement followed by the government was fiercely opposed by Churchill and a handful of cronies in the bitter decade of the thirties. Hitler's actions in 1939, of course, proved appeasement to be foolish but at the time it was very much the most popular policy amongst politicians, military advisers and the general population. No one wanted another war and who can blame them? Churchill, however, was very clear-sighted about Hitler's intentions and vocal about the need to stand up to him. He was shouted down as a 'warmonger', and although he kept his seat as an MP throughout, he held no ministerial position. This was agony for a man who was used to power, having already held several weighty cabinet positions. By all accounts he was almost intolerable to live with in this period and Clementine may even, at least momentarily, have spoken to friends about divorcing him. By 1938, when this novel opens, however, it was clear to those prepared to look at the facts that Hitler was intent on war and Clementine was firmly behind her husband as he grew close, through a harsh set of circumstances, to finally becoming prime minister.

Fire watching, as shown in the opening scene of this novel, is something Clementine really did. The Fire Watchers scheme was instigated in January 1941, at the height of the Blitz. Fire Guards were men aged 16–30 (presumably those who could not/would not fight) and women aged 20–45, plus volunteers of men up to the age of 70 and women 60. Clearly the take-up was not great, however, as in May 1941 Clementine wrote to Herbert Morrison, the Home Secretary, stating that the fire-watching service was woefully undermanned and urging him to ask middle-aged women (35–60) to register for shifts in all heavily bombed cities. She said she would gladly have her name associated with the scheme and signed up for active duty. Her shifts are in her diaries (which can be read in the fabulous archives in Churchill College, Cambridge) and on 8 June 1941, Mary noted that her mother had had an attack of lumbago following 'violent use of a stirrup pump in fire practice'! I can only imagine how tiring it must have been for this woman in her fifties to take night shifts on top of everything else she was doing and feel this service is testimony to her selfless sense of duty to the city she loved and, perhaps more so, to helping Winston win the war on every front.

Clementine's turbans were truly something she adopted, with great flair, during the war, having copied the idea from the factory girls. A quick google will show you pictures of her looking very smart in a range of them, as she had many made to match her various outfits. The one printed with excerpts of Winston's speeches existed, though I confess the hammer-and-sickle one is an invention of my own. Clementine was a very well-dressed woman and the conflict with Jock over whether she should wear her leopard-fur coat to visit a shelter is clearly documented. He thought she was lording it over the people, she felt she was dressing well for them. Queen Elizabeth took the same approach as Clementine and the people, it seems, loved it, so Clementine's instincts, as in so many things, were correct.

The Aid to Russia Fund was an astonishing success. As shown in the novel, it was set up by the Red Cross after many voluntary donations from the British people, who'd seen the suffering of the Russians on newsreels. It is hard, in the current climate, to convey the sympathy that was engendered for the only nation who were truly standing up to the frightening Nazi Blitzkrieg. All other invaded nations had capitulated quickly, but the Red Army kept on resisting, even though the Nazis were merciless to the innocent civilians they met on their way. Villages and towns were pillaged, their people beaten, killed and raped, and the remains torched. The British wanted to help.

Clementine was approached to be a figurehead but swiftly got stuck in, becoming the face of the campaign and the head of their various fundraising efforts. She broadcast radio appeals, attended endless events, wrote articles for the newspapers, and threw herself into this major project, ultimately raising £8 million – a vast sum at that time. The Russian people were very grateful and many wrote to her personally, as shown. The fund also led to the invitation to visit Russia on what would turn out to be an epic trip covering some six thousand miles. Many details of Clementine's trip feature in the novel, including her giving Stalin a gold pen from Winston and him telling her he only ever used pencil! The female council leaders impressed Clementine so much she dwelled on them in a pamphlet about the trip she wrote on her return. She also found out about Roosevelt's death on arrival in Leningrad, and we can only imagine how worried that must have made her feel about Winston.

While we now know that by April 1945, when she set off, the war had only a month to run, that was clearly not known at the time. Once the surrender was announced, Clementine was keen to get home, but Winston felt it important to keep the Russians sweet (he'd always been very suspicious of them in ways that would turn out to be all too correct) and the War Office advised her to stay. Hence, she was not at Winston's side on 8 May but celebrating in the British embassy, ahead of the rest of her host nation (Stalin's petty alteration of VE day in Russia is also true) – and hence my interest in her and, ultimately, this novel! I very much hope readers enjoyed it.

ACKNOWLEDGEMENTS

I love the quiet, solo creativity of crafting a story, but that story would never see the light of day as a novel without a huge team of people behind it, and I am blessed in those who surround me. My agent, Kate Shaw, always has my back and is both commercially and editorially very wise. Thank you, Kate. I'm also hugely lucky in my writing buddies – Julie, Tracy, Debbie, Helen and Sharon – who are always there for advice, support and laughter. Our bi-annual writing retreats are two of my favourite weeks of the year!

As always, it's my pleasure to thank Natasha and the wonderful team at Bookouture, who work so hard to make my books the best they can be, and to promote and champion them in so many clever ways. This time round, I'd especially like to give a big shout out to the brilliant women who labour on the minutiae of my writing – my line editor, Lauren Finger, copy-editor Anne O'Brien, and proofreader Liz Hatherell. Your editing skills make a huge difference to how smooth and precise my novels finally end up and I thank you all.

As a historical author, research is critical to the veracity of my novels, perhaps especially with this one as it follows the lives of such well-known people. This is a fictionalised account of the lives of Clementine and Winston Churchill, and all those around them during the war, but being faithful to history is important to me. The events shown are carefully researched via both historical accounts and personal biographies and as close to reality as possible.

I offer a huge thank you to Churchill College, Cambridge, and in particular to the lovely staff at the excellent Churchill archives where I had a very happy day reading through Clementine's personal papers (diaries, journals, letters, etc), which are available to anyone on request and make fascinating reading. I would also like to express my admiration for Chartwell House, as run by the National Trust. I had a wonderful day there, and spent a long time in Clementine's bedroom getting a really good feel for her, much helped by a long chat with the knowledgeable volunteer on duty. The house is fascinating and beautifully set up for visitors – particularly those with children, which I'm sure Clementine and Winston would have liked – and I'd strongly recommend it for interested readers. Similarly, the Churchill War Rooms, run by the Imperial War Museum, are fascinating. A particular gem, for me, was the series of personal Churchill memorabilia and photographs that really helped me visualise the characters and the events they went through.

The biggest thank you of all for this book, however, goes to Xinran Fan, an utterly brilliant student at Mount Holyoke College, Massachusetts. I became aware whilst researching this novel that Mount Holyoke – Janet Murrow's alma mater – had a collection of her personal papers, in much the same way that Churchill College in the UK keeps Clementine's. As most of my information to that point had come from books on her husband (as usual with so many women in history!), it seemed vital to me that I was able to read her own words, and these inspired the character of Jenny. I had no time to get to New York, however, so was very grateful when Jeremy King, Professor of History there, put me in touch with one of his students, Xinran. Thanks to the joys of modern technology we were able to chat online and Xinran very kindly agreed to go in and read the papers for me. She did a hugely conscientious, sharp and intelligent job of reading and analysing all the journals and letters. She is a talented researcher and I offer her my huge thanks for her help with this novel and wish her the very best in what I'm sure will be a bright future.

Behind all the research and the publication process, however, is little old me! I consider myself so lucky to have been able to pursue my dream of being a writer and have been hugely supported along the way by those I love. I am blessed in my fantastic friends, my gorgeous children and my wonderful new granddaughter, but this novel is dedicated particularly to my husband, Stuart. Right from the start, he has been unfailingly encouraging and supportive of my writing. Many was the time I would have given up without his belief in me and I'm delighted that at last my writing career has come to fruition – not the least because it can now fund our motorhoming research trips!

Stuart and I have found the happiest of life–work balances with him driving 'Norman' to fascinating places whilst I sit in the back and write another chapter. Research has taken us on wonderful trips together so far and I look forward to many, many more. Readers, watch out for novels set in the most exotic of locations…! Seriously, though, I am lucky to have you, Stuart, not just for my writing but for our life with our lovely family and as a couple. I love you.

A final shout out, as always, to my readers, without whom all the research, writing and publication would be pointless. It makes my day when people get in touch with me, so please feel free to do so. Thank you for reading.

PUBLISHING TEAM

Turning a manuscript into a book requires the efforts of many people. The publishing team at Bookouture would like to acknowledge everyone who contributed to this publication.

Audio
Alba Proko
Melissa Tran
Sinead O'Connor

Commercial
Lauren Morrissette
Hannah Richmond
Imogen Allport

Contracts
Peta Nightingale

Cover design
Lisa Horton

Data and analysis
Mark Alder
Mohamed Bussuri